T0355853

FACING
HARD
TRUTHS

FACING HARD TRUTHS

How Americans Can Get Real, Pull Together,
and Turn Our Country Around

STEPHEN J. CLOOBECK

Lifelong busboy, founder, and former CEO and chairman of Diamond Resorts International

DISRUPTION
BOOKS

Washington, DC

Published by Disruption Books
Washington, DC
www.disruptionbooks.com

Distributed by Disruption Books

For information about special discounts for bulk purchases, please contact Disruption Books at info@disruptionbooks.com.

Cover design by Liz Driesbach
Book design by Brian Phillips

Library of Congress Cataloging-in-Publication Data available

Printed in the United States of America

Print ISBN: 978-1-63331-107-7
eBook ISBN: 978-1-63331-105-3

First Edition

For my father, Sheldon H. Cloobeck,
and for Harry Reid, my friend, mentor, and adopted dad.
With love and admiration, infinity.

CONTENTS

"A republic, if you can keep it."

— Benjamin Franklin's response to Elizabeth Willing Powel's question
"Well, Doctor, what have we got, a republic or a monarchy?"[1]

ENOUGH ALREADY

HOW THE HELL DID WE GET HERE?

I ask myself this question almost every day. Making my way around Los Angeles, I encounter traffic-clogged streets, trash-strewn sidewalks, empty storefronts, and tent encampments occupied by the unhoused. I also hear stories from folks I meet about how tough life is today. It used to be that you could work hard and enjoy a reasonably comfortable middle-class lifestyle, even without a college degree. Not anymore. The cost of living is out of control. And thanks to sky-high home prices and an insurance crisis, it's almost impossible for working people to buy a home.

But California's problems don't stop there. What was once was a place of aspiration, immortalized in songs like the Mamas & the Papas' "California Dreamin'," is turning into a nightmare. Rising unemployment.[1] Failing schools.[2] Increasing retail theft.[3] The nation's highest poverty rate.[4] A health care crisis.[5] An enormous budget gap, in the tens of billions of dollars.[6] It's no wonder so many residents have been leaving the state in recent years. As one demographer says, noting the state's population declines, "California is no longer the preferred destination it used to be."[7]

Communities across America suffer from many of the problems that beset California. What I find most frustrating is that it doesn't have to be this way. I still remember what my home state used to be: a place of dynamism and hope, with safe communities, clean streets, and the best schools. During the final few decades of the twentieth century and into the twenty-first, California was a place where businesses thrived and created opportunities for millions. It was a place where hardworking people from other states and around the world came to better their lives and claim their share of the American dream. Growing up, I would ride my bike around my neighborhood in Encino or to my Little League games, just being a kid and never having to worry about my personal safety or whether my family would lose our modest home. I'm sure you, too, can recall better days in the communities where you live.

So, how did we get here? Our country still has the same natural resources it did decades ago. It's still the world's largest economy. It still has deeply engrained democratic institutions. What has changed, as I'll argue throughout these pages, is *us*—both the citizens and the leaders of this great democracy.

As a nation, we've lost sight of how to come together and solve problems for our collective benefit. Politics has become entertainment. It's a place to feel strong emotions, especially negative ones, as cynical politicians vie with one another to take ever more extreme positions. Other politicians today are well-intentioned and public-spirited, but they often lack the moral clarity, strength, and skills to drive meaningful progress. California and communities across America can enjoy better days again, but only if our elected·leaders get serious about making life better, and if the rest of us hold them accountable for doing so.

Accountable. Now, that's a word you don't hear nearly enough these days. It's also a word that carries deep, personal meaning for me.

As a kid in the late 1960s and early 1970s, I spent several magical summers at Brooktrails, a new subdivision of vacation homes being built in Northern California, near the town of Willits. I recall a newspaper advertisement from the era calling the place a "recreational paradise," and it was right. Blue skies, fresh mountain air, babbling brooks, endless acres of pristine redwood forest, friendly people—that was summer at Brooktrails.

In addition to home sites nestled among the trees, we had a big, rustic lodge with a restaurant and bar, a pool, tennis courts, a golf course, and cabins for staff. I say "we" because my dad was the head of sales and marketing for the company that owned Brooktrails. I was, therefore, kind of a big deal.

OK, not really. But at the time, it certainly felt like it! I got to sleep in a bedroom attached to the owner's cabin, where the property managers, Mr. and Mrs. Boltwood, lived. And I got to ride horses. An old black-and-white photo shows me perched on a saddle when I was maybe eight or nine. With the reins in my hands and a big grin plastered on my face, I look proud as heck.

Mainly what I did, though, starting when I was in third or

fourth grade, was work. My dad valued hard work and discipline, and he drummed it into my preadolescent brain that people who earned a paycheck by the sweat of their brow were most worthy of our respect and admiration. I wasn't legally old enough to earn a paycheck, but nobody seemed to care back then.

At first, I served as a busboy at the lodge. I would hustle around the tables, collect the dishes and glasses, and bring them in back to be washed. When I'd proved my mettle, I went on to help out wherever they needed me: as a waiter, a dishwasher, an assistant cook, a substitute front desk clerk, a maintenance guy. Sometimes I did administrative stuff, like add up the punch cards to calculate other employees' salaries. They even let me hang out at the bar and serve as a barback. I was, like, *ten years old*.

It was great earning extra money, but what I loved most was helping out and serving people, proving that I could be useful. I learned lots of real-world skills: how to scoop ice cream for one hundred people, how to paint cabins, how to make the fluffiest of pancakes, how to keep the kitchen properly stocked, how to clean tables and scrub pots so they shine. I also enjoyed making friends with my fellow workers. Although most were much older, they were consistently kind and welcoming. During off-hours when we hung out at the bar, they taught me to play a dice game called liar's poker and made me virgin Bloody Marys with sticks of beef jerky in them instead of celery.

It wasn't all fun and games. I took out my share of stinking garbage, and I came home tired and dirty at the end of each day. I also learned some formative life lessons.

One of the most important was imparted upon me one evening

when I was still working as a busboy. While staggering across the lodge's crowded dining room, struggling under the weight of about two dozen glasses on a massive tray, I either slipped or lost my balance—I'm not sure which. The next thing I knew, my arms gave way and the heavy load came tumbling down to the floor. *Crash!* The glasses were smashed—it was a total disaster.

The whole place went quiet. I could feel the heat rising in my cheeks, and my face turned fourteen shades of red. I was mortified. But as the conversation began to pick back up, I reached for a broom and began to sweep.

Later, my boss and I sat down to discuss the incident. What was I thinking, trying to bus so many glasses all at once? That was nuts—an accident waiting to happen. I needed to slow down and carry only what I could. I promised I would and said that I was sorry, and he accepted my apology. But the conversation wasn't over.

My boss explained that they'd be taking the cost of those broken glasses out of my paycheck. He wasn't trying to be mean, but it was only fair: You break it, you pay for it. That's how life works. Good intentions don't make up for bad results.

Getting my pay docked stung, but the lesson was transformative. I'd never thought much about the principle of accountability before. Now I realized that it made a ton of sense: If you mess up, you own it. You don't blame it on someone else. You don't cry and whine and make excuses. You don't cover up what you did. You take responsibility. You make it right. You pay for any damages. You say you're sorry. You do whatever it takes to make sure it doesn't happen again. You do better.

As I've since come to realize, this isn't just how a well-run business works. It's how life works. And it's how politics *should* work.

Can you imagine how much safer, happier, and more prosperous America would be if we closely tracked the performance of our elected officials and held them accountable to delivering the results they promised on the campaign trail? Or better yet, if politicians held *themselves* accountable? If they offered real, heartfelt apologies when they got it wrong, instead of fast-talking their way through bad press? If they looked upon government service not as an ego trip or a chance to enrich themselves, but as a dignified and honorable pursuit, an opportunity to serve and help others?

Accountability is a fundamental principle of a working democracy. If you live in a democracy, you must hold elected officials accountable at the ballot box for their performance, tossing out those who aren't getting the job done. Otherwise, the political system breaks down and problems don't get solved.

And that's where we find ourselves right now.

It's Time to Get Real

The need for accountability is what I call a "hard truth"—a basic, nonnegotiable fact, one that you might not like to hear but that you ignore at your peril.

If you have $100 to spend, for instance, you can't spend $130 without going into debt. You might *want* to spend $130 and still be debt-free. Others might *tell* you that you can do that. But you can't. The extra $30 has to come from somewhere—and you're the one who has to pay it. That's a hard truth.

Likewise, you might *want* to support poorly performing officials because they're on your political team or because they pander to your emotional response in some way. But you can't do so without paying a heavy price. That's the hard truth—one so foundational, so general, that again we can think of it as an essential principle of politics.

Businesspeople like me know a lot about hard truths, both the big, foundational kinds and the smaller, more specific ones. We face them all the time, notably every quarter as we balance our books. Basic math is nonnegotiable. If we spend more than the revenues we bring in, we lose money. To become profitable, we must slash costs or find ways to operate better and more cheaply. Doing what's necessary to stay profitable isn't easy or comfortable, but we have no choice. If we pretend that math isn't real, then sooner or later we go out of business. One plus one doesn't equal three; it equals two. Acting like it equals three leads to financial ruin.

Our country has neglected a whole litany of hard truths—including some big, foundational ones—for some time now. The consequences are a lot more severe than a tray of broken glasses. Most Americans today believe that our political system is dysfunctional and that our country is on the wrong track.[8] They've lost faith in the American dream: the notion that if you work hard, you can rise up, regardless of where you start or who you are. And they no longer believe in our democratic institutions. Consider that according to a 2023 survey, only 8 percent had a lot of confidence in Congress.[9] I know what you're thinking: *What were those 8 percent smoking?*

Frustration with the status quo helps us understand Donald Trump's startling comeback in the 2024 election. Political strategists will debate ad nauseam how a race that had seemed so tight could have broken so decisively for a candidate with legal baggage, marked authoritarian tendencies, and endless scandals under his belt. But at its core, the question isn't all that complicated. Americans today are pissed off with our national politics. They *want* a proven norm-breaker like Trump to come in and dash it all to pieces. Trump's win is a protest vote against elites and traditionalists in both parties. On November 5, 2024, voters sent an unmistakable message: "Washington, do things differently!"

Make no mistake: I deeply disagree with many of Trump's radical policy stances. But I also reject the idea of unleashing a blanket "resistance" against the new administration, as some on the left have advocated. We needn't kowtow to every radical policy proposal, but we must respect the wisdom and wishes of the electorate, recognizing that the politics of the past just aren't suited to meeting the needs of Americans today. We should be willing to consider the perspectives of those with whom we disagree and recommit ourselves to finding common ground. That means fighting back not just against the excesses of a second Trump administration, but against divisive tendencies on both sides of the political divide. It means doing our best to replace ideological warfare with a new, more centrist kind of pragmatism. It means unifying around a shared resolve to constructively move forward.

For years now, too many of our nation's elected officials have been causing damage rather than advancing the public good.

Declaring war on so-called socialists and immigrants while over-turning centuries of American tradition, populists and nativists on the political far right have sought to establish an authoritarian government. They've challenged and disrupted the rule of law and spouted rhetoric that often seems racist, homophobic, and transphobic. They've also spread misinformation, turning neighbors against one another and undermining social trust. We should continue to fight this in every form.

But right-wingers by no means have the market cornered when it comes to extreme and divisive rhetoric. When criticizing Israel, some far-left voices veer into dangerous anti-Semitism, all while "canceling" those who disagree with them. Likewise, anticapitalists on the left often demonize business and seek to greatly diminish or even do away with our system of free enterprise.

Constant fighting between the extreme right and left has done little except to polarize voters, degrading our democratic system and rendering it incapable of solving urgent problems. As we yell louder, the problems worsen. Across the country, such dysfunction has led to not only political gridlock but debates and policies that border on the absurd and that, frankly, represent a total disdain for hard truths.

Should we *really* be spending so much time arguing about pronouns at a time when record numbers of people are homeless and many Americans are struggling to buy their first houses? Given the need to make more progress addressing retail theft in American cities, is it *really* a good idea to treat many property thefts as misdemeanor offenses (as California does) instead of prosecuting to the full extent of the law?[10]

While we're at it, in our well-intentioned attempts at addressing widespread inequity, should we demonize big business and successful entrepreneurs even though we need their savvy, drive, and ambition to help fuel the economy and generate prosperity for all? Should we promote efforts to build more affordable housing, and then enforce a litany of rules that make such housing all but impossible to actually build? Should we talk about the need to create economic opportunity and then chase businesses away with high taxes and onerous regulations?

I don't know about you, but one word jumps to my mind: *Enough!*

We've got to get real, folks. We've got to move past the wedge issues, the "gotcha" attacks, the unproductive "whataboutism," the media-baiting. We've got to set aside the political theater, face hard truths, and make decisions that might not please everybody all the time but that will set us right. We've got to look beyond our partisan silos and entrenched assumptions so we can reorient ourselves around a common vision.

In the chapters that follow, I set out *seven hard truths* we Americans must face in 2025 and beyond if we're going to finally get real, pull together, and turn our country around. These truths embody the commonsense principles we need in order to solve some of our most urgent problems. We can convey these principles in just a few simple words: *Integrity. Collaboration. Lawfulness. Economic inclusivity. Competence. Public-spiritedness. Trust.* Dedication to these core ideas has defined American politics at its best, and I know those same ideas will work again to get us back on track.

From Busboy to Boardroom

I believe in these principles because I grew up with them and later used them to succeed in business, serve in government roles, and give back to the community. I got started in real estate development, achieved some early successes, moved to Nevada, and built a multibillion-dollar global business in the vacation ownership and hospitality industry. In addition to creating thousands of jobs, I ran a first-of-its-kind tourism board for the United States and found numerous other ways—big and small—to do some real good. Then I returned to the Golden State, bringing all these lessons back home. The seven principles allowed me to defy the odds, fix a company and an industry that others had left for dead, and turn them into tourism powerhouses.

I'll be the first to admit that my journey from busboy to boardroom was wholly unexpected. Although I always will be a busboy at heart, I've done all kinds of stuff in my life, constantly pivoting to follow what my heart and gut told me, and then pivoting some more. I've consistently tackled new and unforeseen problems, arriving at creative solutions that really work and creating opportunities for countless others. The pathway from busboy to boardroom has been anything but dull.

Let me sketch out that pathway for you a little.

As I mentioned earlier, growing up in Southern California was awesome in an ordinary kind of way. I did the kinds of things boys my age did: rode the bus to school, played baseball (and totally sucked at it), joined the Boy Scouts. My dad worked hard and was gone half of every week, but every Sunday evening we had dinner as a family, usually Chinese food or takeout from this local place called Pioneer Chicken. Trips to McDonald's, when they happened, were a big, big deal. Once a week, my grandfather would take my brother, my sister, and me to the batting cages or to a movie, and afterward we'd each get a Slurpee and exactly one piece of candy. We took vacations as a family, but not on fancy junkets to Europe; we hopped in our station wagon and drove somewhere, staying at a Holiday Inn.

Throughout my childhood, I went to a mix of public and private schools. Although I was Jewish and the descendant of Russian immigrants, I went to an Episcopalian school starting in seventh grade. I served as chair of the student congress and trained in public speaking. I seemed to have a knack for it: I won thirteen gavels in six years, the most in the San Fernando Valley. But I had no clue back then that I would build a career in business. I dreamed of becoming a doctor, and more specifically, a heart surgeon.

At age sixteen, I landed a volunteer position at Cedars-Sinai Medical Center, first in the emergency room and then in a department performing cardiothoracic research. From watching TV shows like *Marcus Welby, M.D.* and *Emergency!*, I knew that health care was the noblest, most heroic profession there was. But now I was tasked with doing some pretty gnarly stuff—like handling cadavers in the morgue. On rare occasions, I was allowed to accompany medical staff into operating rooms to observe the heart surgeons at work. It was mind-blowing and awe-inspiring. Back in those days, they didn't have modern, noninvasive techniques. The surgeons were using basic tools and their own hands to fix one of the body's most complex organs and to save patients' lives. I wanted to do *that*.

As it turned out, life had other plans for me. At one point, while talking to the head of the pathology department, I had an idea about how they could use computers to read the test results and then just pop out a treatment recommendation for doctors to use. Bear in mind, this was during the early 1980s. I had the right idea; I just needed the technology to catch up.

"Cloobeck," the department head replied, "you should go into business."

I blew off that idea. I didn't know anything about business—it was the furthest thing from my mind. But that doctor was on to something.

Upon graduating from high school, I spent a year attending the University of Southern California before transferring to Brandeis University with the goal of preparing for medical school. I studied biology, neurology, physics, psychology, and chemistry (both organic and inorganic), returning over the summers to work at Cedars-Sinai. But as the years passed, I had to face two hard truths about my studies.

First, no matter how much I tried, I was a lackluster writer— OK, a crappy writer. This made sense later when I was diagnosed with dyslexia. One of my college professors, Margret Rey, coauthor of the famous Curious George books, was pretty clear about my lack of literary talent. Believe me, when a living legend gives you harsh feedback, it has an impact. Even today, dyslexia greatly inhibits me from reading and writing text. I can't read a script or teleprompter very well—I have a tendency to twist words. On the other hand, I have a photographic memory and can recall even the slightest details from conversations I have. I could author this book only because I had people on my team working with me to capture my ideas on paper, reading portions of text aloud again and again for me to review, all the while keeping track of sources and endnotes.

The second hard truth I had to face was that I didn't have the patience to practice medicine after all. It didn't help that when doing endocrinological research on pancreatic islets at the University of California, Los Angeles (UCLA), I was tasked with experiments using lab rats. No open heart surgery? No time conversing with doctors about how they saw the profession evolving and improving? No ability to interact with real people—not even dead ones? I absolutely hated it.

Not knowing what to do with myself, I decided after graduating with my bachelor's degree in the spring of 1983 to try real estate. My father was in the business, so I had some opportunities there. After five shots on goal, I finally got my real estate license. That summer, I enrolled in Accounting 101 and 102 at California State University, Northridge (CSUN), and started auditing a business class at night at UCLA. Brandeis hadn't offered business classes, so this was my chance to get some valuable background knowledge.

When autumn rolled around, I took a job at a company that developed shopping centers in Orange County, California. Among other tasks, my boss assigned me to drive every street in the five counties of Southern California, taking note of parcels of land where it would make sense to build a shopping center. No joke—I went *everywhere*, from Ventura down to San Diego. Since we didn't have mobile phones or navigation apps back then, I kept track using paper maps, placing little dots on them and writing down the addresses. Then I cold-called the owners of the parcels and asked if they'd be interested in selling.

I enjoyed the work, and it seemed that I was good at it. After a few years, though, I started getting antsy. I wanted more responsibility, but my job had no upward mobility and little opportunity for risk-taking. I yearned to understand every facet of the real estate development business, to make my own decisions. I wanted to *build* something and take charge of my own destiny.

When the company I worked for reneged on a bonus they'd promised me, I decided to leave my job—against my father's advice—and go out on my own. I used every last penny of my savings to start a business in the same line of work: developing shopping centers. As I soon found out, there was something utterly thrilling about having my own shop and being the one to sign the front of the check. Applying what I'd already learned, I wound up putting together a number of deals over the next few years, when I was in my mid to late twenties, developing sites across Southern California. I did very well—except for one deal that nearly killed me.

It was during the recession of the late 1980s, and all the businesses that had signed on to rent space in a shopping center I was building pulled out, citing economic hardship. The builder I hired also went out of business, as did the subcontractors they hired. This is the downside of being in business for yourself: When times get tough, there is nobody else to fall back on.

Although my situation seemed bleak, I got busy. I had minimal experience in construction, but I served as my own general contractor, learning as I went. I had to learn how to read architectural plans, not to mention a thousand other tasks related to putting up a building. I got the place built, even doing some of the work myself to save money. In the evenings, I went out into the market and hustled, signing up a slew of new tenants. I made all kinds of rookie errors—like paying twice for lumber and failing to get the right price on a retaining wall. But in the end, I was able to transfer ownership of the property to a government agency called the Resolution Trust Corporation without having to go through bankruptcy or accruing any other penalties. It was my biggest business blunder, but I survived, and the tremendous practical wisdom I gained would set me up for future success.

I didn't have to wait long to put my newfound construction experience to work. During the early 1990s, I partnered with my father to build a project in Las Vegas called Polo Plaza and Polo Towers. My father had started his own company in the city, looking to get into the vacation ownership business that had been taking off in the United States. To continue to grow, he needed to increase his inventory. Polo Towers, located right on the city's famous Strip near the big casinos, would be his first build and the first high-rise in the country that would be marketed and sold to customers on a time-share basis. It would also be the first high-rise I'd ever built.

While my father took charge of organizing the financing we'd need for the project, I oversaw just about everything else, getting the building constructed and then operating the business.

Running Polo Towers was a massive undertaking. I had to master everything involved in operating a premium vacation resort, from maintenance to food service to all the back-end stuff. And I had to master marketing and sales—a particularly heavy lift. The time-share and hospitality industry back then was known for marginal properties and questionable sales practices. In launching the project, we had to not only deliver a premium experience but persuade customers to take a chance on us. We had to shift their understanding of what time-share and hospitality *could be*: a high-quality, hugely desirable vacation experience that was also a fantastic value. It was tough, but we managed to get people to buy into our Polo Towers dream. Upon opening in December 1992, Polo Towers was a gigantic success that helped to change the meaning of time-share and hospitality in America.

My father helped run the business for a few years. Then, in 1996, he sold his company, in which I had a small stake, and I stayed on as cochair to help run and grow it. I had a knack for the hospitality business—maybe it was the central tenets of service and respect for hard work that I'd learned all those years ago at Brooktrails. I had a vision for the company, and over the next few years I wound up buying out the other equity partners until eventually I owned the company outright. Although I took out a sixty-month loan to make that happen, I'm proud to say I was able to pay it back in its entirety in just thirty-seven months. We were offering our customers great value, and they were snapping up our vacation ownership offerings, making us quite profitable and giving us excellent cash flow.

The tragedy of 9/11 hit the travel industry hard, but we hunkered down and managed to thrive, pleasing customers and continuing to expand our business. Our company was doing so well, in fact, that in 2003 Marriott made an attractive offer to buy it from me. I sold them many of the company's assets but kept Polo Towers and our name—Diamond Resorts.

There was one problem: Retirement didn't sit well with me. I get bored when I'm not actually doing something. So I looked around for a new opportunity. In 2007, I found it. My team and I at Diamond Resorts, along with a group of investors, completed the $700 million acquisition of Sunterra, a struggling time-share and hospitality company with dozens of resorts around the world, creating one of the industry's largest players.

When I say that Sunterra was "struggling," what I really mean is that it was on death's door. You know those patients I saw flat on their backs, being operated on by heart surgeons at Cedars-Sinai? That was Sunterra. The company was not just poorly managed but battered by an accounting scandal; it was hemorrhaging both money and its most talented employees. It had cultural issues, leadership issues, and legal issues, facing no fewer than ninety-nine active lawsuits. Others in the time-share and hospitality business said I was crazy. The company was unfixable and had been for some time. It was unmanageable, unleadable. They gave me six months, maybe a year, before I lost my shirt.

They were wrong. Over the next decade, my team and I turned Sunterra around, branding it Diamond Resorts International and transforming it into an industry superstar. In the process, we bolstered the reputation of the entire time-share and hospitality industry, infusing ethics into the business and innovating in ways that delivered incredible value to customers. It wasn't easy— the Great Recession hit just as we were undertaking significant changes in the company. But we got through it, and between 2010 and 2015, our revenues skyrocketed from $370 million to about $950 million.[11]

By 2013, when we took the company public, we had grown to include over three hundred vacation resorts in thirty-three countries around the world.[12] In 2016, we sold Diamond Resorts International to the private equity firm Apollo Global Management for $2.2 billion. In 2021, Apollo in turn sold the company to Hilton Grand Vacations, which owns it today.

In the pages that follow, I'll expand on certain elements of our success.[13] But basically, it comes down to this: Where nearly everyone else saw a total train wreck, I saw potential. I understood what Sunterra's strengths were, not least its tremendous portfolio of properties. And I imagined what the company might become were it managed properly. To ensure that we *did* manage it better, my team and I carefully studied the organization, listening closely to customers and facing the hard truths about everything that was wrong.

Imagine if our elected leaders did the same with voters, really listening to understand better what they want!

In our case, we realized that customers sought three core elements: simplicity, choice, and comfort. Rather than try some new-fangled management philosophy or look to some technological innovation to solve all of the company's problems, we focused on infusing those tenets into everything we did. In the process, we implemented the basics that every business must get right to sustain itself over the long term. We empowered team members to provide exceptional, over-the-top customer service—what we came to call "The Meaning of Yes." We treated customers, employees, and other stakeholders fairly, working closely with unions, including the International Longshoremen's Association, the United Brotherhood of Carpenters and Joiners of America, the International Brotherhood of Teamsters, and UNITE HERE, both nationally and internationally. We held people in our company accountable. We welcomed everyone in and built trust. We found practical, commonsense solutions to problems. We contributed to the greater good.

It's one thing to turn around a failing company, but how do I know principles gleaned from that experience will also work in the political arena? Well, because I've applied them there myself.

Even before we sold Diamond Resorts International, I notched some early successes as an activist and concerned citizen in Nevada and beyond. I spearheaded efforts to beautify the Las Vegas Strip, prevent Nevada's university system from charging excessive tuition to in-state students, and prevent the federal government from building a nuclear waste dump less than one hundred miles from Las Vegas. I got busy at the grassroots level, participating in community meetings and knocking on the doors of decision-makers. Some might have been surprised to see a young guy like me with so much passion and energy for public service, but I loved the work of collaborating with a diverse array of players to solve problems and improve our community.

During the early 2010s, I served as the first chairman of Brand USA, an innovative public-private partnership that emerged as America's first national tourism bureau, promoting our country to the world as a travel destination. More recently, I served as chairman of the Nevada Athletic Commission and played a key role in the campaign to rename Las Vegas's airport after the great US Senator Harry Reid. I also began a partnership with Los Angeles Mayor Karen Bass to create new affordable housing solutions in the city via an initiative called LA4LA. To succeed in these roles, I did tons of homework to understand the intricacies of legislation, regulation, and adjudication so I could arrive at solutions that not only were effective but required no additional taxpayer dollars. Ultimately, I worked to drive progress by facing—and respecting—hard truths, using them to arrive at real, honest, consensus-driven improvements.

Repairing the Foundation

Facing Hard Truths draws on my experiences to present a powerful formula for turning around our country. The first three hard truths I discuss in this book correspond to principles for improving American leadership and political discourse. In **Hard Truth #1**, I argue for a collective recommitment to the idea of integrity and fighting for what's right. As I relate in **Hard Truth #2**, though, it's important not to take such fighting too far; we must avoid polarization and retain a capacity for healthy collaboration. In **Hard Truth #3**, I assert that we must also stay in bounds legally and ethically, rededicating ourselves generally to upholding values, fairness, and the rule of law.

The next portion of the book moves to matters of policy. **Hard Truth #4** argues for approaches that foster economic inclusivity and raise *all* of us up. Of course, having the right policy notions isn't enough. We also must get far better at executing them—an argument I make in **Hard Truth #5**.

In the final two chapters, I consider how we might rebuild American community. **Hard Truth #6** advocates for more public-spiritedness among both citizens and leaders, while **Hard Truth #7** calls upon all of us to take steps to rebuild social trust. The epilogue brings together these disparate strands, calling for a new era of seriousness in which we come together to revitalize our great nation.

The truths Americans must embrace are indeed hard, but I hope that you'll come away from this book more optimistic and inspired than when you first picked it up. I don't care whether you're liberal, conservative, Black, white, Asian, Hispanic, male, female, nonbinary, urban, rural, young, old, gay, straight, Christian, Jewish, Muslim, green, purple, or—someone has to say it—*orange*. I also don't care whom you've voted for in the past—whether you've been blue state all the way and cast your ballot for Kamala Harris, or whether you've been a red-hatted, Fox News–loving, MAGA machine whose support for Donald Trump has never wavered. I speak to you simply as a fellow citizen, voter, and community member, hoping to enlist your help in a shared project of getting our democracy back on track by bringing commonsense thinking back into politics.

My message, ultimately, is one of love, compassion, and fiscal responsibility, with law and order worked in for good measure. Everybody's welcome in these pages, because we're all Americans, and we all have common interests. I want us to reconcile with one another, take stock of reality, and most of all, get stuff done for our collective benefit. There's plenty today that divides us, but on the most important issues that affect us all, there's *way* more room for consensus than most politicians on both sides would have you believe. When we set aside the partisan rancor and remember some core principles that we all share, the world suddenly seems much simpler and saner.

I know from my experience and from ongoing conversations with my fellow Americans of all walks of life that practical solutions exist across the political divide. There are innovative policies and programs that, if implemented, would make us all safer, more prosperous, and more comfortable in our communities. No, we won't be able to tap these solutions all at once. It took years to turn Sunterra around, and it'll take years to turn America around too. But we *can* get there if we face the hard truths first.

The foundation is cracked, folks—quite severely so in some places. So, let's fix it! By noticing what's wrong and committing ourselves to make it right, we can build a more stable society that allows us *all* to flourish.

LIFE IS TOUGH— GET A HELMET

IF YOU'RE NOT FAMILIAR WITH MY MENTOR, the late Senator Harry Reid, then let me tell you: He was a fighter. There aren't many US senators who once competed as amateur boxers. There aren't many who began their careers risking life and limb to rid their city of dangerous mobsters. There certainly aren't many who racked up an enviable legislative record thanks to their utter mastery of hand-to-hand political combat.

Harry grew up dirt-poor in Searchlight, Nevada, a hardscrabble mining town that was years past its heyday. Truly, the sort of poverty he endured is hard to imagine today. His childhood home was made of chicken wire and railroad ties and could only graciously be described as a shack. There was no money for extras, let alone décor; the one item tacked onto the walls was an aging pillowcase with stitching that read: *We Can. We Will. We Must.*[1]

Harry's father was a miner and chronically short of cash, his mother a laundress for the town's local brothels, including one with a pool where, incidentally, Harry learned to swim.[2] Since his town had no high school, he famously had to hitch rides to Henderson, located about forty miles away, to continue his education. But Harry refused to be defined by his humble origins. He had bigger things in mind for his life, and he knew he could, he would, he must persevere.

After graduating from college and then law school, Harry served as Henderson's city attorney and then as Nevada's lieutenant governor.[3] In 1977, he was appointed to the Nevada Gaming Commission, the body charged with regulating the state's gambling industry. As Harry himself would later admit, he had little idea what he was getting himself into. He had never even gambled before![4] He certainly didn't expect to find himself at the heart of efforts to rid Las Vegas of its long-standing mob influence so the city could modernize and grow. As Harry put it, "I would quickly learn that decisions we made and actions we took would mean the difference between Las Vegas fulfilling its potential as the city of the future or slipping back into its criminal past. And I would quickly realize that there was real danger involved in this job."[5]

Over the next several years, Harry had countless colorful experiences. He helped the FBI bust men who tried to bribe him, participating in a sting operation in his office that ended in their arrest. "It seemed unbelievable to me at the time that this was really happening," Harry later recalled. Law enforcement agents were supposed to burst in when Harry gave a prearranged signal, but the office door was locked. Only when a flustered Harry managed to casually unlatch the door did the agents finally appear and begin arresting the suspects. At this point, Harry let his emotions get the better of him. Furious at what he'd been put through, he grabbed at one of the suspects, shouting, "You son of a bitch, you tried to bribe me!"[6] The agents had to physically intercede to end the altercation.

As a member of the Nevada Gaming Commission, Harry played a role in banning infamous mobsters Anthony Spilotro and Frank "Lefty" Rosenthal from setting foot in Las Vegas casinos. Such episodes led to repeated threats on his life. After the FBI investigation into the workings of the Kansas City mob in Las Vegas became public, a threat directed at Harry was so serious that he had to receive police protection. On another occasion, someone rigged one of the Reid family cars with a bomb; thankfully, Harry's wife, Landra, discovered it before it could go off.

"The death threats seemed to come almost cyclically," he recounted. "Whenever my picture ran in one of the local newspapers, I could expect another series of bizarre letters or phone calls."[7]

A lesser man might have wilted under the pressure, but not Harry. Committed to fulfilling his public service, he didn't think about resigning and walking away. He reacted to the bomb incident by making a practice of always starting his car by remote control, and Landra did the same. Harry also began carrying a gun and "trained in evasive driving maneuvers, so that I might better throw off a pursuer." In short, he was one tough customer, who stood and fought for what he thought was right.

His successful tenure on the gaming commission would steel him for all the political fights he would face in Washington, DC. As Harry would tell me and plenty of others, whenever people remarked on the bitterness of national politics, he would reflect on what he'd experienced in Las Vegas, which was far harsher by comparison.[8]

As Senate majority leader, Harry didn't waver or flip-flop when faced with staunch political opposition. He didn't stand down and make excuses. Democrats and Republicans alike consider him the most effective tactician Congress has ever known. There's a reason that in 2005 he was able to defeat George W. Bush's efforts to do away with Social Security as a government benefit.[9] There's a reason that in 2009 he was able to get all sixty members of the Democratic caucus to vote for the Affordable Care Act.[10] As a former member of his staff shares, "No modern Democrat has understood how to leverage power versus the Republicans like Reid. He never waited around for an epiphany—he attacked and attacked some more—and won most of the fights."[11]

Like any good boxer, Harry knew how to take a hit when it served his ultimate purpose: to win. "He wasn't irrational," his former colleague Senator Tom Daschle says. "He was fearless. After all, how do you convince a person who had to hitchhike forty miles a day just to attend high school that he couldn't accomplish anything he set his mind to? It made him a formidable opponent, but an even better ally."[12]

I had the good fortune of crossing paths relatively early with Harry and watching his political career blossom. We first met when he was a young lawyer, just starting out, working as my father's outside attorney. I followed his career as he became a member of the US House of Representatives, a senator, and then majority leader. As I became involved in Nevada politics, Harry took me under his wing, teaching me everything he knew not just about how to fight, but how to get things *done*. Getting to know him personally, I recognized that he was a striking exemplar of integrity—someone whose deeds always matched his ideals, even when taking a stand was difficult, risky, or otherwise inconvenient. I realized, too, that I wanted to display that kind of integrity, being every bit as strong, fearless, and determined as Harry was.

That aspiration, unfortunately, seems to make me something of an odd man out today. From where I sit, displays of integrity can be pretty hard to find, and I think it has to do with a particular kind of cultural rot that has taken hold. We like to presume that everything is owed to us, and this warped perspective of entitlement leads us to see ourselves as victims of a pervasive unfairness. We mope and whine about how deprived and disempowered we are, taking every microaggression as "proof" that we're being brutally wronged.

Paradoxically, this oversimplified view of the world seems to render us less capable of distinguishing *real* abuses around us and standing up to fight them. We become less inclined to parse through nuance and ambiguity to arrive at clear moral judgments when they count the most. Even when we do possess moral clarity, we too often equivocate rather than stick up for our beliefs. Think of the phenomenon of establishing "safe spaces." I get the impulse behind them: We want everyone on college campuses to feel like they belong. But they come with a hidden cost. Feeling victimized, young people on college campuses shield themselves from hearing other points of view, which in turn can limit their ability to pose critical questions and stand up for others around them.

If we want to put America on a better path, this stance of passivity and inaction simply won't cut it. We must rediscover a sensitivity to actual injustice—and rededicate ourselves to fighting for what's right.

A Nation of Fighters, Not Whiners

As scarce as it seems to be today, a willingness to champion truth, justice, fairness, propriety, and other standards is actually an important part of the American story. I'm not a historian by any means, but please indulge me just a little.

When the British crown decided it would force American colonists to pay taxes on tea—and further, to buy their tea from the officially sanctioned East India Company—the Sons of Liberty responded with a resounding, "*Hell*, no!" They weren't going to quietly agree to indulge a monopoly and pay the royal taxes, cowering over what might happen otherwise. They wouldn't content themselves with philosophizing about why taxes were unjust. They didn't endlessly debate what to do or form a committee to study the issue. No. They took *action*. In the dark of night, dozens of men boarded boats owned by the East India Company and threw the damn tea leaves into the water.[13]

I'm a firm believer in the rule of law, but in this instance the powers that be were abusing their authority, and there was no other recourse than to take a stand. The British monarchy wanted to tax the colonists without giving them any say at all as to how that money was spent. In the eyes of the colonists, taxation without representation wasn't right. Some two years later, when the colonies formally declared their independence, they did it explicitly in the name of rectitude and integrity, pointing to a long history of "repeated injuries and usurpations, all having in direct object the establishment of an absolute Tyranny."[14]

Americans have contested injustice, abuse, and impropriety on many other occasions. We all know or have heard of people in our communities who have stood up to bullies, stopped crimes as they were happening, and provided support to people who were exploited or hurt by others. But this noble tendency seems to have faded lately—a victim of our dwindling sense of civic responsibility generally.

"Sacrifice for the common good feels anachronistic," Connecticut Senator Chris Murphy and his coauthor pointed out. "Everything not nailed down has been commoditized or turned into a source of personal enrichment. The daily 'shout' shows and nonstop social media hostility push us into corners and reward balkanization. Sacrificing personal gain for the common good or treating people with different views respectfully or prioritizing collective success over individual success—it's all for the suckers."[15]

Our dwindling willingness to stand up for what's right takes on a number of guises. We see it in surveys showing that most people wouldn't serve in the military in the event of another war.[16] If Russia were to attack a NATO country unprovoked or if China were to do the same to Taiwan, why would we want to protect *them*? On the streets of our own country, we sometimes see bystanders failing to intervene as an injustice is being perpetrated, preferring to stand by and take video that they can post online. Instead of speaking up forcefully on social media when a vulnerable person is being attacked, we might leave snarky comments under a cloak of anonymity. Sure, we'll take a stand—when we know we won't bear any costs or consequences.

We're not only more cynical today about politics and institutions, but also more fearful, more isolated, and more individualistic,[17] all of which disinclines us to step up when we spot injustices that affect others. But I think our waning refusal to fight for what's true, right, or fair reflects some bigger problems.

First, we've become emotionally distant from the concepts of decency and truth; as I point out later, we're not teaching young people moral clarity the way we used to. But second, and perhaps more important, we've eroded our collective sense of agency—our notion of ourselves as actors in the world. Many of us just don't see much of a connection between our own efforts and actual results in our lives anymore. As a result, we're less motivated to take positive, meaningful action of many kinds, including stepping up and helping others.

Former Secretary of Labor Robert Reich wrote back in 2015 that in his travels around the country, he was "struck by how utterly powerless most people feel."[18] He blamed this on what he perceived as our lack of real options as consumers and workers thanks to consolidation in industry, and on our lack of a voice thanks to the decline of labor unions. The big corporations have more power whereas we have less, and so we feel disempowered and lacking in agency.

Such conditions persist today, but our sense of powerlessness might be even worse as we face additional social and economic pressures that feel beyond our control. In a 2022 study, the American Psychological Association reported finding "a battered American psyche, facing a barrage of external stressors that are mostly out of personal control. The survey found a majority of adults are disheartened by government and political divisiveness, daunted by historic inflation levels, and dismayed by widespread violence."[19] Other surveys suggest stress might be a global phenomenon related to turbulent economic and political conditions and the insecurity they bring. "In the US and some other Western countries," one researcher said in 2024, such conditions have "led to a perceived loss of agency, with consumers feeling powerless in the face of continued uncertainty."[20]

As bad as all this is, I would point to another cause of this erosion of agency, at least in the United States: our fading belief in this country as a working meritocracy. When economic inequality escalates and upward mobility becomes more difficult, as in recent decades, our efforts and talent don't seem to mean very much. The system seems rigged against us, offering rewards to people and organizations that do little to deserve them. In fact, according to a 2024 poll, a sizable majority of people in our country—almost three-quarters—believe the American dream is no longer a viable possibility.[21] So, why even try to move ahead?

Cultural changes, too, have led to the degradation of meritocratic ideas, and with it, the link between personal effort and results in the world. Today, just about every kid gets a trophy academically, whether or not they actually worked for it. You see this at Harvard, where in 2022 over 70 percent of graduating students had a GPA of 3.8 or above.[22] We inflate grades because we want kids to feel good about themselves. Everyone has to be special, unique, exceptional, gifted. That's infantilizing—and grossly unfair. What about the kids who actually worked hard and excelled?

As a faculty member told students in a viral 2012 commencement address at a high school in Wellesley, Massachusetts, "You're not special. You're not exceptional, contrary to what your . . . soccer trophy suggests, your glowing seventh-grade report card."[23] Talk about hard truths! But he had a point. As a consequence of giving everyone a trophy and swearing that everyone is special, we embed in our citizens the idea that you don't have to strive hard to achieve distinction. You can just lie on your couch watching TikToks all day. As the Wellesley teacher remarked, "We have of late, we Americans, to our detriment come to love accolades more than genuine achievement. We have come to see them as the point. And we are happy to compromise standards or ignore reality if we suspect that's the quickest way, or only way, to have something to put on the mantelpiece."

Does this sound familiar? These days, *feelings* matter most—not excellence, dedication, or sacrifice, but the desperate need to feel good about ourselves even when it's not justified. And we wonder why entrepreneurship has declined, why kids today seem so entitled, why performance standards have dropped, why our society in general, to quote common slang, seems sort of "mid."[24]

Obviously, many factors combine to produce social and cultural trends such as these, but a decline in meritocratic ideals is one of them. In a world where everyone supposedly wins, we all suffer a massive loss. Our drive to conquer, to surpass, to excel withers and dies, and so does our broader sense of agency. The message we collectively receive is: *Don't try hard. Don't take action. What you do doesn't really matter.* As the Wellesley commencement speaker put it, "No longer is it how you play the game. No longer is it even whether you win or lose. Or learn. Or grow. Or enjoy yourself doing it. Now it's 'So what does this get me?' As a consequence, we've cheapened worthy endeavors . . . It's an epidemic."

Instead of pulling ourselves up by the bootstraps, many of us—especially those coming from a position of privilege—seem to have adopted a new pastime: whining. We're conditioned to obsess about how *unfair* or *unjust* we think everything is. We've become so entitled that we now expect the bounties of life will be handed to us regardless of what we've done to earn them. When we don't receive what we think we're owed, we become aggrieved and paint ourselves as victims, embracing the characterization as people utterly bereft of agency. As *New York Times* columnist Frank Bruni observed, ours is an "age of grievance" in which nearly everyone seems to think themselves oppressed by someone. "The American soundtrack has become a cacophony of competing complaints," Bruni says. "Some are righteous and others specious. Some are urgent and others frivolous. Those distinctions are too often lost on the complainers. How they feel is all that matters—it's their greatest truth—and they feel cheated."[25]

Grievance isn't inherently bad. If we weren't so aggrieved, we wouldn't have decided to rebel against England and fight a war of independence. "Across the nearly 250 years of our existence as a country, grievance has been the engine of morally urgent change, the principle force in propelling us . . . toward the 'more perfect union' we so frequently invoke," Bruni asserts. The difference now is that grievance has gotten out of hand.

"What happens," Bruni rhetorically asks, "when all sorts of grievances . . . are jumbled together? When grievances become all-encompassing lenses, all-purpose reflexes, default settings? When people take their grievances to extreme and even violent lengths that they didn't before?"[26] The answer: Our commitment to general, universal principles of fairness wanes, replaced by a much narrower concept—fairness primarily for *us* and the people who fit into our narrow identity group.

Meanwhile, as I've suggested, our broader sense of agency and control over our destiny fades, and with it, our inclination to take action. We complain endlessly but don't actually take responsibility and do something about it. When confronted with real abuse, injustice, and impropriety, we don't stand up and fight.

What's the solution? How do we recover a sense of ourselves as moral actors, with a deep and abiding responsibility toward our fellow humans? Here's a thought: Let's stop looking for others to solve our problems, and instead start looking in the mirror.

To my mind, rebuilding our personal sense of agency starts with focusing on working hard and making something of ourselves. We need to rediscover our meritocratic tradition, reconnecting the concept of success with those of grit, fortitude, and ingenuity.

That's easy for a successful white guy like you to say, Cloobeck, you might be thinking. *You are privileged and always have been.* I've heard it before. And to be honest, there's some truth to it. Yes, starting out in the 1980s I had advantages—no doubt about it. I grew up during peacetime, was able to get into great schools, and had a supportive family. But my greatest privilege was a father who instilled in me the value of hard work. Inspired by his example, I started from zero and built up my fortunes through *decades* of near-constant toil. Long nights. Weekends. Exhausting travel that took me away from my kids. Actually, I started from less than zero. During the 2000s, when I was trying to build my business, my dad's business went bankrupt. I bailed him out—to the tune of $20 million. In effect, I started at negative $20 million and went on from there to build Diamond Resorts, a company that we eventually sold for over $2 billion.

I know it's still possible to achieve anything in America, even with all of its flaws, so long as you apply yourself and never, ever give up. Most of all, I know that I can act and have an impact on the world, and not just in my business life. If I see something that isn't right, I have the power to step up, take a stand, and make a difference.

My lived experience exposed me to the joys and rewards of hard work, and it helped me to see the damage that an entitlement mindset can cause to the process of striving and achieving. We must start celebrating hard work again as the pathway to success—and we must take identity out of the equation when making decisions about people. Instead we must select and advance the best, hardest-working, most talented people—end of story.

"No way!" progressives say. "You're just going to fall prey to your own implicit biases and hire more people who look like you." While that's a danger, we shouldn't allow it to limit us. Experience suggests that taking identity out of the picture *can* increase diversity. Here's an example: The best American orchestras used to be populated almost entirely with male musicians. Today, over 30 percent of members are female. Blind auditions, which orchestras adopted decades ago, made the difference. Job candidates now audition behind a screen, so evaluators can't see their identity.[27] Take identity out of the equation, and you can focus more on quality and talent.

Across the economy, we can select people for jobs in ways that check our biases while also upholding the principles of meritocracy and equality of opportunity. I know this because I've done it myself. During my time at Diamond Resorts, I welcomed a diverse group of people to my senior leadership team. Northerners, Southerners, Jews, Christians, Muslims, Buddhists, Blacks, Hispanics, Anglos, gay people, straight people, men, women—everybody had a shot with me. We operated this way not because our company was consciously trying to fill an artificial quota or redress some historical wrong. Diamond just wanted to run the best business it could, and that meant finding the most talented, hardest-working people, whoever they were and wherever they came from.

Americans today aren't just reexamining the concept of affirmative action; many are rightfully advocating for a fuller, more clear-eyed assessment of diversity, equity, and inclusion (DEI) policies writ large. California recently faced backlash after adopting rules for its community colleges mandating that administrators hire and promote faculty in part based on their adoption of antiracist or social justice ideology. Faculty members will be judged "competent" for purposes of career advancement only if they teach and advocate for DEI ideas.[28] Although such measures may be well intended, they fall far short. At best, they don't work. At worst, they hurt the students they are trying to help.

When state bureaucrats enforce a regime of ideological rigidity and conformity, nobody benefits. Let's focus on teaching the necessary curriculum, grading students properly for their efforts, and hiring and paying teachers based on merit rather than on whether they subscribe to DEI orthodoxy.

I'm all for diversity and inclusion—but in *practice*, not as a form of virtue-signaling. When it comes to the humanities, I believe we should tell *all* stories (presuming they're rooted in objective fact) rather than deliberately limiting ourselves to one or a few perspectives. Everything should be on the table, including topics some people don't like to talk about, such as the treatment of Native Americans or the Holocaust. After all, history is history.

We do a disservice to our nation's young people—and thus compromise our country's future—if we try to cherry-pick historical events that suit some simplistic narrative. We need kids to hear how white people perpetuated slavery and Jim Crow, *and* how America's founding fathers established the greatest, most prosperous democracy the world has ever seen. We need students to learn about the great artistic accomplishments of people hailing from all backgrounds, *and* the treasures of the Western literary canon. *That's* true inclusion. Banishing ideology and letting ideas and arguments stand for themselves will reinforce the underlying idea that merit matters, and that individuals and societies can have an impact by virtue of their own efforts and excellence.

I wish we could adopt a specific policy in our schools and

businesses and make historical injustice magically disappear. I really do. But we can't radically reengineer society overnight to redress injustice. Trying to do so has paradoxically disfigured the American ideals of fairness and justice. We can make slower but more sustainable progress by taking a more modest, practical approach.

So, let's implement another kind of "DEI": an emphasis on discipline, education, and integrity. Let's focus on working hard, on making something of ourselves. And let's create opportunities for others to do the same. Let's respect everyone as human beings just like us. Let's treat them equally. And when we see injustice, abuse, or flogging of the truth—whether or not it affects us directly—let's stand up and do something about it. We *can* make a difference.

Leaders, What Are You Waiting For?

I've focused on the "what" behind our current reluctance to stand up and show integrity, but there's also a "who": our leaders. Representatives and leaders of both major US political parties often fail to aggressively pursue fairness and justice in their policy stances. Our political and business leaders need to start digging in, cutting through the layers of bureaucracy, and giving people a fair shake.

Let's start with everyone's favorite topic: taxes. A 2024 survey by the Associated Press and the University of Chicago's Harris School of Public Policy found that most people feel that taxes are unfair—that they pay too much and don't get enough value for their money. Only 6 percent express high levels of confidence that the US government is using tax money responsibly.[29] Were the 1,024 people who participated in this study totally messed up in their thinking? Not at all. Taxes *are* unfair, in any number of respects.

First, the government wastes an unconscionable amount of money—by some estimates, almost $250 billion annually.[30] The government pays out more money than it's supposed to. It also spends money on stuff it doesn't need. For instance, did you know the military forked out $28 million in 2017 to outfit soldiers with uniforms designed with forest camouflage? That would be great—except those soldiers were serving in Afghanistan's desert terrain.

Career politicians are falling down on the job. To them, a $28 million blunder is just budget dust. They're not checking to ensure the government is collecting and using tax dollars wisely. Most of the time, elected leaders have no clue how tax dollars they've allocated are actually being spent. When you ask them, they assure us they'll "do an audit" and find out. Sounds like a responsible thing to say, but having led a company, I can tell you: It isn't. Leaders of organizations must know at all times where the money is going. Some parts of the government can't even pass an audit—like the Pentagon, which doesn't know where $1.9 *trillion* of its money was spent.[31]

If our leaders cared about fair taxation, they'd clean up the federal tax code with reforms aiming to eliminate arcane loop-holes. They'd also do away with special provisions that make figuring out how to interpret the laws on the books so difficult, and enforcement even harder. At the local level, they'd ensure that property values for tax purposes are appraised properly. At present, if you own pricier property, the authorities tend to undervalue it, whereas they tend to overvalue cheaper property.[32] How is *that* fair?

Let's move from taxation to the internet, and in particular, those social media companies that allow misinformation and other harmful material on their platforms. When almost any other kind of company causes harm, victims have a remedy: They can sue and receive compensation for their losses. The prospect of lawsuits protects the public, incentivizing companies to stop harm or prevent it from occurring. Online platforms are different. Thanks to Section 230 of a 1996 law known as the Communications Decency Act, such platforms generally aren't responsible for what third-party users post on their sites.[33] That sounds innocuous, but consider this: Victims of defamation can't sue platforms for hosting that content as they can with traditional media outlets like newspapers or television shows. Victims of terrorist attacks can't sue platforms that hosted material fostering radicalization. Parents of kids who die of drug overdoses can't sue platforms that made it easy for their kids to access the drugs.[34]

How is any of this fair or right?

Meta CEO Mark Zuckerberg apologized during Senate hearings for failures at Facebook, as did Snapchat CEO Evan Spiegel.[35] But these and other social media companies haven't changed their irresponsible practices. Where is the leadership? Why aren't they moving aggressively toward solutions?

Likewise, policymakers in both parties have talked for years about changing the law to treat social media platforms like they do other companies. They haven't done it. They're too conflicted, too weak, too worried about how they might look or which commercial interests they might anger. They delay as they study the issue, hold meetings and press conferences, consult with experts. In the meantime, what incentive do the platforms have to take down pernicious material? None at all, which is why the internet continues to be such a cesspool of poisonous content. And thanks to the proliferation of generative artificial intelligence, the situation will only deteriorate further. If nobody steps up, we'll soon see the problems of social media jacked up on steroids.

A reluctance to uphold standards of fairness and rectitude is broadly visible in government at all levels, extending all the way up to the US Supreme Court.[36] Unbelievably, the Court still has no binding code of ethics regulating the conduct of its sitting justices. You'd think these ultimate arbiters of justice would feel obliged, as a matter of conscience, to zealously embrace a binding code. At the very least, you'd think they'd submit to one out of enlightened self-interest. After all, the Court's reputation has suffered in recent years, and the lack of an ethical code only piles on more damage. But apparently some of the Supreme Court justices care about ethical rigor only when it applies to *other* people. In 2023, in response to concerns about improprieties at the Court, they opted to install a code that is *non*binding.[37] Employees at every other court or agency in our immense federal bureaucracy are subject to obligatory standards, facing sanctions if they step over the lines, but the nation's Supreme Court apparently thinks it's above all that.

This is deeply troubling. We've got wealthy litigants, whose cases are being handled by the Court, giving free stuff to Justices Clarence Thomas and Samuel Alito: rides on private jets, cruises, free tuition for their relatives—all without disclosing it to the public. We've got a Stop the Steal symbol flying on a flagpole on Justice Alito's property—implying support for extremist lies about the 2020 election results—even as he's helping to adjudicate cases related to the January 6 insurrection.[38] And they refuse to submit to a binding ethical code? Where I come from, that's called *corruption*.

At the very least, it's a seriously bad look. As the Center for American Progress argued, "The justices should not be allowed to play by a different set of ethical rules than the rest of the federal government—especially when public trust in the institution is at an all-time low. The [C]ourt is supposed to uphold the rule of law, not flout it."[39] I wholeheartedly agree. And I agree with a 2023 assessment that appeared in *The Economist*: "Now, of all times, America needs a [C]ourt that is spotless and seen to be."[40] We need a court that cares about fairness and that will show integrity in fighting for it.

It *is* possible for leaders to show more integrity and respond more quickly to injustice. I know because that's how I operated throughout my career. Individuals in positions of power should stop hesitating, return to moral obligations and ethical principles, and do the courageous work of applying those principles fairly. That's *true* leadership.

Joining the Fight

Diamond Resorts and the Supreme Court are distinctly different animals, but they have at least one thing in common: They both depend upon their good reputation. In Diamond's case, we needed to prove to our guests that we delivered an absolutely amazing vacation experience that was also a great value for the money. Given the history of shady practices in our industry, we also needed to prove that we adhered to the highest ethical standards, treating guests fairly at all times. And that's precisely what we did.

Shortly after we bought Sunterra, we learned that parts of the company had been mistreating customers. So, we bent over backward to make these customers whole, in some cases refunding their money and voluntarily letting them out of their legal agreements with us—even though their contracts didn't require it, and nobody else in the industry did it. In one instance, I personally spoke with a dissatisfied customer and let her out of a twenty-year-old contract, refunding her money within the space of a couple of days. No big legal fight. No bureaucracy to navigate. The customer couldn't believe I'd treated her fairly, because nobody under the old management had. She was so ecstatic that she told me about going to church and lighting a candle in my honor.

That felt great, but it wasn't necessary. Customers should *expect* integrity and fair treatment, and companies should deliver it. It's the only way companies can build trusting relationships and a strong, respected brand.

Looking at our customer base, we identified other opportunities to stand up and show integrity. It turned out that some of our customers who had been vacation owners for years under the old Sunterra weren't taking vacations with us any longer. Some were too elderly or sick and had trouble traveling as they once did. Others had experienced a divorce or retired from their jobs, and couldn't afford to pay the regular property maintenance fees required under their contracts. Although we had no obligation to let them out of their agreements, we chose to voluntarily do so if they were struggling. The last thing we wanted was to prey on people who were experiencing financial hardship. Instead, we wanted to participate in a mutually beneficial economic exchange, offering an amazing vacation and receiving fair compensation in return. If these customers could no longer use our properties, we'd take them back and resell them to customers who would be able to enjoy them. We wound up letting more than three thousand customers out of their contracts—at no small expense. Showing consumers and our industry that we behaved with integrity was that important to us.

We also sought to protect customers from bad actors in our industry. When customers no longer wanted to vacation with us and were thinking of selling their fractional ownership in a vacation property, they sometimes turned to so-called exit companies. These slick operators offered to facilitate a sale in exchange for a fee that sometimes ran into the tens of thousands of dollars.[41] Customers would pay the money and then find that these companies didn't do a damn thing for them. Even worse, customers would breach their contracts with us under the guidance of these exit companies, in some cases losing their properties through foreclosure. It was a giant scam! Under my watch and even after we'd sold the company, Diamond went after exit companies, suing them for fraud and false advertising. This was the right thing to do, and it was in our interest too. We wanted to be known as a highly reputable company. That was hard if others around us were tarnishing the image of our industry.

We also stood up when companies or individuals targeted *us*, seeking to besmirch our reputation. When I was leading Diamond Resorts, we never settled a lawsuit that affected our reputation or brand. *Never*. We always fought it, even if it cost us more to do so. We felt it was vital to show integrity, and we wanted everyone in the industry (and beyond) to know that about us.

We also felt it was important to show integrity in our treatment of team members. When one of our team members complained that a customer was treating them poorly, speaking rudely to them, or otherwise disrespecting them, I followed up to learn the facts about what had happened. Everyone knew not to mistake my concern for weakness: If the team member had lied or embellished the story, they would be fired. But if their story checked out, we'd suspend the customer's privileges on the spot. If the customer didn't like that, we'd write them a check and cancel their vacation ownership contract with us. Adopting a customer focus is one thing, but fairness also requires that we take care of our team members.

As former Diamond Resorts CEO Mike Flaskey remembers, our practice of protecting team members "earned us an incredible amount of loyalty with the rank and file, the people who were in customer-facing roles. Difficult situations arose from time to time with customers who were behaving unethically, and our people loved the fact that we were no-nonsense in saying, 'Don't treat my team members that way.'"[42]

Doing the right thing in our dealings with team members also meant making sure that they were compensated for their hard work, and that they didn't get stuck shouldering the burden during challenging economic times. The Great Recession of

2008–2009 was disastrous for the vacation ownership industry. At several points, I wasn't sure our company was going to make it. Many in our industry responded by cutting back on labor costs through layoffs, pay cuts, and the like, riding out the crisis on the backs of their workforce. Companies in many industries did the same: Some 1.5 million non-farm workers were laid off in 2008, according to the US Department of Labor.[43]

We took a different tack. We did say goodbye to some employees as part of our ongoing efforts to restructure Sunterra and operate it more efficiently. If previous management had two teams of people at different locations needlessly doing the same work that one team could do, we made sure to rectify that, pursuing such changes with new urgency during the recession. But what we *didn't* do, even when we were teetering on the edge of bankruptcy, was specifically lay people off to shrink our budgets and keep us solvent. In fact, we *boosted* pay for some of our team members during this period.

To help make our budgets work, we enlisted a different constituency to help out: our leadership team. We asked leaders to agree to a temporary 30 percent cut in compensation. We told them that when the economy improved, we'd pay them back this missing money, with interest. In effect, we were asking them to take on personal risk for the good of the company. Highly paid executives taking a financial hit for the benefit of employees: How often do you see *that* in corporate America? It was the right thing to do, and it was good for our business.

Our rank-and-file team members—the housekeepers, front desk staff, maintenance workers, waitstaff, and so on—worked incredibly hard, and they depended on each paycheck to feed their families. A layoff would devastate them, and it would be a slap in the face after all they'd done, day after day, to please our customers. It also would put us in a bad position, eroding the loyalty and morale of our remaining team members and making it harder for us to expand when the economy improved.

Our executives worked hard too, but since they were better off financially, they could survive a period in which their household budgets were a little tighter than usual. Later, as the crisis was lifting, we brought our executive pay back up, and we also were one of the first companies in our industry to bring back bonuses for rank-and-file team members. They had worked so hard to help us get through the crisis. It was only fair that we reward their efforts. Team members rewarded us in turn with their loyalty and dedicated work.

Contrast that with the way many tech employees today feel about their employers. In 2023 and 2024, many companies in the tech industry downsized their workforce, in part to adjust for expected growth that never materialized. These moves, referred to by some as "the Great Betrayal," led to intense dissatisfaction and disgruntlement among employees.[44] The prospect of future mass downsizing thanks to artificial intelligence has only added to the insecurity felt by many knowledge workers, to the point where some have chosen to avoid tethering themselves to any company and instead to work as freelancers. As a writer for *Fast Company* observed, "There's an ongoing shift in sentiment—a change in how workers think about their jobs. Our collective trust in full-time employment is faltering."[45] The uncompromising, unfair use of layoffs as a management tool leads to profound disloyalty and a lack of trust on the part of employees.[46] As well it should.

Our leaders need to start speaking out and taking a brave stand whenever they see people suffering from injustice. Beyond Sunterra, I've advocated staunchly for fairness throughout my political life. During the early 2000s, my friend Steve Sisolak, then a member of the Nevada System of Higher Education Board of Regents, introduced me to a young woman who desperately wanted to attend college in order to build a better future for herself, but couldn't afford to pay the high out-of-state rates. She had lived in Nevada long enough to be considered a resident of the state, yet wasn't being afforded the benefit of the less expensive in-state tuition. Steve was saddened by this woman's story, and appalled that his colleagues on the board weren't taking it very seriously. How could our state purposely impede this woman from getting an education by failing to apply its own policies? And if administrators were doing it to *her*, how many other people were they treating in this way? It wasn't right.

Steve knew that I was active politically and philanthropically, and that members of the Board of Regents would be inclined to listen to me. He introduced me to this woman in hopes of leveling the playing field for her, and I was determined to do just that. Administrators were shafting her—and hundreds if not thousands of other people—because they perceived her to be powerless, unable to advocate for herself. Countless families were not receiving the lower tuition bills to which they were entitled, and having to make up the difference somehow. Basically, the state was padding its budgets by systematically cheating its own citizens. It was wrong. And it had to end.

I joined this woman at a meeting of the Board of Regents, ready to call out the thirteen elected board members and make them see reason. "You're not complying with the law," I said. "If you don't listen to her story and correct the situation, I will see to it that every one of you in the university system is sued." I was serious. If we didn't get the required action, I intended to help facilitate a class action lawsuit, approaching law firms and asking them to handle the case pro bono. I also met with the local media to tell them what was going on. They ran with the story, interviewing the woman and turning this injustice into a major local issue.

My strong words got the Board of Regents' attention. Under pressure, they wound up changing how they interpreted the law governing tuition, granting in-state tuition to this woman and many others. The board also refunded the money they had wrongly collected by overcharging students—a total of $16 million. The State of Nevada also clarified its definition of *residency*. "This really made a huge impact," Steve later recalled. "We leveled the playing field very, very quickly."[47]

I'm sure there have been times when I've failed to demand equitable treatment or stand up for my values as vigorously as I might have. I'm sure that on occasion I've treated people wrongly. But I really do try; and when I mess up, I learn. Integrity matters to me—not just in relation to my personal interests, but in general. That's because I believe in my ability to shape my own future, and to change the world around me. You should too. We should all feel capable of contributing to a society that is fairer, more righteous, and simply *better*.

When we harness the power of our inherent agency, we can push back against the grievance culture and the impulse to reduce our concern for justice and fairness to something that only our own identity groups deserve. Let's become better in our dealings with others by throwing ourselves into the project of rejuvenating our meritocratic system and values from the bottom up. Let's choose to see ourselves as gladiators fighting for what we believe is right, rather than as victims.

It's easy to talk about integrity and then whine when we think *others* don't show it. That's grievance for you. But if we really want a better society, we must concern ourselves with our own integrity first. We must take action, even if that means stepping outside of our comfort zone. We also must elect more leaders who are willing to stand up for their beliefs and for our shared principles. The leaders in our nation's history whom we admire the most—from George Washington to Abraham Lincoln to Martin Luther King Jr.—showed tremendous integrity, even (and especially) when it was hard to do so. They acknowledged the problems around them, and they didn't shrink from a fight when the cause was righteous.

As my mentor Harry Reid once said, "I would rather dance than fight, but I know how to fight."[48]

My attitude is exactly the same. Like Harry, I never look for conflict—I always fire a shot over the bow first, hoping that potential adversaries will get the message. But if they don't, I won't hesitate to follow Harry's lead. I will take many a punch while fighting through to victory. Harry taught me to think both strategically and tactically and to go the distance, and that's what I do. We need a new generation of leaders just like this. People who won't be extorted. Who won't compromise their core beliefs. Who are willing to play the long game. Who never give in.

A TEAM THAT IS DIVIDED CANNOT WIN

I'M NOT EXACTLY A BIG SPORTS FAN. Chalk it up to my childhood baseball failures, which permanently soured me on team sports. In Little League, I didn't cycle through the normal rotation of positions: shortstop, pitcher, first base. I was so bad that I was routinely and summarily dispatched not to left field, but to *left out*.

Sports fan or not, it's hard not to marvel at the performance of the US women's national soccer team. *Wait*, you're thinking, *soccer? Really?* I totally agree, it's not pickleball (a sport I do play quite fanatically). But hey, soccer is way more popular in our country than it used to be. And from what I gather, few teams anywhere can rival the US women's team. As of 2024, the team has won four

World Cup championships (the latest in 2019) and four Olympic gold medals. Their off-field performance has been impressive too, particularly in efforts to advocate for issues such as equal pay for women in sports and to create a market for soccer in a country that hasn't always appreciated it.

What I've found especially inspiring about the US women's soccer team are moments when it has overcome extreme adversity thanks to exceptional collaboration and teamwork. In 1999, when the team hosted the women's World Cup for the first time, it faced the prospect of playing in half-empty stadiums due to lackluster fan interest. What did those scrappy women do? They pulled together and got busy signing autographs, showing up at youth training camps, and appearing at team practices.[1] One member of the squad, Kristine Lilly, remembers it fondly: "We did little sneak attacks. We would go to soccer fields where teams were training and sneak up on them. I remember going to a soccer practice in Boston with Mia Hamm, and the team was like, 'Oh my God' when we snuck up on them. It gave us a chance to talk to them, we signed autographs—we wanted to connect with the fans."[2]

As team co-captain Carla Overbeck recalls, "We were promoters of our sport. When they started targeting the big stadiums, we knew there was going to be work that went along with that to fill the stadiums. Our team genuinely liked being out in public, doing clinics, meeting children. It was second nature to us and it just so happened to help [sell more tickets]."[3]

Such efforts paid off. The women wound up playing in sold-out stadiums, including at the Rose Bowl in Pasadena, California, where they came away with the championship in front of ninety thousand fans.[4] With forty million people across America watching that final game, players like Hamm and Brandi Chastain became household names.[5] President Bill Clinton had watched the game, and invited the team to the White House.[6]

"We felt like the Beatles for three weeks," team co-captain Julie Foudy says. "We had no idea it would take off like that. When we walked into the last week of training in LA for the final, and we'd literally get off the bus and it would be a tunnel of thousands of fans lining the way from the bus to the training pitch, and thousands of fans screaming the entire time, we were like, what is this? We barely even got a thousand people at games before."[7]

As Lilly notes, the team created "cultural change," shifting American attitudes about soccer and also about the participation of women in sports generally.[8] But bear in mind, the successful 1999 World Cup is only one accomplishment among many that the US women's team has come together to earn over the past few decades. As one commentator has remarked, the team "has a long-standing culture of battling for victory not only on the field, but off the field as well. From the historic '99ers to today's team of icons in their own right, and every step along the way, the teamwork and grit of women forged what has now become a national treasure and thriving global industry."[9]

How do you nurture this kind of gutsiness and dedication? Teams so often fall apart when facing adversity. If people have big, out-of-control egos, if they're overly committed to a particular ideology or approach, if they're unable to listen and compromise with one another, the team won't function well. Small disagreements will fester. A spirit of divisiveness emerges, trust breaks down, and people forget the common goals and values that united them in the first place. Rather than working together, individuals end up focusing on achieving wins for themselves. Such teams make little progress on the biggest problems—those that usually require collaboration to solve. Meanwhile, new problems will arise as team members work at cross-purposes with one another. Before long, the team will stall out and maybe even go down in flames.

In *Team of Teams: New Rules of Engagement for a Complex World*, General Stanley A. McChrystal describes teams that manage to not only hang together in times of crisis, but operate at a higher level. The US Navy SEALS accomplish so much not just because individual team members are enormously talented, "but because those members coalesce into a single organism."[10] Unpacking how that team spirit forms, McChrystal emphasizes two factors: First, he describes the bonds of trust that form between team members during SEALS training. And second, he notes the importance of team members' dedication to a common purpose—something else that the training helps nurture. Cultivating these two elements allows Navy SEALS teams to perform better than if they focused on just making individual soldiers as good as they could possibly be. "A fighting force with good individual training, a solid handbook, and a sound strategy can execute a plan efficiently" and probably get the job done under normal circumstances, McChrystal writes. But a team with trust and purpose can improvise when things become unexpectedly dicey. Up against seemingly impossible odds, a team that values trust and purpose can *still* get the job done.[11]

There's a third factor, however, that is related to trust and that defines resilient teams: an ability to solve practical problems, bringing together a range of differing opinions without getting bogged down in conflict.

During the late 2000s, knee-deep in turning Sunterra around in its new incarnation as Diamond Resorts International, we faced immense challenges. It wasn't just a matter of fixing up the company's many far-flung vacation properties, which were poorly run and had only mediocre appeal. The whole operation—including the parts that customers couldn't see—was dysfunctional. And Sunterra had been bleeding money, so we didn't have much time to make changes. We had to move quickly and decisively to solve an array of practical problems, or we risked getting sucked into a financial disaster. Was it kind of like preparing to host your first World Cup and facing the prospect of playing in empty stadiums? Or like participating in a Navy SEALS mission that has somehow gone sideways? Humor me—let's at least say, "Perhaps."

Happily, we succeeded. Many factors helped us win, but one of the most important had to do with the quality and cohesiveness of our team. At Diamond Resorts International, we didn't simply have smart, experienced, talented people on our leadership team. We had executives who knew how to collaborate with one another to *get the job done*.

From day one, our team pulled together around a common purpose: making whatever changes were necessary to provide unparalleled value for our customers, even putting that ahead of turning a profit. We knew that if we could please customers as never before, our business would improve and we'd do well financially. So, any potential changes to our operations were fair game. No existing practice or process was sacred. When a leader on our team saw something that needed fixing—from what kind of pillows we used to how our rooms got cleaned, from who should sign off on spending decisions to how we communicated with customers—we fixed it, even if that meant departing from business as usual.

As we learned to listen to customers and discovered in detail what they wanted, our leaders pulled together around delivering our three priorities of simplicity, choice, and comfort. Critically, the leadership team also committed itself to something we called "The Meaning of Yes": an ethic of empowering everyone at our company, including thousands of frontline team members, to delight our guests by saying yes to their requests even if it entailed going beyond existing policies and procedures. In keeping with this ethic, we committed to collaborating with one another to solve problems. We refused to let our egos get in the way. What mattered most was our shared ambition to delight customers.

With time and hard work, our team spread this ethic of collaboration across the company on behalf of our shared purpose. The mantra that came to define our culture was *Collaboration, communication, and no stagnation.* In many organizations, people become siloed in their particular department or specialty. Not at Diamond Resorts. Instead of a typical executive management team with a handful of leaders, we created our "E-team," bringing together over two dozen leaders, from across every area of the company and from around the world, to solve operational issues of every kind. We had our head of marketing talking to our CFO, and our head of operations connecting with our head of global sales. We also went one level down in each department and brought those leaders to the table too.

This was revolutionary. In many cases, these departments had never worked together before. By encouraging collaboration not just across silos but throughout entire business units, we adopted an intensive open-door policy and the promise of transparency. Collaboration at this broader scale was never easy; given the geographical spread of our team members, for instance, some of us had to get up at 2 a.m. to participate in meetings. But it was worth it. Anyone at any level or in any corner of the organization could come to me to share their concerns or great ideas. And repeatedly, they did so.

I don't mean to suggest we had no tensions or differences of opinion. Of course we did. But that was the beautiful thing about the E-team: Our meetings became a venue to air out our differences and hear everyone's opinions, always in a civil way. Let me be clear: We didn't communicate for the sake of allowing everyone to feel "heard." In a serious business, there's no time for fluff or pandering to people's feelings. Instead, the E-team made space for real debate that focused on important topics, with an eye toward the three Rs of business: *respect*, *responsibility*, and *results*. Our exchanges were vigorous and intense, but divisiveness and conflict never became entrenched within Diamond. We had healthy debates that always ended when I, as the CEO, made the final decision. Upon leaving our E-team meetings, leaders left the debate behind too, and aligned their teams around the decisions we made.

Patrick Duffy, our former chief experience officer, remembers these meetings well. "We would all get into a room maybe once every couple of weeks," he says, "and that's where the feathers could fly."[12] Sometimes sales and accounting would go at it, other times accounting and operations. I required that everybody do their homework in advance of the meeting, reviewing what we'd already done regarding the topic at hand, including what had worked and what hadn't. That way, we could set a baseline and hold ourselves accountable for achieving results. Leaders would have a chance to explain their points of view in detail to others who, by virtue of their roles, might have had little direct knowledge of what they were doing. If anybody seemed like they were sanitizing their opinions or trying to be politically correct, I would quickly call them out on it. As Duffy once observed, "Being PC is like TP. You wipe your ass with both of them." I couldn't have put it better myself.

Again, my aversion to political correctness didn't imply a license to be rude, or to stick your thumb in the eye of another. On the contrary, it reflected my belief in meaningful debate where *ideas* are the focus. It's hard to have a debate with others when you're virtue-signaling or tiptoeing around to avoid causing even the slightest offense or discomfort. Taken too far, the fear of saying the wrong thing—or saying the right thing in the wrong way—makes it that much harder to get real work done. Who has time for that? The best way to show genuine respect for our colleagues, companions, and teammates is to say what you really think, trusting that your colleagues, companions, or teammates will be smart and well intentioned enough to receive it as intended and to share their honest thoughts in return.

Challenging leaders to speak frankly allowed us to get to the root of issues and handle them quickly. In fact, we were almost always able to resolve disputes amicably, leaving all parties feeling like they'd won. When leaders returned to their teams, they didn't dwell on the fight that had transpired. They got *busy*. You know that phrase *What happens in Vegas stays in Vegas*—well, it was kind of like that. As Patrick recalls, "When we left that room, and when you went back to your department, it was important that that department not even be aware of what might've transpired in the E-team. Because really what the E-team was all about was a micro dispute resolution pool."

In leading these discussions, I did my best to hear people out while also wielding authority decisively. I had a point of view, and I didn't hesitate to share it. But because of the no-holds-barred approach we'd established—and more important, the trust—others on my team didn't hesitate to say what they thought either. And I listened. When an executive felt strongly about a position that conflicted with mine, I'd sit with their argument for twenty-four hours before making a decision. Even when I disagreed with a point others were making, I sometimes relented and let them run with their idea anyway. Who knows—maybe they were right! If that turned out to be the case, great; our company would benefit. If it didn't, then our team would be more likely to pay even closer attention to my thinking going forward.

Our leadership team was incredibly effective because we could debate critical issues and not get bogged down with infighting. We came together, assessed the available evidence, made decisions, and solved problems. Then we aligned behind these solutions to execute them well. We improved our business and won over customers. And that's how we became the best damn vacation ownership company out there.

A House Divided

Here's a hard truth, and a foundational principle in business, politics, and life alike: To drive progress, *we must be able to come together despite our differences to solve problems.* It's common sense, right? Certainly we all can and must pursue our individual interests and stick to our own strongly held personal beliefs. But at a certain point, we've got to sit down with our opponents to work for the public good. As the Bible tells us—and as President Abraham Lincoln remarked when the nation was heading toward the Civil War—a house divided cannot stand. We've got to trust and respect one another, setting aside discord and looking for areas where we can make progress together for everybody's benefit.

To move forward and achieve the best possible outcomes, we can't attack, insult, or otherwise disrespect our opponents. We can't talk past one another, sticking to extreme, polarized positions and refusing to deal with other perspectives. We can't demonize those who disagree with us, labeling them as "the enemy" or "traitors." We can't spread rumors and lies in attempts to discredit the other side. And we certainly can't resort to political violence. In short, we can't treat politics as scorched-earth warfare. If we do, our "team"—in this case, the entire country—breaks down.

Sadly, that's where we are these days in America. Real, honest debate about issues that matter is scarce. Instead of elected officials working together to solve actual problems, we've got discourse that is largely performative, meant primarily to entertain the true believers. Instead of reality, we've got politics-as-reality-TV, in its crassest and crudest form.

Divisiveness in our politics is now so intense that large segments of American society—47 percent, in one 2024 survey—see a civil war brewing.[13] That's half the country! People who study civil wars for a living are ringing alarm bells. In her book *How Civil Wars Start*, Professor Barbara F. Walter of the University of California at San Diego argues that when you look at the data, "the United States, a democracy founded more than two centuries ago, has entered dangerous territory." She cites survey data showing that about a third of Democrats and Republicans now see their potential use of violence as "somewhat justified." And she warns that "America's extremists are becoming more organized, more dangerous, and more determined, and they're not going away."[14]

The potential for violence starts with the wholesale degradation of political discourse, a scenario that has become disturbingly familiar in the United States. In the early days of the run-up to the 2024 presidential election, if you visited a rally for Republican candidate Donald Trump, you'd see children walking around with shirts that read *FJB*. *JB* stands for *Joe Biden*—I'll let you imagine what the *F* stands for.[15] President Trump himself has routinely demeaned not just former President Biden but all of his opponents, both online and off. This is to say nothing about his willingness—and that of others on the far right of the political spectrum—to spread outright lies intended to discredit Democrats, most notably "the big lie" that the 2020 election was stolen.

The idea of the big lie originated in Nazi Germany, where spreading the notion that the Jews had betrayed Germany during World War I was a convenient way to underpin the regime's genocidal ideology.[16] Unable (or unwilling) to recognize the parallels with fascism, right-wing idealogues have made countless other outlandish claims in recent years—for example, arguing that President Biden's immigration policies amount to "a conspiracy to overthrow the United States of America"; that the government intentionally spread Covid-19 to induce Americans to get vaccinated; that musician Taylor Swift has been working for the Pentagon to manipulate the public; and the list goes on.[17]

Anyone can shout, "Make America great again!" all they want, but these divisive attitudes are not helping our nation make progress or reach greatness in any way. On the contrary, sowing discord instead of reaching out to build consensus only makes problem-solving and general success more difficult to achieve. We see similarly divisive attitudes among some on the left. At the rallies that roiled college campuses in 2024, students and faculty espousing extreme far-left views physically prevented supporters of Israel from entering parts of their own campus, simply on account of their differing beliefs. All too often, the anti-Zionism espoused by these protesters—some of them making statements or wearing clothes that glorify the terrorist group Hamas— became full-fledged anti-Semitic hate speech.

Likewise, rather than talk civilly to those with whom they disagree, virtue-signalers on the left rush to "cancel" them. This is a shame. As Columbia professor John McWhorter reflects, "We should be able to evaluate various figures, past and present, by noting their indecorous or hateful views and continuing to appreciate, even celebrate, their achievements without making them candidates for cancellation."[18]

I'll tell you one thing: If members of my team at Diamond refused to hear opposing viewpoints, spewed hate, shut down honest debate, and lied in order to get what they wanted, they wouldn't have done so for very long—at least not as employed members of Diamond Resorts International.

Americans of all beliefs and political persuasions deserve better than politicians who knowingly spread polarizing, fanatical views. They deserve leaders who are serious and who double down on the issues most people care about rather than those that engender the most outrage. Those unifying concerns, shared by Republicans, Democrats, and Independents alike, are kitchen-table issues like jobs and the economy, the lack of affordable health care, the drug epidemic, and the state of our democracy.[19]

Too many elected leaders look past the real issues that supermajorities of Americans care about to focus on wedge concerns. When they *do* get the topic right, they often get the tone wrong. They fail to talk in serious ways designed to build consensus. Rather, they seek to inflame the complaints of their constituents, encouraging us to feel aggrieved and victimized thanks to those villains on the other side—what some have called the "oppression Olympics."[20] We see plenty of such demagoguery in political campaigning today, which has become much more negative than it has been in recent decades as politicians seek to fire up partisan outrage. Back in 1960, just a sliver, 10 percent, of the political ads fielded by presidential candidates were negative attacks.

Fast-forward to 2012, and the situation was reversed: Only a sliver of ads, 14 percent, were inspiring and positive.[21]

All the fanaticism, outrage, and performativity in politics has rendered our governing institutions increasingly dysfunctional. US Congress, for instance, has become notorious for soap-opera dramas, not progress toward helping the American people. When you have extremist members of the Freedom Caucus appealing to their most extremist followers by killing off useful legislation that members of their own party championed, you're just not going to get much done. And Congress, in recent years, hasn't: In 1975, our national legislative body passed 649 laws; by 2023, that number had dwindled to just twenty-seven.

No wonder Americans feel stuck! Far from consistently taking bipartisan action to pursue the public good, Congress these days can barely even keep the federal government funded. Every year we see fiscal crises and the threat of government shutdowns. As Democratic Congressman Derek Kilmer put it, "I don't think it's a secret that Congress is a fixer-upper."[22]

Our politics is so bad that we can't even work together to defend ourselves against serious threats. A good example is the Covid-19 pandemic. In 2020, instead of unifying to fight the spread of a lethal virus, the country fragmented. So-called red and blue states split over issues such as vaccinations, mask wearing, and economic closures. Because the country couldn't manage a unified response, people died. Some citizens learned from irresponsible politicians that the virus wasn't that bad and that government masking guidelines and other public health recommendations were attempts to take away their freedom. They heard from these sources that vaccines were not to be trusted. As a result, they didn't take the proper precautions, and the virus spread. As one academic study concluded, "the catastrophic death toll in the United States was largely preventable and due, in large part, to the polarization of the pandemic."[23]

The polarization that has become so destructive nationally has seeped into local politics too. Coming together around a local project that benefits the community should be relatively easy and noncontroversial, because the interests of local players tend to be closely aligned. And yet, a recent survey of local government officials found that almost 70 percent saw polarization as a problem, with 80 percent citing the destructive impact of misinformation on their communities. Polarization in turn is making local governance harder, eroding public trust and triggering greater expenses when it comes to financing projects.[24] As the authors of one academic study concluded, "The costs imposed by political polarization have larger implications for the welfare of the residents."[25]

We all know polarization is a complex phenomenon with many causes and damaging effects. Yet we continue to feed the breakdown of unity, respect, and civil discourse when we defriend someone with whom we disagree; tell our kids not to marry someone who does not align with our beliefs; or leave a red state to resettle in a place that conforms to our blue-state beliefs, and vice versa.[26] Social media companies feed this harmful trend by failing to police the misinformation on their platforms and by deploying algorithms that, in a bid to keep our attention, send us only content that affirms what we already think.[27]

But in fact the biggest culprits may be our nation's political leaders, operators, and experts. Here's a surprising fact: Research shows that most Americans aren't nearly as polarized on the issues as we think. On many of today's important issues, we basically agree. Consider how many voters in November 2024 split their tickets, casting their ballots for both Democratic and Republican candidates in different races. In North Carolina, a battleground state that swung early for Trump, the Democratic candidate for governor, Josh Stein, beat the Trump-endorsed Republican candidate for governor, Mark Robinson, by nearly a 15-point margin.[28] That simply couldn't have happened if the electorate was ideologically divided! That other states saw similar results suggests that it's our *politicians* who are ideologically polarized, not us. They seek political gain by whipping up hatred toward perceived enemies, which increases the potential for political violence.[29] These leaders must tone down the rhetoric—*now*. Over the longer term, we owe it to ourselves and future generations to elect more leaders who are unifiers, not bomb-throwers.

How Government *Used* to Work

What we need most in politics today are good-hearted, *pragmatic* leaders. We need a government that is willing to focus on the most important issues, tell us the hard truths, and build consensus around workable solutions. We need leaders with the balls to guide us back to sanity again, pushing back against the radical left and right and their divisive agendas.

America's greatest historical leaders have understood the fundamental principle of building consensus around the common good. Our founding fathers strongly distrusted political parties and the passions they aroused, which is why they made no mention of them when drafting the US Constitution. They were focused on *results*, on moving the ball forward. They set up our whole system of self-governance not to advance a particular ideology or set of policy solutions, but to provide mechanisms for coming together to solve our shared problems.

Just look at the preamble of the Constitution, the words that founding father (and later president) James Monroe called the "key of the constitution":

> We the People of the United States, in Order to form a more perfect Union, establish Justice, insure domestic Tranquility, provide for the common defense, promote the general Welfare, and secure the Blessings of Liberty to ourselves and our Posterity, do ordain and establish this Constitution for the United States of America.[30]

Note that opening phrase: *We the People*. Not *we the Republicans*. Not *we the Democrats*. And certainly not *I*, as in the autocrat's motto: *Only I can fix it*.

We.

Our founding fathers didn't design our governing institutions to serve as a venue for lurid political theater or the perpetual airing of grievances. They forged this revolutionary political system to help Americans get stuff done for their collective benefit. The well-being of all Americans rests on fundamentals like the rule of law, peaceful communities, a military capable of repelling threats from abroad, and protections for basic liberties. Our ground-breaking government institutions were designed so Americans could work through their differences and unite around practical measures for the good of all. They were intended to provide for "a more perfect Union" and support "the general Welfare."

President George Washington, in his farewell address to the country, warned future generations against the passions of political parties and urged them to resist demagogues who would spew lies to stir up internal resentments. As he wrote, "One of the expedients of party to acquire influence within particular districts is to misrepresent the opinions and aims of other districts. You cannot shield yourselves too much against the jealousies and heart burnings which spring from these misrepresentations. They tend to render alien to each other those who ought to be bound together by fraternal affection."[31] Sounds like a pretty good description of what is going on in our society today.

You don't have to look all the way back to our nation's founding to remember a time when politics was far less divisive and unpleasant than it currently is. During the 1990s and 2000s, when I was building my business and becoming active in Nevada politics, I had a chance to get to know Nevada Governor Kenny Guinn. He and I didn't agree on everything: He was a Republican, and I was a Democrat. He opposed government recognition of gay marriage, and I supported it.[32] I'm sure if you had sat us down in a room and peppered us with questions, there would have been a few other areas where we didn't see eye to eye.

But our opinions on specific issues and our differing political loyalties didn't matter as much as what we shared in common, most notably our devotion to our community. Guinn and I were on friendly terms, and we respected one another. In 2004, he showed his respect for me by appointing me to my first formal government role: membership on the Standing Committee on Judicial Ethics and Election Practices. That's right, Guinn made me—a proud member of the opposite party—a judge of judges. He gave me authority over *election practices* in the state. Can you imagine this happening in today's political landscape?

But just a few decades ago, this was the way it was. For much of my political life in Nevada, people holding diverse views had warm relationships with one another. This was *normal*. I was friends with Bill Raggio, a Republican leader in the state senate, and with Joe Dini, a Democratic leader in the state assembly. We belonged to political parties, but we always saw ourselves first and foremost as fellow citizens.

Yes, we cared about our side winning elections and enacting policies that reflected our beliefs. But we weren't idealogues. We knew we didn't have everything figured out. We looked at politics primarily as a chance to advance the public good, not our own careers. We respected people who came to different conclusions about important issues. We didn't attack one another, calling one another insulting names and engaging in vitriolic debates. We didn't focus on the most divisive issues in a bid to earn approval. We had a baseline trust in one another. We cared about working together to get stuff done for everybody's benefit.

This pragmatism and awareness of the common good tran-scended party affiliations, allowing us to make progress and advance the public interest. If you walk along the Las Vegas Strip today, you'll find palm trees and areas of lush tropical greenery alongside sidewalks and in view of pedestrian bridges. It's a beautiful and welcoming environment—something you'll remember when you think back on your visit to the city. That beauty is there because of work that we did during the mid-1990s. It's there because we were able to transcend our differences and solve problems for the community.

Back then, the Strip was expanding commercially, but it wasn't at all pleasant to walk or drive among the casinos—you felt like you were in a harsh concrete jungle. The Strip was developed haphazardly, a legacy of the early gaming industry's entrepreneurial, Wild West quality. Hotel owners, seeking to evade municipal taxes, built properties there because the Strip technically falls outside the city limits, on unincorporated land.[33] Competing for business and thinking about their own interests, they focused on bettering their own properties and getting rich. They had big egos and larger-than-life personalities, and they didn't come together very often to pursue shared interests, including how they might make the entire Strip more visually appealing as a tourist destination.

By the 1990s, however, that everyone-for-themselves kind of approach wasn't cutting it. As former Nevada Congresswoman Shelley Berkley remembers, "Everybody on the Strip knew we had to do something to make it look nicer. I mean, it's our bread and butter here in Nevada. There wasn't a controversy about whether or not we should do it. It was more about what to do and how are we going to get it done." In other words, what exactly would a beautification of the Strip entail, and who would pay for it?[34]

Given that the state's economy depended on the hotels and

casinos located along the Strip, beautifying the area wasn't simply a nice thing to do. It was an economic imperative, something that would contribute to everyone's prosperity and well-being. But someone had to light the fuse, bringing all these competing hotel and casino owners together to work toward the common good. That someone turned out to be me.

We created a community-based initiative called the Las Vegas Beautification Project, convening a steering committee of representatives from all the important hotels and casinos. As head of the recently opened Polo Towers project located just off the Strip, I volunteered to chair that committee. In this capacity, I met with senior leaders of the major hotels, getting their input and building consensus around a way forward. Berkley (who served on the committee representing the Sands Hotel and Casino) remembers, "Everybody wanted to play a role in this and make sure that it turned out nicely and that their particular part of the Strip looked good."

Thanks to hard work, lots of listening, and a willingness to collaborate, we were able to work together to find common ground. I literally went door to door, asking to meet with folks. In the end, we got roughly one hundred local property owners to agree to fund a $13 million project to improve the Strip, at no cost to the public. We planted tens of thousands of palm trees, flowering bushes, and other foliage, creating a setting so pleasing that it has been named a Nevada Scenic Highway.[35] As James Murren, former CEO of MGM Resorts International, recalls, "It was quite a feat to get Las Vegas people to cooperate on anything, but of course it benefited everybody once the project was done."[36]

If you haven't visited, I invite you to spend an afternoon strolling the Vegas Strip. I think you'll find it pretty magical. The work we did back then to beautify the Strip didn't just benefit us economically; it helped to set the tone for politics in Nevada, establishing a spirit of collaboration that continued to yield results. As Murren reflects, "The beautification project encouraged stakeholders in Las Vegas to think more broadly than the contours of their own resorts, to continue to invest in the destination and improve its attractiveness for everybody. We started a changing of the guard, from being very myopic and very insular and very selfish to more of a desire to work for the common good."[37]

Nevadans since then have benefitted from that collaborative, pragmatic spirit on any number of occasions. In recent years, local interests have come together to invest in projects for the public benefit, such as the expansion of Las Vegas's convention center and airport. Collaboration has also allowed Nevadans to respond well in response to external threats to their well-being.

During the early 2000s, the federal government seemed poised to bring in seventy thousand tons of nuclear waste from around the country and dump it in a facility at Yucca Mountain, located about ninety miles from Las Vegas. I'm not at all against nuclear energy, particularly when powered by Gen IV reactors, which are more secure. But Nevada at the time didn't get any of its power from that source. Why should the country expect us to store all of its waste? Not only that, but of all the places the government could have chosen to store nuclear waste, it chose one within spitting distance of Nevada's main population center and economic lifeblood. We'd have trains carrying radioactive material from other states streaming through our communities. One accident was all it would take to destroy the tourism industry on which Nevada depends.

As I realized, the government's plans for Yucca Mountain were a clear and present danger not just to big hotel and casino owners, but to the hundreds of thousands of people whose livelihoods depended on tourism and who called the greater Las Vegas area home. So, I got busy as a grassroots activist, rallying local opposition and creating a group called Save Nevada.[38]

To educate myself, I took a government tour of the Yucca Mountain storage facility and learned in painful detail about the engineering specifications of the proposed storage site. I wasn't exactly heartened by what I saw. So, in an op-ed, I asked my neighbors to join me in pressuring our leaders to speak up against the government's plan. As I wrote, "I ask—no, I plead with—every Southern Nevadan to get involved in the Yucca Mountain fight. Make your voices heard. I urge you to send letters of opposition to the governor, the mayor, or the Board of County Commissioners."[39]

We talked to everyone as part of our advocacy efforts, including players who didn't always see eye to eye on other issues: organized labor, the big gaming companies, politicians, and other local industries like banking and communications. We managed to arouse incredible public support, including from the gaming companies.[40] This was truly an all-hands-on-deck moment. To this day, thanks in part to our determination to raise our unified voice, the government hasn't stored nuclear waste at Yucca Mountain.

During the pandemic's early days, Nevada again saw local groups rally to protect the community against a threat. States were fighting one another for desperately needed personal protective equipment (PPE) to stem the virus's spread, and Nevada was struggling to muster resources to protect our population. When then-Governor Steve Sisolak asked community leaders to form a Covid-19 task force, with James Murren serving as chair, our citizens put any differences aside, understanding that they were all Nevadans first. In five days, the task force raised $13 million to procure PPE and mobilized the procurement departments of several gaming companies and other big employers to source it from around the world. The task force also worked with the National Guard to distribute the PPE and helped arrange internet connectivity in local school districts to allow for online learning.[41]

Murren, for one, was awed by the community's capacity to work together and deal effectively with a crisis. As he said at the time, "I have always been so proud to call myself a Nevadan. When the call goes out, it is answered tenfold. Nevada has seen its share of adversity in the last few years—but each and every time, we fight with that Battle Born spirit, and we face the challenge head on, with creativity and determination."[42]

This community spirit and willingness to collaborate is still evident in Nevada, but it's getting tougher to muster as political divisiveness in our society intensifies. Across the country, the story is depressingly similar: Our differences seem to loom larger than what we hold in common.

Although polarization has been building for decades, our country took a sharp turn for the worse when President Barack Obama was in office, and some felt the administration veered too far to the left on sensitive issues related to identity politics. The first four Trump years in turn saw a backlash from the right, putting us where we now are: on a doom loop to nowhere.

It's Time to Reverse the Doom Loop

We have the power to heal our country. We can do it as voters by supporting pragmatic leaders who will put country ahead of party, and we can do it in our personal lives by reaching out across the political divide. Building on the spirit of bipartisanship I saw in Nevada, I continue to count many Democrats as friends, including New Jersey Senator Cory Booker, former President Bill Clinton, and Governor Sisolak. But I remain genuine friends with leaders on the Republican side too, including former Congressman and House Majority Leader Eric Cantor, former Congressman and House Speaker Kevin McCarthy, and former Senator Roy Blunt.

Politics doesn't always have to come first. When I encounter these individuals at social events, we chat amicably and catch up on what's happening in our lives, with our kids, and in our communities. We know that we can call one another up and ask for opinions and advice whenever we'd like. We might disagree on certain issues, but we always remain civil with one another. There's a baseline respect and trust.

I'd like to challenge all of us to have more frequent and civil conversations with people who harbor different political loyalties. You won't agree on everything, but chances are that you'll find more common ground than you might have imagined. You might learn something, correct your unexamined assumptions, and even find yourself tempering your more extreme views.

The mantra that worked so well for Sunterra—*Collaboration, communication, and no stagnation*—can work for America too. And what's the alternative? If our team at Diamond Resorts International hadn't found ways to transcend differences and collaborate, our competitors would have benefitted. Likewise, America's adversaries today—including China, Russia, and Iran—will benefit if we can't get along with one another better and put our affairs in order. The leaders of these countries know that a house divided cannot stand, which is why they're sowing so much division in America by constantly pumping out disinformation on social media.

Letting our political adversaries around the globe divide us would have disastrous consequences for the United States. We must remember who we are: Americans first, and members of political parties only second. Let's inject more seriousness into politics. Let's demand less reality TV in our political discourse and more real problem-solving. Let's exhort our elected leaders to focus on the issues the majority of us care about, and to work toward commonsense solutions. Let's get things *done*.

RULES ARE RULES

———————

IN 2023, A SAN DIEGO TEEN NAMED DESSA KURITZ was driving her 2006 Honda Civic through a parking lot when another car backed into her. Thankfully, nobody was hurt. As police quickly concluded, Dessa wasn't at fault—the other driver had backed carelessly out of their parking spot. Dessa legitimately expected, as any of us would, that the other driver or their insurance company would compensate her for the damage—which amounted to more than $4,000—so she could fix her car.

But that's not what happened. You see, the individual who dinged Dessa's car wasn't an ordinary person but a government employee driving a government-owned vehicle. When Dessa contacted the General Services Administration, the agency charged with administering federal property, they elected not to compensate her. In fact, the agency had the audacity to charge *her* for the damage sustained by the government vehicle. When she tried to resolve the incident, they refused to communicate with her.

Six months later, Dessa still couldn't afford to fix her car. As she remarks, it seemed that the government had been purposely steamrolling her and avoiding accountability for the accident—indeed, that doing so was "routine policy." The government was refusing to do "what it demands we all do—take responsibility when we hit someone with a car." Noting that she would soon take part in her first election, she wondered, "What am I supposed to think about all this, as a young citizen just getting to know how my government works?"[1]

It's a good question. If Dessa's account is accurate, then the government agency giving her the runaround should be ashamed of itself. Instead of setting an example of responsibility for others to follow, the agency is modeling the opposite. But they're hardly the only ones that deserve censure.

Dessa's experience points us toward a fundamental problem in American life today, one that is every bit as serious as grievance culture, polarization, and the breakdown in problem-solving and collaboration. I'm talking about the eroding respect we have for laws, rules, ethics, and established norms of conduct. This problem is evident in small lapses that arise in our everyday lives, such as the one Dessa experienced, but it also expands outward to pervade our homes, our schools, and public life in general.

Rules matter. This is a critically important hard truth, one that underlies our fundamental status as a country of laws, and one that we should all accept regardless of party or ideology. We all have an obligation to uphold the formal, legal kinds of rules as well as commonly held ethical codes. We also have an obligation, as the diplomat Richard Haass has suggested, to value and uphold social norms that might be informal or unwritten.[2]

Rules of all types embody a collective agreement we've made to govern how we interact with one another. They reflect an image of society at its best: civil, fair, orderly, safe. Without rules in place to help determine how individuals, families, communities, and the country at large should behave, we'd be forced to figure it all out as we go. We wouldn't know what to expect from one another, and we wouldn't be able to make decisions with any confidence or plan for the future. Chaos would reign as everyone started to behave as they saw fit. We'd all live in a state of constant fear and uncertainty.

In fact, the very minute we start to act as if rules don't matter—by bending or breaking them with impunity, by neglecting to enforce them, by normalizing illegality, dishonesty, impropriety, or evasion of responsibility—the rule of law starts to break down. We often presume that small infractions like driving 80 mph in a 65 mph zone are insignificant, and superficially (depending on the situation) they might be. On a deeper level, though, even small misdeeds signal to others that they can't rely on you, that you'd rather deal with chaos than hew to the limitations we've placed on everyone for the collective good.

Our misdeeds encourage others to break rules, including ones that we view as important but they don't. This is how, little by little, society degrades and we all become worse off. If anyone can simply damage our property at will, and there's nothing we can do about it, then what incentive do we have to work hard and invest in buying and improving property? Why should we spend our time and money creating economic value if someone can come along and, with no impunity, snatch it from us?

We need not look far to see what happens when rule-breaking goes unchecked for too long. In Vladimir Putin's Russia, the law of the strongest reigns, and those in power take advantage of their position to do as they please without consequences. For years now, Putin has jailed his political enemies, permitting only the vague appearance of a fair trial. Trust in Russian institutions has evaporated because outcomes depend on a single individual's whim, not collectively established principles. With no norms to keep the powerful in check, dissent and free thinking of all kinds have withered.

We shouldn't presume we're immune to tyranny. The United States may not be Russia, but in our country, too, people and institutions feel increasingly free to bend, break, or ignore the law when it serves their interests. The most obvious example might be then-President Trump's attempts to foment an insurrection and delegitimize the 2020 election—an alarming disregard for laws and long-standing democratic norms that mirrors authoritarian leaders around the world.

President Biden acknowledged Trump's lawlessness in his 2023 proclamation to mark Law Day, set aside by Congress annually to celebrate the rule of law.[3] Biden noted that "our nation and world are at an inflection point. At home and around the globe, autocrats and dictators threaten the rule of law. Our democracy is under strain, with people's rights, including the sacred right to vote, at risk. We face a choice between moving backward—unraveling so much of the progress our nation has made—or moving forward toward a future of possibilities and promise."[4]

For all its merit, Biden's diagnosis of the problem was incomplete. The decline of respect for laws and rules is more far-reaching than the challenges that exist to voting rights, as pernicious as those are. It extends beyond the other issues referenced in Biden's proclamation, such as "equal access to justice," the rise of hate crimes, and unjust invasion of sovereign nations, such as Russia's attack on Ukraine.[5] Virtually everywhere we look in our domestic political life, we find a disrespect for law and order.

Elected officials deal corruptly and behave as if they're above the very standards they seek to impose on others. They refuse to enforce laws that are already on the books. They—and we, in our capacity as voters—even pass laws and regulations that specifically empower people to violate basic legal and ethical norms. If you want to understand why we have so little faith in institutions of all kinds, and why local communities are falling apart from within, consider this failure to behave lawfully a big underlying cause. Collectively, we're forgetting the spirit of our founding fathers, who sought to create, in the words of statesman John Adams, "a government of laws, not of men."[6]

Tolerating Illegality

In my home state of California, one of the most damaging examples of the decline in our respect for lawfulness is Proposition

47, a progressive law approved by voters in 2014 that reclassifies
the theft of anything valued at up to $950 as a misdemeanor.[7] It's
true that California's threshold is not the highest among the fifty
states. In Texas, for instance, you'd have to steal $2,500 worth of
merchandise before being charged with a felony. But if you walk
into a Walmart in California today and steal, say, $500 in jewelry,
you'll be charged with a misdemeanor, which means the maximum
punishment you could possibly face would be $1,000 in fines and
six months in county jail. In all likelihood, however, given our
overburdened legal system, you'd get just a slap on the wrist—if
anyone bothers prosecuting you at all. Compare this with the law
in New Jersey, where stealing something worth just $200 will
bring down felony charges.[8]

On the face of it, raising the threshold as California and Texas
have done might seem to make sense. By defining felony offenses
less stringently, we can keep people who commit less serious
crimes out of prison, saving the government money and reserv-
ing prison space for more serious offenders. Many people who
shoplift are addicted to drugs, and some citizens feel that society
can deal with them more efficiently and effectively, with no appre-
ciable increase in crime, by treating their addictions rather than
locking them up.[9]

Proponents of Proposition 47 argue that the law has saved
California money.[10] Looking at the bigger picture, however, I'd
say the measure is an unmitigated disaster. Proposition 47 has
contributed to a massive spike in retail crime, hitting the state's
brick-and-mortar businesses hard. Police no longer pursue shoplifters as aggressively as they might, since they know prosecutors

won't bother prosecuting. Big retailers tell their employees not to physically prevent shoplifting for fear of violence. It's almost as if everyone is just throwing up their hands and declaring a free-for-all. And criminals are getting the message. Between 2019 and 2022, shoplifting in California rose by 29 percent. Some areas saw an increase of more than 50 percent during that time.[11] In Los Angeles, shoplifting was up by 81 percent in 2023 compared with the year before.[12]

California has also seen a rise in organized retail crime by theft rings. According to the National Retail Federation, Los Angeles, San Francisco, and Sacramento all rank among the top ten cities in the country for organized retail crime.[13] The situation is so bad that some retail stores have taken to outfitting staff with body cameras to prevent shoplifting.[14] Some people question whether Proposition 47 has indeed caused the spike in crime, but California's district attorneys know better—which is why, a decade after Proposition 47 was passed, they have joined the mayors of cities like San Francisco and San Jose in seeking to crack down on people who commit these offenses.[15]

In August 2024, California Governor Gavin Newsom signed legislation cracking down on retail theft, including by increasing penalties and making it easier for police to arrest suspects.[16] A November 2024 ballot initiative would roll back Proposition 47, including by allowing prosecutors to charge those who steal less than $950 with a felony if the suspect previously committed multiple thefts.[17] These are good steps, but they don't go far enough. I believe that the threshold should be *zero*, not $950.

Think of the message that Proposition 47 sends: *If you steal* *less than $950, well, that's not too bad. You won't face any serious conse-quences. Yes, you're breaking the law, but it's just not a big deal.* Apparently, these days, it's OK to steal. Just don't take too much at any one time.

I mean, what?

A principle should be upheld, irrespective of the dollar value involved. Stealing is wrong, period. This can't be controversial! If you take something that isn't yours, you should face consequences. We should be sending a message that *all* theft is morally and legally unacceptable and needs to be treated as such by society. The notion that we should tolerate *some* theft is completely ridiculous. It bespeaks a tired, flimsy society that equivocates rather than stands up for what is just.

Proposition 47 is just one example of how wobbly we Americans are getting about the rule of law and our sense of what we can expect from one another. There are myriad others.

Take immigration. Yes, we're a country of immigrants, and we should welcome and accept others who are different from us and can contribute to our society. But a basic principle of national sovereignty is control of borders. Without that, we're not a nation at all. So, how we admit others into our country matters. We must do it in a lawful and orderly way, with intention and accountability. Today, unfortunately, we often don't.

Tougher controls at the Mexican border allow us to intercept a much greater proportion of the migrants heading illegally into our country.[18] The problem is that we've constricted legal options for entering the country and allowed our asylum system to decay. We also have failed to adopt policies that might improve conditions in nearby countries, thus encouraging more people to stay put rather than try to enter the United States. As a result, the throngs of people who do make it across our borders and claim asylum are thrust into a prolonged legal limbo.[19] We're left with millions of migrants living in our cities with no clear legal status.[20] Because they can't legally hold jobs, they drain public resources, don't pay taxes, and must work under the table. But instead of doing what it takes to reach some workable compromise on immigration policy, our elected leaders seem willing to tolerate a situation of massive illegality that benefits no one.

As a society, we're also tolerating an erosion of basic property rights. In California and other areas of the country, squatters can occupy your empty home and then claim that they own the place. You might be able to evict them eventually, but it could take months or even longer. If you own a rental property, your tenants could stop paying rent and become squatters, and it might take you a year or more to get them out.[21]

In Washington state, a renter paid nothing to his landlord for nearly two years, owing rent to a tune of about $80,000. Yet landlord Jaskaran Singh couldn't get this unscrupulous squatter to leave. Would the police help him? Nope. In fact, the squatter got a restraining order against Singh, preventing him from coming close to his own $2 million property! Singh was left with no recourse except to hold protest rallies and appeal for support via GoFundMe.[22]

Imagine that: You scrimp and save to buy and maintain a property, and somebody just takes it from you—and you have no choice but to fight a protracted and stressful legal battle. The situation is so bad that some landlords and investors are abandoning opportunities in California, looking to buy properties in locations where they won't have to worry about squatters as much.[23] Clearly, homelessness and the high cost of housing are forcing some desperate residents to become squatters, but that's no reason to tolerate lawlessness. Instead, it should prompt elected officials to do what it takes to fix our homeless problem and respect the sacred rights of property owners. Anything less, and our society starts to devolve into chaos and the law of the strong.

Our weakening approach to upholding the law and ethical rules is apparent also in the anti-Israel demonstrations that shook university campuses across the country in 2024. Students have a historic right to free speech, and the United States has a proud tradition of demonstrations on our college campuses. But when demonstrators spray property with anti-Semitic hate speech, glorify terrorist groups, and threaten the physical safety of students, as anti-Israel protestors often have, then administrators have an obligation to shut it down.[24] At Columbia, protestors displayed a banner that read *Intifada*, advocating violent attacks against Jews. One protestor, who thankfully was suspended by university administrators, said on video that "Zionists don't deserve to live."[25] I'm no lawyer, but this isn't protected hate speech—it's harassment and incitement to violence. If someone told *you* in a charged public setting that you didn't deserve to live, I think you might take that as a threat.

Unfortunately, many university leaders have been weak and hesitant in dealing with such frightening excesses. UCLA, to take but one example, was way too slow to shut down the encampments built by anti-Israel protestors, even when Jewish students at this public university were prevented from entering university buildings where they had every right to be. And when a mob violently attacked the anti-Israel demonstrators, authorities were late in intervening.[26] This is what happens when you don't clearly enforce legal and ethical rules from the beginning. You get chaos.

We as a society must do better. We can't just say we're against hate speech but then fail to take action when slurs and threats are shouted at a group we're charged to protect. We can't get bogged down in legalities, as the presidents of several elite universities shamefully did before a congressional committee, when it comes to protecting students from those who would advocate genocide against them.[27] Congresswoman Elise Stefanik asked former Harvard President Claudine Gay a simple question: If somebody called for genocide directed at Jews, would it violate her university's rules? This wasn't a trick question. It was easy—or should have been. Gay's answer should have been an immediate, unequivocal, "Yes." Instead she said that the answer "depends on the context."

What kind of statement is this from someone chosen to lead a respected institution in a lawful and ethical manner? If you call for the extermination of an entire people—some of whom are also members of your community—the community leaders better consider that harassment and forbid it. Isn't that obvious? And forbidding harassment should include *all* harassment, whether it's directed against Jews, Muslims, women, gay people, Black people, Asian Americans—whomever. As a nation and as a population, in every community in the entire country, we must *always* respect and vigorously enforce our rules and laws.

Every time we hold someone accountable for breaking the law or violating an ethical standard, we affirm our system of laws and rules. Every time we don't, the rule of law decays further. That's not to say we should worry less about treating people justly and compassionately. Of course we must ensure that people receive proper adjudication, including an opportunity to defend their conduct. We should give people second chances when they mess up, and offer our forgiveness whenever possible. We should also address underlying social and economic problems—such as drug addiction, poverty, and systemic inequities—that can contribute to lawlessness. Ultimately, we should care for people and their basic needs. But when we start to equivocate on our system of laws—that essential blueprint of the kind of country we all want to live in—something is broken and we must fix it. And our elected leaders especially have an obligation to do so.

We Want Leaders, Not Scoundrels and Liars

If you occupy a position of power, you must enforce the law and apply it fairly and transparently. You also must abide by the law yourself. When you make a mistake or violate a rule of any kind, including basic ethical standards, you must acknowledge it and hold yourself accountable.

Given how obvious this principle is to anyone who respects the rule of law, the Supreme Court's 2024 decision in *Trump v. United States*—to provide presidents with immunity for deeds they committed as official acts—is deeply damaging.[28] Why should presidents be able to use the powers of the Oval Office to violate the law, and then not bear the consequences? As Justice Sonia Sotomayor writes in her scathing dissent, the court "effectively creates a law-free zone around the president, upsetting the status quo that has existed since the founding." She notes the great irony at play here: "The man in charge of enforcing laws can now just break them."[29]

Leaders serve as role models for others. This means they must act in a law-abiding way themselves if they're requiring others to abide by the law. They have a duty to demonstrate to the public that the laws apply equally to everyone, no matter how wealthy, prominent, or connected you might be.

Sadly, too many leaders today fall far short of the mark. In 2020, with the Covid-19 pandemic raging, Governor Newsom and other leaders admonished California's people to take sensible precautions, including wearing masks and avoiding large social gatherings. And yet a few months later, amid a spike in Covid-19 cases, photographs emerged showing Newsom enjoying dinner with others at an exclusive restaurant—indoors, no masks, no social distancing.[30] Ordinary Californians who played by the rules were going stir-crazy in their homes, but apparently holding a position of power allowed Newsom to avoid playing by those same rules. The governor eventually acknowledged making a "bad mistake," but he also misleadingly claimed that the dinner was held outdoors. *The New York Times* scolded him for this instance of "do as I say, not as I dine,"[31] and one observer described this as "Newsom at his worst," showing "a nagging lack of judgment and an overinflated sense of entitlement in the service of double standards that apply to him [and] a chosen few in his circle but not the rest of us."[32]

Newsom seems to have displayed similarly questionable judgment on other occasions. In 2023, the California Assembly passed a law establishing a $20 an hour minimum wage for the state's fast-food workers. The measure promised to help out folks working in these jobs, but it seemed poised to hurt businesses that depended on hourly labor, including many restaurants. The law had a strange exception written into it: "Chains that bake bread and sell it as a standalone item" didn't have to abide by the new minimum wage regulations. And exactly which chains do that? Well, Panera Bread bakes and sells bread as a standalone item.[33] It might be a coincidence, but the guy who owns some two dozen Panera Bread restaurants in California is one of Newsom's friends and campaign donors.

Although Newsom's office denied any wrongdoing, some observers found that connection curious.[34] We should also wonder about the confidentiality that surrounded the making of this law—participants who took part in negotiations had to sign a formal agreement stating they wouldn't blab about it.[35] Is someone trying to avoid accountability to the public here? What ever happened to transparency?

Newsom's behavior is troubling for the message it sends, but at least there is no direct evidence, so far as I know, of explicit illegality. Many people in positions of power *do* wind up breaking the law, however. We can start with President Trump, who in May 2024 was convicted of thirty-four charges relating to a hush money cover-up surrounding his 2016 presidential campaign.

Jurors found him guilty of fraudulently misstating expenses and falsifying his records, violating New York State election law in the process.[36] But the sad reality is that an unacceptable number of high-profile leaders in both parties have been charged with crimes in recent years, including Democratic Senator Bob Menendez, Republican Congressman George Santos, Republican Congressman Jeff Fortenberry, and Republican Congressman Duncan Hunter.[37] Corruption is also present at the local level. In 2023, the US Department of Justice (DOJ) obtained eighty convictions of local officials for corruption.[38]

You might look at a statistic like that and say, *Hey, at least we're catching and convicting unscrupulous leaders!* Indeed, it is some reassurance that the rule of law still matters. But our country is pretty crappy at holding leaders accountable. Did we ever put in jail all those CEOs who brought the 2007–2008 banking crisis upon us? What about the leaders who took us to war in Iraq under dubious pretenses or knew about torture perpetrated by the US government abroad?[39] Today, despite efforts to convict public leaders who are behaving improperly, our country is still scandalously corrupt. According to Transparency International, a group that tracks corruption globally, the United States ranked as just the twenty-fourth least corrupt country in the world in 2022, behind Estonia and Uruguay and just above Bhutan and the United Arab Emirates.[40]

Every time an ethical scandal breaks involving a leader who holds the public trust, it damages our faith in institutions and the rule of law. And it seems we can't even trust those in the role of enforcing the law to discharge their duties honorably. In 2023, the DOJ obtained convictions in forty-four cases related to corruption by federal law enforcement officials.[41] That sounds substantial, but it begs the question: How many officers committed offenses and *didn't* get convicted?

As a matter of fact, the United States seems to have a terrible record of holding accountable those with powerful roles in the justice system. Reporting by *Reuters* between 2008 and 2019 uncovered thousands of instances where judges abused their authority, yet in 90 percent of cases, judges found their way back to their posts, essentially receiving just a "tsk, tsk." These cases included judges who sent sexually explicit pictures, had sexual encounters in their chambers, were involved in early morning fights, and wrongfully put underprivileged people in jail for overdue traffic fines.[42] As one judicial oversight expert noted, "When you see cases like that, the public starts to wonder about the integrity and honesty of the system. It looks like a good ol' boys club."[43]

Many Americans are indeed wondering. Less than half of the country claims to trust the federal government's judicial branch—a new low, according to Gallup.[44] Trust in state courts also seems to have been declining in recent years.[45] And in 2022, less than half of Americans in a Gallup poll had confidence in the police, another new low.[46]

Given the messiness of daily reality, it's not always easy for people in positions of power to uphold laws and ethical rules, or even to hold themselves accountable. But leaders simply must find the strength, wisdom, and courage to do so—or risk allowing the United States to become a nation governed by scoundrels and liars.

As of 2024, bipartisan legislation is pending that would make it illegal for members of Congress as well as their close family members to trade on the stock market.[47] Of course, we shouldn't need a law to prevent such unseemly conduct—elected officials should refrain on their own. They have no business trading stocks, given that these lawmakers are privy to all kinds of sensitive information that might move markets and that their decision-making itself can impact companies' stock prices. The potential for impropriety is too high.

And the standard our leaders must live up to isn't simply behaving legally and ethically. They also have a duty to avoid the *appearance* of impropriety, even if they technically haven't violated any law. Perhaps you've heard the old saying that those in a position of leadership must be "like Caesar's wife, above reproach."[48] In other words, it isn't enough for a public servant to be virtuous— the company they keep must be trustworthy as well. That used to be the standard for those charged with the public's business, and it must be again. No special perks. No conflicts of interest. No suspicious conduct of *any* kind.

When I served as chairman of Brand USA, the innovative body that serves as our country's national tourism board, some on the board wanted the government to reimburse them for travel or meals they might have paid for in connection with their roles. My response: No friggin' way. Their request wasn't illegal or even, strictly speaking, unethical. But it conflicted with the spirit of what we on the board were supposed to be doing, which was to volunteer our time and expertise for the public good. The last thing I wanted was for the public to learn about a board member who had expensed a lavish hotel stay, living large on the public dime. That would tarnish the whole organization and make our work more difficult. I told our board members, who were senior leaders at major companies in the hospitality and travel industries, that their respective firms had to pay their expenses. If they didn't like it, they could leave the board. I also made it a policy to personally review any agency expenditures over $25,000 to ensure that they were legitimate.[49]

As it turned out, a number of board members didn't like my strict governing style. They let me know by trying to oust me in a palace coup. That's right, they tried to "coup the Cloo"! The plan was to call a surprise vote at an upcoming meeting and kick me to the curb. However, these schemers hadn't read the text in our charter very carefully. Those rules said that I, as chairman, had to call a meeting to order; otherwise it wasn't legitimate. Without my assent, the meeting couldn't occur. Catching wind of their intentions, I squelched them by declining to call the meeting; then I set about getting the plotters to give up their plans. Not only did I uphold the rules, but my intimate knowledge of them—and my insistence on sticking to them—paid off. If you try to coup the Cloo, watch out: You're going to get beat!

When Governor Steve Sisolak appointed me to chair the Nevada Athletic Commission, I likewise took a firm stance when it came to ethics and legality. From the very beginning, I disclosed every potential conflict of interest I could fathom. Nevada's attorney general said I was going overboard, but I wanted to be transparent. I also didn't hesitate to make decisions that were ethically necessary—even if they would upset powerful people.

In 2021, a young college student named Nathan Valencia was tragically killed while participating in an informal boxing match held by a fraternity to benefit charity.[50] Thanks to a crazy loophole in the law, my commission had no jurisdiction over amateur fights that involved students exclusively. After the fact, though, local police had an obligation to investigate thoroughly what had happened and determine whether to bring any charges. As far as I could tell, a thorough investigation didn't happen—and I spoke up about it.

A serious investigation would have entailed collecting the other combatant's gloves as evidence. That didn't happen here, even after the commission pressed for it not once, not twice, but three times. Police investigators didn't look at photos showing the referee holding a canned alcoholic beverage. And while police queried whether the venue involved had proper permits, they never sought to open a murder investigation or to hold anyone accountable. They simply determined that the young boxer's death was "not criminal" and moved on. At the end of the day, Joe Lombardo, the county sheriff at the time who has since been elected Nevada's governor, just didn't seem interested in getting the investigation right.

I wasn't alone in my criticism. Responding to public outcry as well as my requests, Nevada's attorney general looked independently at how the police handled the case. In a comprehensive, 158-page report, the attorney general's office concluded that the police contention that no crime had been committed had indeed been too definitive and "premature."[51] Although I helped shine a spotlight onto this situation, bringing public pressure to bear,

I lacked the power to force the sheriff to uphold the law as I believe he should have. Having concluded that no crime had been committed, he never sent a case over for the district attorney to prosecute.

To this day, I remain convinced that justice wasn't fully served in this case—that the local leadership succumbed to the moral flabbiness that afflicts so many of our country's leaders. Hoping to prevent future harm, the Nevada Athletic Commission pushed for a new regulation—called Nathan's Law—expanding its regulatory powers to include oversight in cases such as this.

You might wonder if I apply rules and ethics as stringently when running my own businesses. The answer is a bright, flashing *yes!* At Diamond, ethical conduct was always critically important and in fact a guiding principle. Our team members knew that our leaders had zero tolerance for misdeeds. If you treated your colleagues or our guests poorly once, maybe I'd give you the benefit of the doubt. But if you did it again, you were gone. And if you stole from the company, you were not only gone—we might file charges against you, as we had to do on occasion. This was a signal to our thousands of workers that our rules were there for a reason, and that we'd enforce them vigorously.

And don't even think about lying! In my book, that's a fireable offense too—no second chances given. Even today, I will fire anybody I work or partner with on the spot when I uncover lies. Telling the truth is *everything*. It's fundamental. It's absolutely nonnegotiable. This might be surprising given today's post-truth society, but a person who lies can't be trusted—and trust is necessary for any healthy relationship, community, or company to function. I deal honestly with people at all times, and I demand honesty. The minute I learn that someone is purposely trying to deceive me or others around me, we're done.

Many CEOs think their position shields them from upholding laws and rules and from being held accountable. I think the opposite: The more power you have, the more you should accept accountability. When I was running Diamond, I called guests and personally apologized when, say, a housekeeper had an off day and didn't clean a room properly.

"Your housekeeper made a mistake," they would say.

"No," I would say, "I did. I'm the housekeeper."

In this vein, I did something that very few CEOs in the history of big business have ever done. When entering one of our properties, right at the front desk, you would see business cards with my personal contact information and an invitation to get in touch if something about your vacation wasn't right. In other words, I made myself personally accountable to every single customer for our company's performance.

Leaders at other companies thought I was nuts. I'm sure some people in *our* company thought so too. Remember, Diamond Resorts had a multitude of properties around the world and hundreds of thousands of vacation owners. People insisted that I'd be deluged at all hours with phone calls or emails.

Well, I thought, *we'll cross that bridge when we come to it*. For me, being accountable to our customers was vital, and it set an example for everyone else in the company.

As it turned out, hundreds of people *did* contact me. And each time, I responded personally and copied my team so they would understand just how seriously I took my responsibility to our guests. This extra work was manageable for me, and it allowed me to learn of any problems we had and ensure they got fixed. Trust me, when you practice that kind of accountability, you're not going to make many mistakes.

That's not to say I'm perfect—I'm certainly not.

When I chaired the Nevada Athletic Commission, I agreed to allow Dana White, president and CEO of Ultimate Fighting Championship (UFC), to go forward with a new league called Power Slap. If you haven't heard of slap fighting, that's probably a good thing. The league oversaw this new "sport," if you want to use that word—basically, it's badass dudes and dudettes taking turns slapping the heck out of one another to see who falls first. I was assured that slap fighting was safe, and organizers claimed that the fighting would be well regulated. They had reputable sponsors lined up. Everything seemed to be in order for Nevada to allow this new, innovative sport. But as I've since realized, it's not as safe as they said.

You might be thinking, *Duh*. And I don't blame you. Reports about slap fighting, and videos of competitors getting the crap beat out of them and suffering concussions, changed my mind. I realize now that doctors who had criticized slap fighting were right, and that the long-term effects of receiving blows to the side of the head are unknown. I regret allowing slap fighting in the state of Nevada, and knowing what I now know, I would decide differently.

I've publicly admitted making a mistake and using poor judgment in that instance.[52] And I take comfort in the fact that at least I owned up to it. I won't suck up to Dana White or corporate sponsors who support slap fighting by doubling down on my misstep. In order to live with myself, I had to take responsibility. That, in my view, is what a leader does.

And that's what I want to see more leaders do, at all levels—take responsibility for mistakes and commit to telling the truth—not to save their butts or salvage their reputations, but because they believe in the rule of law and feel morally obliged to serve the public with integrity.

A Little Discipline, Please

Like the transformative lesson about accountability I learned as a kid working at Brooktrails, my broader obsession with truth, ethics, and lawfulness started early. Once as a young boy, I don't remember exactly how old, I told my father a lie—not a big lie, just something stupid or silly. My father might have calmly lectured me on why lying was wrong and given me a warning of future punishment, as parents sometimes do today. That wasn't exactly his style. He took off his belt and slapped me hard on the ass with it, old-school style. It wasn't pleasant; I would never do this to my kids or endorse this sort of discipline. But it's what happened to me, and you better believe I got the message: *You don't lie. Ever. You tell the freaking truth.*

My dad was tough with me on other occasions when I stepped out of line in some way. He raised his voice. He didn't coddle. He told me, "Because I said so." None of this was abusive, at least not as that concept was defined back in the day. It was well-meaning parental discipline. My dad was not my friend growing up. He was an authority figure who took seriously his responsibility to teach me right from wrong. And I learned. It became really clear that rules were rules, and you needed to abide by them.

I didn't resent my dad for his toughness. On the contrary, my dad eventually became my best friend and business partner. I felt *grateful* to him. He disciplined me because he loved me, and his tough love made me better, turning me into the person I am today. How can you possibly repay someone for that?

I tried my best. Later in his life, when he was suffering from Alzheimer's disease and had trouble caring for himself, I brought him into my home and provided for his every need, often attending to him myself. When he died in 2018, I felt the greatest sorrow I've ever experienced. I never have loved another person like I loved him, even though he was tough on me. *Because* he was tough on me.

Raising kids today, we're far more aware of the mental impact of various kinds of discipline, and that's a good thing. We move forward. We get better. But we can't just blame our leaders for ignoring the hard truth that rules and laws matter. We must also blame ourselves for softening up in our concern with laws and rules—not only when it comes to public life, but to what and how we teach our children.

We do ourselves a disservice when we equate discipline with punishment. They are *not* the same. Discipline is about establishing healthy boundaries and useful expectations. And that's something our parents, our schools, and our society could do more to instill.

In recent decades, administrators have watered down rules and standards as part of restorative justice approaches to education.[53] While it's vital for schools to adopt inclusive policies and treat all students fairly, teachers in some states have protested and even walked out because schools are failing to satisfactorily address problem behavior in the classroom.[54]

"Too many administrators ignore the minutiae of behavior codes, such as the need for a uniform policy," one education expert says. "Why enforce attendance or discipline a child for talking out of turn when there's a fight in the cafeteria? 'We've got bigger fish to fry!' But if school staff do not hold the line on small fights, bigger fish come along."[55] This is exactly what I've been saying: When we don't respect rules, we get chaos.

Many of our schools also aren't enforcing academic standards. They're certainly not teaching civics: According to the Institute for Citizens & Scholars, only about a third of Americans today have the basic knowledge required to pass a citizenship test.[56] And as I've suggested, grade inflation has run rampant in recent decades. By 2016, almost half of high school students received A grades. Yet during the preceding two decades, grade point averages rose while SAT scores declined, suggesting that kids aren't actually doing better work to justify those higher grades.[57] Apparently the goal is to help students *feel* like they're the best, the smartest—to make sure everybody wins a prize. The underlying message is clear: *You can decide to break the academic rules, or fail to study hard and turn in your assignments, and not have to suffer the consequences of a lower grade.* These days, people argue that allowing kids to turn in late assignments is a *good* thing since "flexible due dates" reduce stress.[58] Call me an old fogey, but a little motivational stress is *good* for you.

Look, I know kids are suffering from higher rates of mental illness.[59] But isn't it plausible that teaching kids to be fragile is contributing to those upticks? During adolescence, we prepare young people to function in adult society—and in real life, you don't get an extra day just because you feel you need it. Someone *else* will land the big client. Someone *else* will get the coveted job. That's the hard truth.

Rules, boundaries, and restrictions are real. If we don't help our kids understand and respect this reality, we're setting them up for failure. We're compromising America's future. We're imparting the same logic that says, *You know, it's not so bad if you steal something worth $100*, and that says, *Hey, it's not so bad if I'm in a position of power and behave unethically.* We need to take responsibility for preparing kids for life, not just blame them once they reach adulthood and can't function as productive members of society. That means teaching them to respect the rules while they're young.

Getting Our Act Together

Transgressions small and large *are* bad. But even worse is that we as a society have lost sight of that hard truth. Gallup surveys have shown a decline since 2002 in how people rate the state of morality in our country.[60] Although some point out that people *always* seem to think that morality is declining, other data suggests that accountability and standards of behavior really might be getting worse.[61]

Opinions on the ethics and honesty of members of various professions—law, medicine, business, engineering—are down across the board.[62] Research shows that citizens might be especially willing to overlook lying on the part of politicians if those leaders happen to agree with them on the issues.[63] Americans also allow themselves to behave dishonestly and unethically in all kinds of small ways: by lying on dating websites, puffing up résumés, stealing from employers, ghosting potential employers when applying for jobs, and so forth.[64]

These are troubling trends. How can we continue to live in an orderly, trustworthy society when we write a lack of accountability into our laws, when leaders behave improperly and buck responsibility, and when we ourselves grow mushy on morality in our own personal lives?

We've got to get our act together. We've got to shape up. And by *we*, I mean each and every one of us. Let's take the rule of law more seriously than we have been—and demand that our leaders do too. Let's uphold rules and ethical principles in our own conduct, even when other people aren't looking. Let's impart on our kids a stricter sense of right and wrong. Let's elect leaders who not only share our viewpoints on specific issues or belong to our political party, but care about the rule of law and honor it in their own conduct.

The women's rights activist Elizabeth Cady Stanton once remarked, "It is very important in a republic, that the people should respect the laws, for if we throw them to the winds, what becomes of civil government?"[65] The answer, unfortunately, is becoming clear in our own society. But if we all pull together to reaffirm the role of laws, rules, ethics, and accountability in our public and private lives, we can help put America and our local communities back on a better track.

THE BEST ECONOMIES BENEFIT *EVERYONE*

IF YOU'RE A FAN OF MEXICAN CUISINE, you might have heard of Ruiz Foods. This family-owned firm, which sells frozen burritos, taquitos, and other products under the El Monterey and Tornados brand names, is a classic California success story—but to ensure its continued success, the company was forced to take some of its business elsewhere.

The company's cofounder, Louis Ruiz, emigrated to the state in 1923 as a small boy, escaping the tumult of the Mexican Revolution.[1] His family settled in Los Angeles before relocating to Tulare County. In 1964, when his son and cofounder Fred Ruiz was in college, the two of them began making frozen Mexican food in a warehouse in Tulare, California. Louis would sell their products and make deliveries. Fred remembers that when he was first developing the company's products, he'd race samples over to his mother's workplace so she could offer direction: *Add a little more of this, a little more of that.* Years later, Fred's daughter Kim Ruiz Beck joined the business, eventually serving as chairman of the board. To date, four generations of the family have worked at the company.[2]

Early on, Fred had big dreams: He wanted one day to build the firm to $3.5 million in revenues.[3] Boy, did he exceed that goal. A decade into it, Ruiz Food was bringing in *$50 million* in annual revenues, and consumers coast to coast were enjoying the company's products.[4] In 1983, President Ronald Reagan honored Fred and Louis as US Small Business Persons of the Year. In 2005, the company was doing so well that it expanded to a factory in Texas; nine years later, it started manufacturing products in South Carolina.[5] All along, the company's California presence remained strong. Long headquartered in Dinuba, a small city about forty miles southeast of Fresno, the company had a flagship production facility there that was home to some 1,600 employees as of 2019.[6] Today, Ruiz Foods is the largest maker of frozen Mexican foods in the United States, with annual sales that surpassed $1 billion as of 2021.[7]

In the strictest sense, though, Ruiz Foods is no longer a California company. In 2024, the firm celebrated the grand opening of a new headquarters—in Frisco, Texas, a town located about thirty miles from Dallas.

Moving to the Lone Star State made good sense. The new location would allow Ruiz Foods to better access its far-flung customers and factories. Being close to Dallas also offered Ruiz Foods access to a larger talent pool than they'd had back in Dinuba.[8] There were hints that an unfavorable business climate in California might have factored in, if only secondarily: As Kim Ruiz Beck pointed out, Texas currently is friendlier to businesses than California. It probably didn't hurt that the city of Frisco chipped in $250,000 in incentives for hiring local employees.[9]

The relocation of Ruiz Foods' headquarters is part of a larger flight of companies, jobs, people, and wealth away from the burden of high taxes and overregulation in states that are not particularly business-friendly. Over 350 companies moved their headquarters out of California between 2018 and 2021, including big names like Tesla, Charles Schwab, and Hewlett-Packard—in fact, no fewer than eleven Fortune 1000 companies in about the same time frame.[10]

To fuel economic growth and increase broad-based prosperity, state and federal government institutions must do what's in their power to welcome entrepreneurs and businesses of all sizes. We can't vilify them, treating them as enemies and regulating the crap out of them. Nor can we view them as bottomless piggy banks to be tapped for tax dollars. We must understand their needs and incentivize them to grow—and to start additional companies, bringing expanding prosperity to all.

Strong, prosperous, sustainable economies aren't divisive, favoring one group at the expense of others. They're *inclusive*. We need sound policies that deliver this inclusivity, not just more empty rhetoric. That's the hard truth, and one we desperately need to hear—and deserve to see in our own backyard.

Chasing Away the Wealthy

Individuals, especially the wealthier and better educated, are also leaving California in droves. In 2023, the state population suffered a net loss of more than seventy-five thousand people; by one count, the previous two years' loss was about ten times that.[11] During those years, the average income of a person fleeing California for states like Texas, Florida, or South Carolina was $137,000, well above the 2024 national median income of about $60,000.[12] From a revenue standpoint, at a time of astronomical budget deficits, losing wealthier taxpayers is the last thing California needs.

In fact, departures of wealthy Californians might have contributed to an anticipated drop in the state's personal income tax proceeds of 25 percent.[13] In 2023, California ranked as the state with the largest net outflow of wealth—a number pegged at $343 million. Other blue states like New York, Illinois, and Massachusetts also ranked high on this list.[14] Meanwhile, red states like Florida and Texas have picked up billions of new taxable wealth as people of means have moved in.

Why are so many people heading for the exits? California, after all, has so much going for it: amazing weather, unparalleled natural beauty, a diverse economy, world-class universities like Stanford and the University of California, Berkeley. A good part of the answer has to do with California's elected officials and their misguided policies. The many social problems that plague California, like homelessness, the housing crisis, and crime, make it an unattractive place to start a career or raise a family, and it's a travesty that the state's elected leaders haven't yet provided effective solutions. Add to those challenges an unfavorable business climate that makes it difficult to start and grow a company, and consequently, difficult for people to find good jobs.

When researchers ask business leaders which states are worst for business, they typically shout, "California!"[15] Like other blue states, the state has failed to provide the kinds of economic incentives that businesses need to prosper. Worse, it has discouraged business and wealth creation by penalizing companies with high taxes and burdensome regulations. No surprise that companies like Ruiz Foods aren't going the extra mile to stick around.

But left-wing extremist policymakers in California and elsewhere haven't simply scuttled economic growth by making life difficult for businesses. They've also seemed eager to push wealthy individuals out the door. As of 2024, if you earned $1 million or more and you happen to live in California, you had the privilege of paying a 14.4 percent state income tax—the nation's highest.[16] Layer that onto federal taxes, and you have top earners—the drivers of the economy—often paying more than half of their income to the government.

In an effort to help reduce yawning wealth inequalities, progressives want to tax the very wealthiest even more. One 2023 measure introduced in California would have had people with assets of $50 million or more paying a special tax of 1 percent; billionaires would have paid 1.5 percent. Although it might seem fair to ask the extremely wealthy to pay more than they already do, in reality these measures are bad policy. Rather than generate more tax revenue as the policies intend, they encourage the wealthiest to move to lower-tax states like Montana, Texas, or Nevada, taking their tax payments with them.[17]

In some localities, the tax burden placed on the wealthiest is even heavier. In April 2023, the city of Los Angeles imposed a special 4 percent "mansion" tax on the sale of luxury homes selling above $5 million; if your home was worth $10 million or more, the tax rose to 5.5 percent. Such policies might generate funding for the state, but they crimp the economy by incenting wealthy Californians to keep their homes off the market and rent them out rather than sell and face a hefty tax bill. For some wealthy Los Angelenos, this measure has been the final nudge they've needed to leave the state.[18]

In what world does it make sense to tax wealthy people so much that it prompts them to pick up their roots and move on? As Richard A. Epstein, a professor at the New York University School of Law, remarks, "Pro-growth policies make sense, by making everyone better off. Tax gimmicks don't."[19] What California should be doing is providing incentives to form and fund new businesses that benefit more people. Instead of hammering wealthy people with taxes to the point where they're itching to leave, make it attractive for them to stay, generate value, and create jobs.

A number of states, for instance, allow entrepreneurs and investors to avoid taxes on up to $10 million in capital gains, assuming that they meet various requirements. Being allowed to keep more of the value you create is a huge incentive to start and grow a business. California used to allow for this kind of tax relief via a qualified small business stock (QSBS) exclusion—but unfortunately it has been repealed.[20]

California continues to consider cutting financial support to small business to help make up for the state's massive budget shortfall.[21] Another bad policy! California would be better off aggressively using the tax code and government spending to *encourage* small business formation, mindful of the jobs these companies bring as well as the opportunities for employees to enjoy upward mobility.

In considering incentives for wealthy individuals and businesses to create wealth, remember that some of California's biggest industries took root in the state because of its more favorable business climate. During the early twentieth century, filmmakers migrated to Hollywood because of the fantastic weather and the state's geographic diversity, but also because its non-union labor was cheaper than what producers would have to pay on the East Coast. As one historian relates, "The pro-business orientation of the courts and city council helped local employers undercut the strength of organized labor."[22]

Hollywood has served for over a century as the global center of filmmaking, but much of that business has drifted elsewhere in recent years. States like Georgia have drawn film production away from its iconic home in Hollywood by offering billions in tax incentives, just as California does.[23] In terms of labor, the tables have turned: Now Georgia's workers are largely non-union and earn less, making it more attractive for film producers to do business in the state.[24] And local leaders in Georgia go out of their way to welcome film productions, making sites in their jurisdictions accessible to film crews.[25] Georgia in 2016 accounted for more big feature films than California did and is now known as the "Hollywood of the South."[26]

California's shrinking film production is more than just a

cultural bombshell; it's a blow to the state's economy. Each day of a film's production can pump over $1 million into a local economy. When the movie *Black Panther* was made, about 3,100 Georgians—not Californians—brought home paychecks totaling over $26.5 million.[27] As one observer writing in the *Los Angeles Times* lamented, "There's no business like show business—but in Los Angeles, it feels like there's no business at all." Film production has been drip-dripping out of California for decades, but as this observer noted, at a certain point the state risks a collapse of its industry: "If productions in Southern California dip below a critical level for too long, the industry's essential talent will drift away along with enormous sums of revenue."[28]

Employees deserve to earn a good, living wage, but there's also enormous value for everyone in making a state economically competitive. As the state of Georgia has decided, it's better to have decent jobs, even if they pay a bit lower, than no jobs at all.

The surest path to generalized prosperity is to avoid extremes and instead take a commonsense, *moderate* approach. We must take steps to create *shared* prosperity that benefits people at the top as well as those further on down the ranks. That means embracing pro-business, pro-growth policies that create jobs, but also tempering these policies to avoid social and environmental harms and to ensure that *everyone* benefits—people and businesses alike.

Giving Business the Middle Finger

How, you might ask, have wayward policies tended to discourage business and wealth creation? Let's start with high taxes—and for simplicity's sake, I'll keep my focus on California, mindful that similar arguments hold for localities elsewhere.

Every year, a nonpartisan think tank called the Tax Foundation puts together its State Business Tax Climate Index, a measurement of how business-friendly states are in their tax policies. (Yes, there are tax wonks out there who obsess about this kind of stuff.) Guess where California ranks on the index? Forty-eighth.[29] At least it's not fiftieth—that's an honor reserved for another deep blue state, New Jersey. But California suffers from corporate, sales, and personal taxes that are among the highest in the country, and also among the most complex.[30] If you're a business, tax policy makes it significantly harder to operate profitably in California than in, say, Texas, which ranks thirteenth overall on the index and where taxes are lower.

Regulations and government red tape in California also make the business environment more difficult for many companies. Legislators in the state seemingly haven't found a business regulation they don't like. Labor regulations, environmental laws—there are so damn many of them! As the California Policy Center, a group that takes aim at public-sector unions, has remarked, "Across every sector, businesspeople are trying to cope with the harmful impact of labor laws, environmental regulations, high taxes, and a byzantine array of often indecipherable and ever-changing rules from dozens of oversight agencies."[31] If you run a restaurant, for instance, your employees must take breaks every four and a half hours—even if they'd rather just keep working so they can leave early. You also have to have a test kit on hand at your bar so concerned patrons can check if someone has put an illegal drug in their drinks. And you can no longer tack on minor surcharges to your patrons' bills without disclosing it in advance as part of the price, a tactic that restaurants sometimes deploy so they can afford to provide health care for their employees.

These sorts of regulations might sound like good ideas, and perhaps some of them are, taken individually. But we don't live in a utopia where regulations are cost-free; we live in the real world. When you pile on restrictions and micromanage compliance, you make it extremely hard for entrepreneurs to run a profitable business, especially in a sector like food service, where margins are frequently razor-thin. Often, restaurants are forced to respond by simply increasing the prices paid by consumers, potentially lowering demand.[32]

Excessive regulations can not only prevent economic activity but exacerbate other social problems. Real estate development is a good example. The California Environmental Quality Act (CEQA) mandates that anyone who wants to put up a new building has to file a report with the government laying out the environmental impact. That sounds like a good idea. Who doesn't want to protect the environment? In practice, though, neighborhood groups, unions, and others have exploited the law, using it not to protect the environment but to achieve other objectives, like gaining leverage in negotiations. A union might tell a developer they'll sue under CEQA if the developer doesn't hire unionized employees. The developer must either give in or spend time and money fighting the lawsuit in court. According to a 2015 study, just 13 percent of CEQA lawsuits were filed by legitimate environmental advocates.[33]

Abuses of CEQA make it impossible to strike a sensible balance between development and environmental protection. The result has been terrible for California. A 2023 *Los Angeles Times* editorial observed that although the law "has improved countless construction projects," it has "also too often been used to thwart progress on the state's most pressing needs by stalling or blocking important projects."[34] If you're wondering why the state has a housing crisis (which has helped propel many of those educated high earners to other states), this is a big part of the answer. As urban planner M. Nolan Gray has remarked, "One of the main effects of CEQA has been to exacerbate the state's crippling housing-affordability crisis."[35] In some cases, a single individual filing (or even threatening to file) a lawsuit is all it takes to derail a housing development project that otherwise might have greatly benefitted a local community.

Elected leaders in California understand CEQA's flaws, but they haven't moved quickly enough to remedy them. As the *Los Angeles Times* editorial page complained, "There isn't the political will to get it done. There are too many stakeholders, particularly labor unions, that don't want to lose the leverage CEQA gives them and too few lawmakers willing to take on those interests."[36] While elected officials dither, development projects are going unbuilt, and businesses and people are leaving.

Sometimes the best way that government can have our backs really is by getting *off* our backs. My experiences growing a successful business in the hospitality industry have sensitized me to the problem of excessive regulations. Tourism is a $156 billion business in California, so why does the state make it so hard for developers to build new hotels?[37] If you want to put up a hotel along the coast in California or expand an existing one, you might have to pay millions to create affordable housing or provide for other public goods. You might also have to allocate a percentage of your rooms to be priced for low- and middle-income guests.[38]

Regulations and restrictions arise at the local level too. In Los Angeles, anyone who wants to build a hotel must commit to replacing any housing units that are put out of use as a result of the project. Meanwhile, work rules dictate operational minutiae such as how many rooms an individual housekeeper can maintain without having to be paid double-time wages.[39]

The intentions of such policies might be laudable, even reasonable on a case-by-case basis. But the sheer piling on of universal regulations makes hotel construction uneconomical for developers, preventing new hotels from being built. "The weight of all that together, it just crushes," says one California developer. "It doesn't make economic sense [for the business] anymore, and so there's no new hotel. That's what happened to us. We ended up selling it and got out of it. . . . The problem is, it's not just one cut. It's death by a thousand cuts."[40]

And the developer isn't the only one to lose out when a project is canceled. Local economies miss the jobs and other economic activity that a new hotel might have generated. Lodging prices rise due to lower supply, perhaps leading some consumers to skip a vacation in the area and go elsewhere. Municipalities also lose the tourism-related taxes they would have collected—revenue that normally helps them to fund their budgets.

Roger Dow, former president and CEO of the US Travel

Association (a lobbying group for the hospitality industry) sees diminishing prospects for growth in the tourism industry in California if the state doesn't curb its excessive regulation. "I've talked to almost all the major hoteliers," he explains, "and they say to me, 'We're probably not going to build another big box hotel—one with a thousand rooms—in California.' It no longer pencils. It no longer makes money. The work rules, all the criteria, all the regulations we have to do—it's basically impossible to develop in California."[41]

Hearing Dow's assessment, I doubt it would have been possible to build a large, thriving hospitality company like Diamond Resorts if I were starting in the state and conducting most of my operations there. The legal impediments to growth would have been too great.

The knee-jerk tendency to regulate reflects an underlying suspicion of business interests, a perception that businesses are an enemy of the people. Politicians like Senator Bernie Sanders say the quiet part out loud, calling Wall Street, for instance, a "fraud."[42] Although I absolutely sympathize with the little guy and want to see everyone get a fair shake, this is not a good-versus-bad situation. Demonizing business is wrong. Companies and investors can sometimes go too far in pursuing profits, but they're not the enemy—they're an asset to society, thanks to the innovation and economic growth they foster. If we punish businesses by saddling them with excessive regulations, we're not just hurting them; we're holding back progress for all of society.

The New York Times columnist Nicholas Kristof, in a 2024 opinion piece lamenting the excesses of West Coast progressives, noted that "one element of progressive purity is suspicion of the private sector, and this hobbles efforts to make businesses part of the solution."[43] Kristof points to a long-standing rule in Portland, Oregon, that prohibits members of the city council from earning outside income—a restriction that, in practice, requires candidates who are also entrepreneurs to give up their businesses before taking office. That's ridiculous! We should be *encouraging* business leaders to run for elected office, where they can harness their rich operational and organizational knowledge for the public good. If we had more successful business leaders in office at every level, believe me, our government agencies would be run far more efficiently and responsibly than they are today.

But the costs to society when we demonize business run deeper than a city council bereft of active business leaders: Regulations forged at all levels of government without the participation and foresight of business leaders can cause unexpected problems. Missed opportunities for creative public-private partnerships can mean the difference between success and failure in addressing the serious problems communities face. I know that such partnerships can make that difference because I've been involved with them myself.

One of my passions as a philanthropist and activist is finding solutions to the housing crisis, both in California and in my city of Los Angeles. I'm drawn to the issue more and more because it's a seemingly intractable problem that California hasn't been able to address effectively, despite spending $24 billion on it (more on that in the next chapter). Why not use my business and government experience to shake things up and get officials to focus on real solutions?

To that end, I've helped sponsor LA4LA, an initiative championed by Los Angeles Mayor Karen Bass that seeks to disrupt the status quo on this issue by bringing together philanthropy, business, and government. The initiative identifies barriers to development and works to solve them by creating new financing arrangements, and by unearthing affordable housing projects that have stalled but could be quickly unlocked.[44] LA4LA not only seeks to attract philanthropic interest in addressing the housing scarcity issue, but also invites the public to propose ideas for new projects and to volunteer their time.[45]

In 2024, our work with LA4LA resulted in the completion of a fifty-eight-unit affordable housing project in the city's Koreatown section, called the Eaves Development. That's potentially hundreds of people saved from homelessness, and it contributed to the first drop in homelessness in Los Angeles in six years.[46] It's a small victory, and it never would have happened without Mayor Bass being willing to partner with business leaders.[47]

Another private-public partnership I was privileged to be involved with operated on a much larger scale: Brand USA. Recognizing the economic value that tourism brings, many countries around the world have set up formal agencies dedicated to promoting themselves as travel destinations. Prior to 2009, when the legislation passed that would create Brand USA, individual US states had tourism boards, but the United States lacked an organization that promoted the entire country. Brand USA was designed to fill this gap.

Funded by private companies, and with the federal government chipping in matching dollars, Brand USA coordinates with the travel industry as well as with federal agencies that include the Department of Homeland Security, the Department of State, Congress, and the White House. The organization has been enormously effective in driving new tourism, in turn helping to build our nation's economy. Since 2013, the promotional activities of Brand USA have led to $28.8 billion in spending from international visitors. In 2023 alone, Brand USA created almost thirty-two thousand jobs in the United States thanks to its promotional activity, representing $1.5 billion in earned income. Our federal, state, and local government entities took in almost $700 million in tax revenue.[48]

It's extraordinarily difficult to start an organization like Brand USA; the logistics and legal hurdles are enormous. Seeing the partnership continue to thrive in 2024, fourteen years after its founding—using the standard operating procedures we originally created—is incredibly gratifying. Brand USA is a perfect example of how working energetically and creatively with business, as opposed to simply trying to regulate it, can yield economic victories for everyone.

The Need for Balance

Although we should create an economy that encourages the contributions of the wealthy rather than antagonize them, we must not do so to the exclusion of other priorities. We need *some* regulations to ensure that, for example, our natural landscapes aren't ruined forever and our workforce isn't unfairly exploited. And basic fairness suggests that businesses and the wealthy should pay a reasonable share of taxes. The problem isn't that we have laws like CEQA on the books—I'm glad we do. It's that we haven't updated and fine-tuned such laws or used them judiciously to allow for a *balance* between incentivizing and supporting business and pursuing other social priorities. Likewise, I'm not claiming that we should avoid taxing businesses. But we should avoid taxing them too much, without regard to their economic realities and society's strong interest in fueling economic growth.

You know what isn't healthy? A government that's utterly unable to regulate properly, and that as a result will let business run rampant in polluting the environment, exploiting workers, taking advantage of consumers, and letting the poor and the disadvantaged fend for themselves. Unfortunately, that's what the United States may soon have, thanks to the Supreme Court and its misguided 2024 decision *Loper Bright Enterprises v. Raimondo*.

The decision ended something known as the Chevron precedent, which said that federal agencies could interpret the law using their subject-matter expertise when devising specific regulations. It makes sense to allow, say, the Environmental Protection Agency to figure out what Congress meant in passing a law intended to protect the environment, since such regulations often are highly technical in nature. But instead, the Supreme Court has ruled that the courts are ultimately the deciders. Somehow, the Supreme Court thinks justices and judges know how to handle technical matters better than the actual scientific experts do.

This court decision sounds like a boring, bureaucratic matter: Who cares who gets the last word interpreting the laws passed by Congress and signed by the president? As legal experts have pointed out, however, the effects of the *Loper Bright* decision will be far-reaching. In effect, the Supreme Court has rendered it much easier to challenge thousands of existing regulations issued by government agencies in areas like consumer protection, the environment, labor law, and more.

As an example, the Federal Trade Commission (FTC) recently proclaimed that employers can't make you agree to a noncompete clause when you sign a contract to work for them. Employers like those clauses because they prevent employees from amassing knowledge or client contacts at their company, and then quitting and going to work for a competitor. The FTC's ruling was a win for employees, who gained more freedom in the labor marketplace as well as leverage over their employers when seeking improved working circumstances. But thanks to the *Loper Bright* ruling, as some legal experts have observed, this employee advantage is now more vulnerable.[49] Already, a federal court has held that the FTC's rule is unenforceable (a decision that is under appeal as of 2024).[50] Soon, you might have to sign a noncompete clause after all to secure a job.

Prepare for all kinds of important regulations to become tied up in court, and for some or many of them to be overturned, as a result of the *Loper Bright* decision. Prepare, too, for government to simply regulate less. The ruling puts pressure on lawmakers to be far more precise in the language they use when drafting laws—a task that becomes especially hard in our polarized political environment. It's impossible for lawmakers to account for every possible situation in which a law might be applied, so regulations will now be much more easily challenged in court from various angles.

Government agencies will also be more timid about regulating, even in cases where scientific or technical considerations warrant expert involvement, or where citizens need crucial protections, as they'll fear being taken to court. Why put the time and effort into proper regulation when they'll end up forced to expend valuable resources fighting off court challenges—and rewriting rules if those challenges succeed?[51] All told, it's a historic neutering of the administrative state and a giveaway to the libertarian far right. Companies will win—at least in the short term—at the expense of Americans and the public good. As Georgetown Law professor Lawrence O. Gostin put it, the Supreme Court's decision was "a gut punch for health, safety, and the environment in the US. There'll be no area where agencies act to protect the public's health or safety or the environment that won't be adversely affected by this ruling."[52]

In addition to reining in capitalist excesses and requiring that businesses contribute their fair share in taxes, we must take care to protect the underprivileged and underserved in society and make sure that our economy benefits them too. If progressives demonize business, far-right conservatives often do something similar to those of lesser means. They're content to slash the social welfare programs that people on the low end of the income spectrum rely on, often insinuating that poor people are to blame for any economic misfortunes they're experiencing and therefore should be left on their own to pull themselves up out of poverty.[53] According to many conservatives, providing food stamps, welfare payments, and other benefits only serves to discourage poor people from working, making them lazier.[54]

This kind of thinking goes back decades—think of President Reagan's disparagement of "welfare queens."[55] In such a view, the only real solution to poverty lies in the private sector; the government bears no responsibility for helping people up. To combat poverty, conservatives suggest, the government should focus on deregulating businesses so they can prosper and (hopefully) create more jobs for those people. Critiquing the Obama administration, former Republican Congressman Dave Camp remarked in 2014 that "the formula for beating poverty is a job. This administration has no real focus on job creation—they are really focused on how long [unemployment] checks are being received."[56]

Notwithstanding what many Republicans seem to believe, in the vast majority of cases, poverty isn't a choice people make because they're unwilling to work hard.[57] Although individual initiative, talent, and industriousness obviously matter, myriad other factors can hold people back, including unexpected health crises, a lack of educational opportunities, structural racism, caretaking obligations, and yes, plain bad luck. We can't just tell ourselves that these individuals must be responsible for their own lives, that they've gotten what they deserve, and then instruct government to ignore them. These are *people*. Instead, we must take a balanced, moderate approach to poverty, fostering a work ethic and adopting pro-growth, pro-business policies while also making sure nobody gets left behind.

One policy that states across America should consider to make our economy more inclusive is instituting a universal basic income. Conservatives oppose this idea, arguing that it's unaffordable and will leave people with no incentive to work. Some liberals oppose it too, claiming that people need the meaning and purpose that a job provides, and that implementing a universal basic income will deprive people of that by removing the incentive to get a job. These objections are wrong. As research shows, universal basic income doesn't lead most people to stay at home and sit on the couch all day long.[58] Instead, it eases suffering among low-income folks and puts more of them on a path to getting jobs and achieving stable lives.

It's profoundly wrong to demonize those who are in crisis and struggling with issues like poverty, addiction, and homelessness. But taking such a hard-line approach to poverty isn't just heartless; it's also shortsighted.

In Denver, a program that gave cash payments to eight hundred unhoused people found that 45 percent of them obtained housing and that recipients in general spent less time in hospital emergency rooms or jail. Many used the money to help them get jobs and establish careers. The savings to taxpayers: over a half-million dollars.[59] Programs in other localities have yielded similar results.[60]

The lesson: When we give people the means to provide for their basic needs, they do better, and society wins too. And I know the value of giving people a helping hand because I've seen what happens when we do.

Not Handouts, but a Hand Up

In 2020, during the pandemic, entertainment journalist Jason Kennedy and I had a little bet going: He thought he could do more push-ups than I could. No chance of that! But my son and I challenged him to a push-up contest, with the loser making a donation to the winner's favorite charity. Well, I ended up "letting" Jason win. He did fifty-one push-ups that day, so I made a donation of $51,000 to the Los Angeles organization he chose, called the Dream Center.[61] I soon became fascinated by this organization and the good work that it did, and I've been involved with the Dream Center ever since. Who knew that a silly little bet could lead to such a wonderful and productive relationship?

Founded in 1994 by Pastor Matthew Barnett and his father, Tommy, the Dream Center offers outreach programs designed to help people in crisis fulfill their basic needs and stabilize their lives. Serving fifty thousand people a month, the center provides disaster relief; distributes food, clothing, and other essentials in local neighborhoods; and arranges transitional housing for unhoused people seeking to overcome addictions, mental health issues, and other challenges. Recipients can access mentorship, job training, and other support to help them turn around their lives.[62]

Since first donating to the Dream Center, I've gotten to know Pastor Barnett, and I've met individuals benefitting from its programs, talking one on one with them and asking for their best thinking on how best to address homelessness and related issues. I've heard many inspiring stories from people whose lives have been ruined by abuse, addiction, or a mistake they've made. For these folks, getting a hand up from the center is critical as they build themselves back up, one step at a time. They're people like Stirling, a young man who wound up unhoused after struggling with drug abuse and depression, but who now has a home of his own and works as a drug counselor.[63] And Sarah, a young mom who left her alcoholic husband and found refuge for herself and her two kids on the Dream Center's family floor, learning life skills that gave her a foundation for a healthier, more stable future. Once her husband joined her on the family floor, she was even able to begin to repair her marriage.[64]

I've been so impressed by the Dream Center as a faith-based model for raising people up that I've made it the core of my philanthropic efforts to combat homelessness, giving about $1 million to date. For each of the past four years, I've financially supported forty-two families at the center. I'm happy to give in part because the center is so results-oriented and diligent about tracking its impact. In 2023, its outreach programs served over sixty-five thousand people, while temporary housing and recovery programs helped hundreds of people and families get off the streets, get the addiction treatment they need, and transition back into stable lives.[65] These are just a couple of the many profound contributions the organization has made to the local community—so that community members can continue making their own contributions to our society.

As they say at the Dream Center, everybody deserves a chance to dream. Isn't chasing dreams what America is all about? That's why, in our policymaking, we must lead with love, respect, generosity, and understanding for *all* people. Rather than wash our hands of individuals in crisis, we must create pathways for them to rebuild their lives so they can pull themselves up. It's the compassionate and humane thing to do.

It's also sound policy that will lead to a healthier, safer, more prosperous society. The strongest economies are inclusive ones, with leaders who refuse to portray certain groups as evil or worthy of contempt, and instead help and incent people across the socioeconomic spectrum to get ahead. To achieve this goal, we need to strive for more balanced policymaking: an approach that unleashes business and wealthy people to create jobs while also providing for those who lack resources. This idea is deeply meaningful to me, in part because of a man named Kenny Williams.

I first met Kenny during the late 1980s when he came into the Jockey Club, a vacation ownership property in Las Vegas that my father partially owned. A young man at the time, Kenny came in looking for a job, but the company wouldn't hire him. He'd been incarcerated for having been an accessory to a murder, and our president and others at the company saw him as risky and undesirable to have around. Many bosses today would agree with that, which is why so many convicted felons have trouble finding work upon release from prison. I saw it differently.

Kenny had tremendous drive and a desire to turn around his life. Although he wasn't a conventional hire, I thought he had the potential to be a great one. Yes, he'd been involved in a crime scene, but he hadn't pulled the trigger himself. Rather, he'd hung around bad people and gotten drawn into a criminal lifestyle. I wanted to give him a chance and see what he could do.

I fought hard to get Kenny hired, and in the end my father—a big-hearted man—agreed to give him a job as a porter. Kenny worked hard cleaning the floors and helping the bellmen at our property bring our guests' bags to and from their rooms. He proved himself a good, diligent, hardworking team member. Soon we made him a housekeeper, and then we promoted him to head porter. Eventually, Kenny decided to go off and start his own business cleaning and buffing marble floors in the big Las Vegas hotels and casinos. He wanted to build something, take charge of his own destiny. As I had sensed when I first met him, he had dreams and the will to make them reality.

We wound up hiring Kenny's company to clean our floors, as did many other establishments. Over time, his company became the largest marble-cleaning and buffing vendor on the Vegas Strip. That's saying something—if you've been to Las Vegas, you know how many acres of marble floors there are in the city! Kenny also founded a separate business that sold cleaning supplies. He became tremendously successful while finding happiness in his personal life, getting married, and having kids.

Kenny's journey from ex-con to successful business owner continues to inspire me, and perhaps it will inspire you too. It confirms my firm belief that our free-market system is the best ever devised for the creation of broad-based prosperity. It provides opportunities for Kenny and others who've caught a bad break to make something of themselves, for immigrants like Louis Ruiz to come to this country and realize the American dream, and for dyslexic kids like me to start with nothing and eventually transform an industry.

Those who struggle aren't lost causes; they're merely successes waiting to happen. We must recognize that struggling individuals can't always grasp those opportunities on their own. Mindful of poverty's systemic roots, we must hold out the prospect of a second chance and sometimes even a third. We must provide pathways up, equipping individuals with the necessary skills, resources, and opportunities so they can work hard, live their dreams, and help build a better future. And when people *do* make it, we should celebrate their accomplishments, not disparage them or try to punish their success.

An inclusive economy and a balanced, moderate approach to regulation are vital to turning this country around. To achieve more prosperity for everyone, we must nurture free enterprise and ensure that our industries and businesses are thriving. We must implement the right policies, including some that not everyone is going to like. The solutions are out there, but we must be bold enough to implement them.

That's the hard truth.

LEADERSHIP IS ABOUT COMPETENCE, NOT CELEBRITY

IN APRIL 2021, GOVERNOR GAVIN NEWSOM announced that the California Correctional Center (CCC) in the small, rural town of Susanville, a municipality nestled in the Sierra Nevada Mountains, would close its doors.[1] Local residents greeted the news with anger and alarm. Susanville was also home to another correctional institution, the High Desert State Prison, and these two facilities were the town's economic lifeblood. In this town of about fourteen thousand people, about 40 percent were inmates; most of the others either worked at one of the prisons or had some connection to them.[2] With more than a thousand jobs at the CCC hanging in the balance, some community members were so upset that they apparently broached the idea of renaming the local landfill after the governor.[3] Susanville Mayor Mendy Schuster predicted that the CCC's closure would "affect the whole town. I don't want to imagine what that would be like."[4]

Mayor Schuster wouldn't have to imagine for long. Although the town sued to block the state from going through with its plan, the prison ultimately closed in 2023.[5] In the aftermath, one resident claimed the governor was "persecuting" their rural county—a belief that seems to have been shared by other locals. In Lassen County, considered "California's Trumpiest region," more than 70 percent of voters supported Trump in 2016 and 2020, and over 80 percent voted to recall Governor Newsom in 2021. So, to many, it seemed more than plausible that closing the prison was a form of political payback, an easy way for Newsom to punish his critics and detractors, even if they were also his constituents.[6]

On the face of it, closing prisons in California isn't necessarily a bad idea. During the 2000s, the state went overboard incarcerating people thanks to "tough on crime" policies, so much so that its prisons became overcrowded, leading to a deterioration in conditions for inmates. After a 2011 US Supreme Court decision forced the state to reduce prison overcrowding, California voters affirmed measures that would reduce prison populations by moving inmates convicted of certain crimes into local jails.[7] Other ballot initiatives approved by voters kept offenders out of prison by lowering penalties or allowing for quicker parole. More recently, the state released thousands of prisoners early in response to the Covid-19 pandemic and as part of a focus on rehabilitative justice.[8]

All told, the prison population in California *has* dropped—from 165,000 prisoners in 2006 to just 93,000 in 2024.[9] That's a reduction of over 40 percent! With fewer inmates, California doesn't need as many prisons as it used to, making closures attractive from a budgeting standpoint. Indeed, when announcing that the CCC would close, the state suggested the move would be financially responsible, amounting to a cost savings of $122 million each year.[10] Governor Newsom also appears to be an advocate of a reduced prison footprint for philosophical reasons. As one expert, Michael Romano of Stanford University, explains, Governor Newsom "has a long track record of being on the progressive side of criminal justice. His belief that we can reduce prison populations and improve public safety is achievable. That's the core of his goal."[11]

We can debate elsewhere whether our society should be tough on crime and emphasize imprisonment as a legal penalty, but here let's focus on policy *execution*. If leaders in California were set on a policy of shuttering prisons, did they think through and execute their policy carefully and competently enough? I have my doubts, on at least two counts.

First, whether the Susanville closure represented political payback or not, it was announced without much planning or care for how it would impact the local community. Critics have regarded the CCC's closure as "arbitrary and confusing"—and they're right.[12] As a commentator in the *San Francisco Chronicle* noted in 2022, the CCC hadn't been on the chopping block prior to the announcement of its closing, like other facilities had. One facility, the Riverside County prison, was decrepit and almost closed in

2016—but somehow Susanville's prison got the ax, without any real explanation as to why.[13] The state gave Susanville $1 million to help ease the impact of the prison closure, but besides that it seems to have done little to keep the town alive economically.[14] That's simply not right. California has a responsibility to care for everyone who calls the state home. People who disagree with those in charge are citizens too, and seeing to their economic well-being is both good policy and the right thing to do.

There's a second problem, one that goes beyond Susanville and the CCC. These prison closures and the cost savings they're supposed to provide come in the context of a staggering budget crisis in California: in 2024, a deficit of roughly $45 billion.[15] To close that massive gap, the governor has envisioned dipping into state reserves but also implementing painful spending cuts. Shutting prisons is part of the answer. As of 2024, California has either closed or planned to close four prisons, with an anticipated cost savings of $3.4 billion by 2027.[16] That might sound like a big number, but the state could be doing much more to save money on incarceration. Indeed, at a time when the prison population is falling and California is facing an economic crunch, the state is actually spending *more* overall keeping Californians locked up.

In 2019, the state funneled $15.7 billion into its prison system. In 2024, Newsom's budget allocated $18 billion. It now costs California over $130,000 to keep a single person in prison for one year, almost twice the cost a decade ago.[17] Fewer inmates yet significantly greater cost—what kind of government does *less* with more taxpayer dollars? You don't have to have spent decades running companies to know that something doesn't add up. As one analyst colorfully put it, "The math isn't mathing."[18]

So, why not?

Some of the additional costs reflect the state's efforts to provide better health care to inmates—a laudable goal that is indeed quite expensive. But the state is also paying more for labor in its prisons, thanks to lucrative union contracts it negotiated.[19] We should certainly support correctional officers with the resources they need to be safe on the job, but we should also be careful to use taxpayer resources as efficiently as possible.

Others might wonder why California isn't closing even more prisons to reap even greater cost savings. Given how steeply the prison population has fallen, the state could viably close five more facilities, saving $1 billion annually and using that money to avoid other budget cuts—for example, in vital social services programs.[20] But as of 2024, there were no such plans, leaving the state paying for fifteen thousand vacant prison beds.[21] Once again, leaders seem to be responding to political pressure, not just from the prison unions but also from local communities.[22]

Instead of just shutting facilities with a cavalier attitude toward the communities affected, California could also be taking steps to make prisons run more *efficiently*. Has anyone in charge methodically examined the prison system, looking for potential synergies? If the prison system were run like a well-functioning business, that's exactly what leaders would do. They'd scour for potential changes in policies and processes that could cut cost without compromising quality—indeed, that in many cases could *improve* quality.

Some inefficiencies that have come to light suggest that leaders haven't evaluated the prison system carefully enough to ensure that we're using taxpayer money efficiently and effectively. For instance, California might have fifteen thousand vacancies, but concentrating these in certain facilities would leave the state able to close others.[23] Also, the state relies excessively on outside contractors to provide mental health services to inmates, a practice that costs more than retaining enough medical professionals on staff while also leading to poorer-quality care. Because there is little transparency here, the true fiscal costs are at present unknown.[24] Couldn't we improve that part of how the government is delivering service? We could—if we cared to poke through the system with an eye toward making it run better.

But it's easier just to have the prison system do what it has always done, tacking on additional funds to the budget each year. It's easier to give more to unions without requiring them to help you meticulously search for efficiencies and build an improved system. It's easier to shutter individual prisons rather than research and develop a comprehensive plan that delves into all facets of prison operations and management across the statewide system. And that, my friends, is how you wind up with a prison system that, during a fiscal crisis, houses fewer inmates but costs billions of dollars more.

Here's the hard truth: If we want to turn around struggling and failing communities across the country, we need leadership that is willing to come down from their ivory tower, roll up their sleeves, and get into the weeds of our most pressing issues. We need leaders who are committed to handling taxpayer money as carefully as they would their own—and who are *equipped* to deploy taxpayer money wisely. We need leaders who know how to frame policy effectively, execute it competently, and run complex government bureaucracies efficiently.

We need leaders who can get shit done.

Understanding the Full Picture

Perhaps you think the California corrections system is just an isolated instance of good intentions gone awry. But you don't wind up with a $45 billion budget deficit without implementing a whole slew of flawed policies. In far too many domains, across the country and at all levels of governance, we find a train wreck of ill-advised, shoddily implemented policies and unintended consequences that, in turn, require even more policies—and more taxpayer money—to fix.

Even when politicians do cut budgets, they all too often are swayed by anecdotes rather than sticking to hard data. They make decisions based on emotion rather than on metrics that are meaningful and measurable. They simply aren't accustomed to looking at the full picture.

That's not because leaders are malicious or corrupt—plenty of smart, well-meaning people support ill-conceived policies. It's because they aren't experienced enough in or knowledgeable enough about execution and governance. Governor Newsom spent four years in business, founding the PlumpJack Group in 1992, before starting his political career in 1996, which he's been pursuing ever since. He's an intelligent, well-intentioned guy and good in front of the cameras, but he didn't spend decades responsible for the fiscal success and growth of large organizations.

As someone who did, I can tell you: However hard you think it is to run a large organization, multiply that by a factor of ten. Whether you're leading a business or a government agency, you must confront the reality that many areas of economic and social life are interconnected. Every decision or policy change you make comes with a set of far-reaching consequences—some you can anticipate, and others you can't. As leader, your goal is to make decisions that take into account and anticipate as many potential consequences as possible. Along the way, you also must build coalitions of people who see your broader vision and will work hard to achieve it.

Unserious leaders look at decisions or policy matters simplistically, thinking about just one or a few possible first- and second-order consequences. When they make a decision or implement a policy, they pat themselves on the back for delivering on a priority that investors or taxpayers care about. Capable leaders, on the other hand, think through many of the consequences, recognizing that they must keep many balls in the air at once. Or to use a different metaphor that my mentor, Senator Harry Reid, taught me, they're like chess players, thinking ten or fifteen moves ahead. When they make a decision or implement a policy, it's more comprehensive and thoughtful, and less likely to lead to unintended consequences that then take time and money to unravel.

So many policy decisions reflect an inability of elected leaders to think past their particular priorities and consider the bigger picture. Trying to reduce California's prison population, for example, is great. But what of the burden on local communities when you send many of those prisoners back to local jails to serve their sentences? In California, local jails have struggled to accommodate the influx of inmates from state prisons, leading to more violence. As *ProPublica* has reported: "The state handed the county sheriffs a huge problem and shifted billions of dollars to help them fix it. But some have viewed the changes as a burden, not an opportunity. They aren't separating violent mentally ill patients from the general population. Their jails lack adequate health care."[25]

Furthermore, if we're releasing more prisoners onto the streets, have we ensured that these people can provide for their own basic needs? California hasn't, and as a result, judicial reform has contributed to the state's burgeoning homelessness crisis, creating what some have called a "prison-to-homelessness pipeline" that might be making our cities and towns less safe.[26]

We see this same failure to think through the consequences in other policy areas. Consider electric vehicles. In 2020, California mandated the total elimination of sales of new fossil fuel-powered cars and trucks by 2035. The measure aimed to help the state move toward a carbon-neutral economy by 2045.[27] Tackling the climate crisis by taking the economy carbon-neutral is an incredible goal, but it's also resorting to an incredibly heavy-handed mandate. Shouldn't consumers be able to choose what kind of car they want to buy? Why should political leaders decide this for them?

Furthermore, I'm not sure leaders were pragmatic in adopting this goal. If there are 12.5 million electric vehicles zipping around California in 2035, as state officials anticipate, we'll crash the power grid at its current capacity. State officials reassure the public that the future grid will be able to handle it, but as one commentator observed, their assessments reflect "a best-case—some say unrealistic—scenario: massive and rapid construction of offshore wind and solar farms, and drivers charging their cars in off-peak hours." Bear in mind, at the same time as the state is transitioning to electric vehicles, it is also transitioning to renewable energy and phasing out nuclear energy. Some experts question whether the state has done what's required to get enough clean power in place by the deadline.

"We're going to have to expand the grid at a radically much faster rate," says David Victor of UC San Diego. "This is plausible if the right policies are in place, but it's not guaranteed. It's best-case."[28] Shouldn't state leadership have thought through all this at the outset, so we're not relying on a hopeful, fingers-crossed, best-case outcome?

Another problem to think about concerns California's roads. The state maintains its roadways by collecting a tax on the sale of gasoline and then sending money back to county governments to fix all those potholes.[29] In 2024, 80 percent of all money spent repairing California roads came from this tax.[30] When the vast majority of cars on the road are electric vehicles, those tax funds will dry up. How will California replace them? The answer remains unclear.

The state has been trying to figure out an alternate way of generating the funds for the past decade.[31] On top of this conundrum, electric cars weigh about 30 percent more than their gas-guzzling counterparts on account of the batteries they truck around, and so they potentially damage the roads more than gas-powered cars.[32] Any new taxation regime must account for these complexities. Again, you'd think policymakers would have pondered these issues and had clear policy recommendations ready to go before simply launching such a radical policy.

The issue of transitioning to a carbon-neutral economy is obviously complex, involving many important issues and consequences. Rather than simply tossing out a mandate, leaders should have methodically addressed the complexities of actually executing the proposed policy. Then they should have transparently communicated these nuances to voters, walking them through the various far-reaching implications of the policy, and asked what *they* think.

So much policymaking takes place in back rooms, without public consultations that would help reveal the full picture. Leaders need to trust and engage the public more, asking: Are voters really OK with this policy once they know all that it entails? If so, great. If not, then try taking a different tack. Just like companies must listen to customers to understand and deliver on their needs, elected leaders must consult with the people who pay their salaries—the taxpayers.

The failure to work through the complexities of policies and their execution helps explain why California faces a fiscal predicament and stagnation today. Consider the state's policy of extending generous social benefits to undocumented migrants. If you're a migrant and you cross the southern border into the United States, you'd be crazy not to come to California, where any living, breathing human being qualifies for all kinds of benefits. You get free health care under California's Medi-Cal program, free food assistance under the state's Women, Infants, and Children (WIC) program, a driver's license, and even potentially in-state tuition at public colleges and universities.[33] You may or may not pay income taxes like Californians who reside and work legally in the state do, but either way, you get more social benefits than in other states.

Listen, I'm all for treating people compassionately, and I'm also a strong proponent of immigration. As the descendant of immigrants, I think the infusion of people from other countries and cultures has helped make our country the world-class economy it is today, to the benefit of all Americans. In fact, the data shows that immigration—including the rise in undocumented migrants—has benefitted California's economy in recent years, and that undocumented migrants contribute billions in tax revenue of various kinds.[34]

As I've learned while working with the United Farm Workers in California to help migrants secure deferred action classifications and work permits—which can help protect them and their families from exploitative employers and other harms—there also are often good policy reasons for providing specific benefits. California's streets might be safer, for instance, if migrants have licenses, since at least this way we can ensure that they have the skills required to pass a driver's test. And yet, we need to balance such considerations with the significant negative consequences to providing generous social services to undocumented immigrants.

First, as discussed in an earlier chapter, undocumented migrants are breaking the law by living and working here. What kind of message do we send by bestowing the same benefits that law-abiding, documented immigrants receive? If migrants aren't paying income tax, it's also unfair to channel the bounty of other taxpayers' money toward them in the form of benefits.

An enormous wave of migrants also represents a fiscal strain. California spends billions providing benefits to undocumented migrants—the free health care alone costs over $6.5 billion a year.[35] How is that sustainable for a state that faces a $45 billion shortfall? The problem escalates because by offering social benefits that exceed what other states provide, California has become a beacon for even more migrants, increasing the already massive burden on its system. It's like California has erected a blinking welcome sign: *Please come to our state!* Unfortunately, that translates to some combination of reduced services and higher taxes for citizens, which (if past history is any guide) will make the state even less business-friendly. Its economy will be facing even greater headwinds on growth, and California's brand as a state that's open for business will become even more tarnished.

It feels good to provide generous services to the needy. But elected leaders in California aren't working with their own money. They're allocating taxpayer dollars. And that means they have a fiduciary responsibility to look at the bigger picture and consider what the state can afford. They must act in taxpayers' best interest, not in their own political interests or in service to some ideological agenda. In a utopia, we'd provide for everyone's needs, regardless of whether they contribute via taxes. There would be no limit on the public pocketbook. I wish we lived in such a place, but we don't.

Besides shortsighted policies that contribute to other problems, we often find our communities hamstrung by laws that are hastily written, precisely because officials haven't sufficiently pondered the executional realities. To cite but one example, in July 2024 California enacted a law that made taking a basic financial literacy course a graduation requirement in the state's public schools. That's a policy that promises great value: Research has shown that by taking just one semester of personal finance, a student in California will be $127,000 richer over their lifetime.[36] But if you look a little closer, you find the law is not all that it could be.

First, the requirement doesn't go into effect until the 2030–2031 school year.[37] Why wait so long? Pennsylvania, which in late 2023 passed similar legislation, put its measure in effect starting in 2026—just three years later.[38] You might argue that it will take time for education officials in California to nail down the curriculum requirements, but couldn't legislators have put in place some kind of interim measures? And couldn't the bill have incorporated some specific curriculum requirements? It's not as if this would be the first personal finance course available to US students—California was the twenty-sixth state to require such a course.[39] Legislators could have researched what has worked and what hasn't in other states and written at least an outline of curriculum into the law. Anyone could've gotten a running start on this research just by hopping online for an hour or two.[40]

As far as I can tell, the bill also doesn't include mechanisms to hold school districts accountable for providing quality instruction. Wouldn't it make sense, for example, to have students take a basic financial literacy test before and after taking the class, to see if they're actually learning anything? And shouldn't districts have to collect and report that data to the state? In this case, and in countless others, lawmakers needed to immerse themselves in the details of execution to ensure that understanding is reflected in the laws themselves.

It's not just legislators' responsibility to do a better job with executing carefully planned policy. The executive branch plays a role too. Governors should work with legislators to ensure that laws are as concise, comprehensible, and well-written as possible. They should use all the resources at their disposal to coach and counsel lawmakers, serving as a guide with no pride of ownership and giving legislators the trophy when it's well deserved. They should analyze the far-reaching consequences of policy and help communicate complexities to constituents for maximum transparency. If you really want effective and efficient government that uses taxpayer dollars wisely, such engagement is vital.

Doing Our Homework

The executional care and precision I'm advocating requires a commitment to doing your homework and knowing the details. In fact, when it comes to an ability to execute, a willingness to do your homework as a leader might even be more important than past experience. If you don't research the issues and closely understand the organization you're leading, you might not be ready to take the keys of the castle on day one—or to handle that critical 3 a.m. call when it comes in. When you're serving in elected office, there's no time for on-the-job training. You simply must know your stuff.

If you're prepared to really dig in and learn, you can lead organizations successfully even when gaps in your experience exist. In November 2019, when I was first appointed to serve on the Nevada Athletic Commission, I knew little about the organization and virtually nothing about the sports that it regulated. I wasn't a boxing fan, nor did I watch mixed martial arts. I could have just shown up at the meetings and tried to do my work blind, like most of my predecessors had. Worse, I could have viewed this as an opportunity simply to have fun, go to events, and phone it in. But I had other ideas.

Before beginning the work, I immersed myself in boxing and mixed martial arts. I also showed up at the commission's office and interviewed every single staff member I could, asking questions exhaustively: What did they do on the job? What were the commission's policies and practices? What did they like and dislike about how the commission operated? How did they think the commission could improve? In just a few months, I became familiar with everything I needed to know to make smart, sound regulatory decisions. I'm not saying all of my decisions were perfect; I made my share of mistakes. But my mistakes were fewer than they would have been, because I'd taken the time to learn.

I can't emphasize enough how important due diligence is for leaders. Throughout my career, I've been shocked at how many leaders *don't* do their homework. When I was running Brand USA, I found that many members of Congress—lawmakers responsible for America's position on the world stage—hadn't traveled much internationally. Some didn't even have a passport. They didn't understand the relevant geography and history, nor did they have an appreciation of national cultures. How can you vote on, say, our policy toward China or Russia if you lack that sort of knowledge? Are you going to rely on the research of some staff member in your office, who might never have visited these countries either? That's no substitute. Unless a congressmember has spent time actually researching an issue, including by putting boots on the ground and speaking with real people who possess firsthand knowledge, they don't have the perspective required to cast an informed vote. Likewise, if you're voting on a bill related to fiscal matters, you must be able to read a balance sheet and an income statement. You must understand subjects like interest rates, key economic indicators, and how markets work. If you don't have that knowledge, then go out and get it before voting. Otherwise, you won't be able to come to an informed judgment.

I wonder how many members of Congress could even tell you where China is on a map—or India, or Russia, or Ukraine. Although new congressmembers attend a legislative orientation when they assume office, how many could pass the test we give to new immigrants applying for citizenship? Do today's elected leaders know basic facts about our political system and our history? A strong case can be made, I think, for instituting some kind of basic requirement—a test of fundamental, relevant knowledge in civics, business, history, and more—people need to pass before they can run for Congress. The foreign service has an exam it administers to applicants. The armed services give physical tests to recruits, weeding out those who don't make the cut. Students seeking admission to college take tests like the SATs. Why shouldn't aspiring political candidates take a test establishing their basic competency? You needn't have attended a fancy college, or any college at all, to pass the test. Maybe life experience taught you the basics. If not, you could brush up on what you need to know. That way, when you entered Congress, you'd be better able to handle the public's business.

Possessing relevant knowledge is especially important for leaders trying to deal with turnaround and crisis situations. It's impossible to fully see the big picture without first taking the time to get a grasp of the details. Before we bought Sunterra and began operating it as Diamond Resorts, I researched the crap out of that company. Imagine a car enthusiast taking a 1957 Chevrolet Bel Air apart piece by piece, taking time to inspect each part and understand its condition. That was me with Sunterra.

As David Palmer, the CFO and later CEO of Diamond Resorts, remembers, we spent over a year performing three separate forms of due diligence. First, Sunterra had been under investigation in Europe for fraud, so we strove to understand the nature of the fraud and the extent of the company's legal exposure. Second, to obtain bank financing and receive approval for the deal from the Securities and Exchange Commission, we pored through the company's financials—which were a total mess—and actually *redid* the recordkeeping.

Taking personal responsibility for the books was a highly unusual move. Palmer and I promised to perform a forensic audit once we completed the acquisition, with the understanding that we would pay a steep financial penalty if we later discovered that our initial numbers were less than 95 percent accurate. They wound up being *over 99 percent accurate*—that's how closely we'd scrutinized the numbers.

"The diligence was extraordinarily important," Palmer says. "We had to really feel very confident that we had asked all the right questions and that we had really pressed everybody as professionally but as diligently as possible to make sure we weren't missing anything."[41]

Our third form of diligence was to go through the nooks and crannies of the company's operations. I visited every one of Sunterra's properties, speaking to staff on the ground about their work and the problems they encountered on the job. I emphasized that I valued their opinions and wanted to learn from them, and I took notes on what they told me. I did the same with executives at Sunterra and with the company's investors.

Working with all this data, I pieced together a rich, nuanced picture of this large global company. I began to understand in precise detail all that was good about the company and all that needed fixing. As you can imagine, the opportunities for improvement were *enormous*. In fact, as I did my research, and before we even completed our purchase, I compiled an extensive list of all the changes I would make to reduce costs, operate more efficiently, provide more value to customers, and turn the company around—things like centralizing our procurement of supplies, consolidating our many reservations systems, unifying two different accounting systems, better managing our energy use, getting rid of organizational silos, and approving a whole slew of upgrades to the properties.

Many corporate leaders, when acquiring a company or making some other big change, might call in business consultants to do the work. Indeed, once our deal to acquire Sunterra went through, as head of the company I inherited a $500,000 research report that the previous management had commissioned from a top management consulting firm. You know what I did with it? I tossed it in the trash. Because that's where it belonged. The report was totally superficial, with lots of business jargon tossed in. It was full of facts but included very little deep understanding of what made the business tick—and what didn't.[42]

Instead of relying on that report, I continued to do my own research, focusing on understanding our guests. I became a one-man qualitative research machine, visiting our properties around the world, observing our operations, and speaking to as many guests as I could. Once again, I took notes to keep track of any insights I uncovered. I also commissioned Frank Luntz, the noted pollster and communication expert, to perform an exhaustive study of our guests and their desires: What did the perfect vacation look like to them? Why had they bought one of our vacation properties? What did they like to see in the properties they visited? What *truly* mattered to them when it came to vacationing with us? The answers gleaned from this study would go on to inform our strategy, ultimately contributing to our signature mission of delivering The Meaning of Yes.

As a leader, I could rely on gut instinct all I wanted, but without taking the time to painstakingly learn about the company, I never could have helped it grow. For that matter, I never would have been able to lead the company successfully through the Great Recession, which materialized within just eighteen months or so after our purchase, as we were still executing our turnaround. Imagine you're running a business that's already on the edge, and consumer demand for your product tanks overnight because suddenly everybody's deeply anxious about their jobs and finances. Imagine, too, that banks are no longer in a position to loan you money to operate. To be more specific, imagine you had a $500 million line of credit in place, and all of a sudden it completely evaporates, leaving you without enough cash to pay salaries and other critical month-to-month expenses.

What would you do?

Many companies would go out of business. In fact, some operators in the hospitality industry did, including those that were saddled with debt and lacked the cash to service their loans.[43] We survived—and actually *increased* our earnings—by doing what some in our industry thought was impossible: moving to an all-cash finance model. Here again, my up-close knowledge of the business paid off. Since we could no longer rely on credit, we went through every corner of the business again, looking for ways to cut costs and increase revenues.

Think of the business discipline this instills. We analyzed our properties and our back-office operations, and if a given process or procedure wasn't necessary, we cut it. If it *was* necessary, we considered how to do it a bit more efficiently. We also scrutinized our contracts with our partners to see if we were receiving all the fees and other revenues to which we were entitled.

In many instances, cost-cutting at companies erodes the quality they deliver. They do *less* with less. At Diamond, we did *more* with less. Simultaneous with our belt-tightening, we became obsessed with improving the quality of our guest experience, focusing on delivering The Meaning of Yes. We developed a whole series of behind-the-scenes systems and procedures—accompanied by a $50 million investment in information technology—that let us provide exceptional vacations at lower cost. For instance, we had a system that tracked all of our guest interactions, including every keystroke our guests made on our website. This allowed us to know their needs and desires, to understand whether we were really delivering on them, and to offer personalized service across all of our resorts—something even the biggest names in our industry weren't doing.[44]

I was right there with my team as they did this work, helping make decisions based on our homework and ensuring we were doing everything possible to delight our guests. Because I was personally involved, I could communicate what we were doing to our team members, and I could handle incoming guest requests through the customer service systems we'd implemented, including having my business card available at every property. This helped me deliver on anything I'd promised to guests—and helped keep employee morale high as we navigated the turnaround. One initiative managed to tick both boxes: I ensured that all of our resorts had an Unexpected Delight Fund—cash they could use to provide small surprises to guests as they saw fit. Imagine the impact when a guest who was celebrating a birthday showed up to find, say, their favorite cupcakes in their room waiting for them. It was huge!

Thanks to our operational efforts, Diamond Resorts didn't just survive the turnaround. We emerged from the Great Recession as our industry's strongest company and were well positioned to grow in the next few years. During the early 2010s, we completed nearly a dozen acquisitions of troubled vacation ownership companies, paying pennies on the dollar. In each case, we did a fine-toothed-comb analysis of the acquired company, stripping it down and building it back up. By introducing the behind-the-scenes systems and procedures we'd already built, we enabled the company to work more efficiently and effectively to serve guests. As our former CEO Mike Flaskey remembers, we were "capable of going in and fixing things that other people didn't want to mess with. And it catapulted our company tremendously in terms of growth in a very condensed window of time."[45] All told, we spent about $140 million acquiring companies that collectively brought in $210 million in pretax earnings.[46]

Across the United States, businesses like Sunterra and our other acquisitions are dealing with severe, perhaps even existential crises. How long can they shoulder massive deficits before they go bankrupt? How long can they survive by blindly cutting costs to narrow these deficits? What we've seen in California essentially has been a two-sided disaster. On the one hand, our leaders have conducted a gigantic, failed social experiment, implementing a host of individual policies that are often well-meaning but clumsily considered. On the other, the state's government bureaucracy doesn't budge much from the status quo despite operating inefficiently. How is this supposed to help anyone get anything accomplished?

What's required is disruption, the kind of wholesale reimagining and retooling that my team did when acquiring Sunterra and riding out the Great Recession. Business as usual won't get us through. We need elected leaders to roll up their sleeves and write precise, effective legislation that accounts for the many wider impacts it will have. And we need them to go through every corner of every government agency, looking for blatant instances of waste—and rethinking policies, processes, or organizational structures so that governance can be *better*, not simply cheaper.

In short, we need a level of seriousness we seldom see in government today, anchored by a knowledge of conditions on the ground, the perceptions and needs of voters, and how governing actually works. We've had enough of the platitudes and photo ops. What we need is substance.

The Three Rs

During my years in business, I came up with three principles that get to the essence of strong, competent leadership—the three Rs mentioned earlier in this book: *respect*, *responsibility*, and *results*.

First, leaders must show *respect* for the people who depend on them and pay their salaries. In the case of businesses, that means investors, employees, and other stakeholders. In the public sector, that means the general public, specifically voters and taxpayers. Political leaders must approach what they do with the constant recognition that they work for the citizenry, not the other way around. They must commit to having the public's back, making sure government serves the common good without unduly encumbering individual citizens.

Showing respect means consulting closely and on an ongoing basis with taxpayers, getting to know them and requesting their input. It means emphasizing transparency, clearly outlining the implications and consequences of proposed laws. Rather than looking down on voters, leaders must respect their individual and collective intelligence, not assume they know better than their constituents. By showing this respect, leaders will engender the same from those they serve. That's how it should work—even if it didn't in Susanville, California.

Leaders who know how to execute also show a strong sense of *responsibility*. Leaders have a duty to taxpayers, as fiduciary stewards of our hard-earned dollars. Elected leaders must ensure they're spending funds wisely and not wasting them. They must know where the money is going, and why—that's their job. When they don't know, they must own up to it. They must also take responsibility when setbacks occur under their watch. It's not someone else's fault way down in the organization. It's *their* fault for not making sure things got done right the first time.

Elected leaders should be held responsible for delivering greater or equal value for each taxpayer dollar they're handed. Why should this be any different from the responsibility that CEOs have to shareholders? If we held elected leaders to this essential standard, they would spend countless hours doing their homework about specific policies, discovering what's worked and what hasn't, and retooling government bureaucracies from top to bottom. They would become pragmatic problem-solvers in their policymaking instead of idealogues, because they'd feel a responsibility to deliver great value.

Research has shown that many Americans *don't* feel that they are getting good value from their government. At the local level, for instance, a 2023 poll indicates they feel that they're paying too much in property taxes and getting too little in return.[47] A 2024 survey confirms my suspicion that a large slice of Americans feel that way about taxes in general.[48] Our elected leaders must do better!

Leaders who display the first two Rs are in a better position to also emphasize the third: cultivation of a strong *results* orientation. From an economic standpoint, a state like California is very much like a business: It must grow its economy, just as a business needs to grow its revenues and profits to be successful. To do that, leaders must have mechanisms in place to generate sufficient resources from taxpayers, and they must allocate those resources efficiently and effectively. If they become lax with taxpayer resources—lavishing them on social experiments that may or may not work, and lazily allowing government bureaucracies to keep anachronistic and wasteful processes in place—sooner or later the state's economy pays the price.

Any competent CEO will be able to tell you in broad terms where their company is deploying capital, and what kind of return it's getting for its investment. The same principle applies in government: An elected leader should be able to tell you quickly what their agency is spending money on, and what the performance data is telling them about the return on investment. If they can't, something is wrong—almost certainly, taxpayers are being poorly served.

A May 2024 audit found that California had spent $24 billion trying to address its homelessness crisis between 2018 and 2023, and yet had no idea whether that spending was making any difference. That's because officials *weren't tracking performance data* on programs receiving billions of dollars in public funding. In a letter to the governor, the auditor argued that the "state must do more to assess the cost-effectiveness of its homelessness programs."[49] Some have spoken of a "data desert" when it comes to the homelessness issue in California, and others have wondered if organizations and agencies fighting homelessness in the state were more interested in emptying the public's wallet than actually solving the problem. But leaders shouldn't have needed an audit to tell them how well California was executing its homelessness policies. They should have known all along where the money was going and what, roughly, the state was getting in return. This significant blind spot shows a glaring ignorance of what it means to have a results orientation. The objective of the program may be sound, but as we see time and again, good intentions aren't an excuse for lack of impact.

If you respect those whom you serve and feel a sense of responsibility to them, you're going to want to make sure you actually deliver for them. That means reporting transparently on how well the policies, laws, and regulations that you've put in place are working. It means writing laws that provide explicitly for accountability, including policy goals that the legislation hopes to achieve; what meaningful, relevant metrics the government will use to determine whether the legislation is succeeding; and how and when these results will be reported.

Leaders must also make metrics visible to constituents in simple, straightforward terms: Did a law achieve the social good that legislators intended? Was there a return on the capital the state invested? What results did a law produce one year, three years, five years after its passage?

Finally, leaders must hold themselves responsible for results. What if Newsom had to pay some kind of financial penalty for losing track of $24 billion? For that matter, what if he bore personal responsibility for ensuring citizens' safety, or providing a good education to their children, or delivering a certain amount of economic growth for the state's economy? For instance, what if an elected official's failure to account for a certain amount of taxpayer money or to meet certain educational goals meant forgoing their government salary for a year? That would be a symbolic penalty in many cases, given that at the local level salaries are often nominal, but it would still send an important message and encourage leaders to take a personal stake in what they're doing. Without some kind of enforcement, there is no accountability.

In every company or organization I've been a part of, I've placed a strong emphasis on results, and I've held others accountable for doing so too. As chairman of the Nevada Athletic Commission, I closely tracked revenues from each major sporting event, getting the numbers in real time rather than waiting for bureaucratic reports. As a result of that diligence, we knew throughout the year how we were doing. When it came time to ask the state for the following year's budget, we didn't have to undergo much legislative scrutiny, because legislators knew all along that we were surpassing expectations. Our intense focus on the bottom line helped to build an environment of trust: Legislators felt that we had a shared sense of purpose. Like them, we wanted to bring in revenues for the state and save money by operating efficiently.

Today, results are still the first thing I inquire about in business meetings: What funds have you allocated, and to where? What's the return on invested capital? What are the latest customer satisfaction numbers? What returns are we delivering for stockholders? How many views or likes did the most recent marketing campaign generate? What does the latest employee survey tell us about the state of morale inside the organization? I expect simple answers to questions like these—the relevant numbers in black and white, not a colorful, fifty-page PowerPoint. If you try to obfuscate or dodge the question, I'll call you out so fast, your head will spin. My father drilled it into me: As a leader, you must know your numbers, and you better make sure others know their numbers too.

It might seem that I'm demanding a lot of our elected leaders. Can they really deliver all this? Abso-friggin'-lutely. But if they don't serve the public respectfully and take personal responsibility for producing the necessary results, they aren't competent leaders. Strong governance takes talent and experience, but primarily it takes work—lots of it. And it's not a life for everyone.

Real Leaders Never Sleep

When I took over Sunterra, some who had been at the company for years wound up leaving because they couldn't handle the pressure. In declaring my expectation that they help drive change in the company, I was asking them to work twice as hard—maybe even more—than they had been, putting in many long nights and weekends. But some company leaders were content to simply do what the company had always done, even giving up lucrative bonuses that had been promised to them. They were afraid of putting in real effort.

If you were a manager at Diamond Resorts responsible for a particular property, we expected you to be available twenty-four hours a day. If I called with an urgent issue at 1 a.m. and a manager didn't pick up—and if they didn't have a good excuse—we had a problem. Likewise, among our executives, I had a rule: If you got an email, text, or phone call about an issue, regardless of what it was, I expected a response within twenty-four hours. And if you received that message between 7 a.m. and 11 p.m., you had to respond within thirty minutes.[50] People knew I meant business because when leaders didn't show this level of commitment, I didn't hesitate to show them the door.

I wasn't trying to be mean. I enforced this type of effort because it was necessary. Our guests' lives were on the line 24/7. Whether it was a hurricane, a tsunami, or political unrest, we received security reports at our resorts at all hours, and we had to take swift action to make sure our guests were safe. "We took this very, very seriously," David Palmer says, describing our attitude toward safety. "No matter what is happening in your life, you have the lives of other people in your hands and have to focus on their well-being."[51] In addition, we dedicated ourselves to providing an exceptional vacation experience. If a guest had an issue that needed solving right away, we couldn't wait until a property manager arrived at 9 a.m. or until an executive returned a call three days later. We needed it done.

One reason managers and executives were willing to treat their jobs as a twenty-four-hour commitment is because they knew that I did too. My attitude was one of direct personal responsibility, as if *I* were the housekeeper, the front desk clerk, or the security guard. This is the kind of commitment you need to excel in business. And it's about time that we started to see more of it in government too. Cities, counties, and entire states don't sleep any more than hotels do.

Leadership in the political realm can be glamorous. You get to hobnob with wealthy donors and celebrities. You get to appear in the media and be the center of attention at events. Everybody wants to hear what you have to say, and a wonderful life awaits you when you exit public office: a cushy job at a law firm or public affairs shop, reaping millions via a book deal or by working the speaking circuit. But that's just the shiny veneer.

Real leadership—the successful execution of policies and the efficient, effective operation of government agencies—isn't glamorous. It's about geeking out on the details and the numbers. It's about really listening to people, even if they're not happy or don't agree with you. It's about reaching tough compromises that balance competing priorities, and then explaining those compromises to the public. Ultimately, it's about putting in the hours, not getting a trophy. Struggling states and communities across the country can make comebacks every bit as dramatic as Sunterra's, but they need serious, committed, knowledgeable people in charge to make it happen. They need leaders who, in effect, never sleep.

Think back to Susanville, that small California community that saw its prison close, leaving local residents in the lurch. If officials had put in a little more thought and done more homework, perhaps they could have devised a way not to punish, but to pivot. In the course of closing the correctional center, perhaps the state could have also made investments to help this community write its next chapter.

As Courtney Hanson, a community organizer who works with the California Coalition for Women Prisoners, remarks, "We don't agree with the argument that a prison should stay open—human cages should stay open—because that's the only way to run an economy. But we do believe that the state of California and the California Department of Corrections [have] a responsibility to work with those on the ground in these communities, and particularly those incarcerated in these communities, to envision and implement alternatives."[52]

In Susanville, the state might have retrained thousands of people—from janitorial staff to guards to vendors—to help with forest management, given the state's increasing problem with wildfires. Or it could have leveraged the area's high desert topography to assist with California's ambitious clean energy goals. In this situation and others like it, the possibilities were—and are—many. But we need leaders to imagine them, and then to work their tails off each and every day to make them a reality.

TRUE SUCCESS REQUIRES PUTTING "WE" BEFORE "ME"

IN 2004, A REALITY TV SHOW DEBUTED that changed the course of history. Bringing viewers into the rough-and-tumble world of American business, it featured a group of contestants vying for a lucrative job working for a seemingly successful, hard-nosed billionaire. "Seemingly successful" because behind the "reality" of reality TV, his businesses were barely solvent. "Hard-nosed" because this businessman delighted in teaching tough life lessons to losing competitors, kicking them off the show with his iconic phrase, *You're fired*. As this businessman later remembered, "the place just reverberated" during the first episode when he said those words. "People were screaming. They were shouting. The crew! The makeup people! Everyone was watching it. There were hundreds of them, and they went crazy."[1]

I'm talking, of course, about *The Apprentice* and its larger-than-life star, Donald Trump. The show paved the way for Trump's political rise, transforming him into a household name and an aspirational figure for millions. Were it not for the show's success, it's hard to imagine Trump could have obtained the Republican nomination and won the presidential election in 2016, repeating the feat in 2024. An ex-producer of the show, writing after the nondisclosure agreement he'd signed had finally expired, put it this way: "By carefully misleading viewers about Trump—his wealth, his stature, his character, and his intent—the competition reality show set about an American fraud that would balloon beyond its creators' wildest imaginations."[2]

Research subsequently documented that the show caused right-leaning voters to trust Trump more and believe him over his critics, which helped him during the 2016 Republican primaries.[3] Pretending to be a singular business mastermind also boosted Trump's finances, apparently earning him nearly half a billion dollars. He apparently incurred over $70,000 in hairstyling expenses, which he wrote off on his taxes.[4] Those are some pretty pricey haircuts.

I, too, have appeared on reality television in my capacity as the leader of a large business, but thankfully my experience was very different, as was my hair. In 2012, I appeared multiple times on *Undercover Boss*, a show that featured a senior leader at a company on each episode, who went in disguise to visit the company's frontline operations, interacting with on-the-ground employees and learning uncomfortable lessons about their business. During my episodes, camera crews filmed me visiting properties and call centers that Diamond Resorts operated in places like Sedona, Arizona; Williamsburg, Virginia; Scottsdale, Arizona; Los Cabos, Mexico; Brian Head, Utah; and Miami, Florida. I interacted and worked with a number of our team members, including customer service personnel, maintenance staff, front desk clerks, and spa attendants.

Unlike Trump's businesses, my company—Diamond Resorts— really *was* profitable when I appeared on these episodes; the show didn't misrepresent our success. Unlike him, I didn't behave like a harsh, uncompromising authority figure, looking over people's shoulders to criticize their work and kicking to the curb those who weren't performing well. For much of these episodes, I wasn't a boss at all—I was posing as a trainee or novice who wanted to learn the ropes.

My objective in appearing on *Undercover Boss* wasn't to beat up people. I knew they were working extremely hard and doing their best to serve our customers. Rather, I wanted to learn from them. By walking a proverbial mile in their shoes, I hoped to spot systemic problems—such as unhelpful processes or poor oversight on the part of managers—that were preventing team members from delivering exceptional vacation experiences. At the time, we were acquiring new resorts around the world, properties that had been struggling under their prior owners. Perhaps there was more we could do to get these properties up to our standards and turn them around.

I never imagined I'd appear on reality television, nor did I ever harbor a dream of becoming famous, but I was surprised at how personally rewarding I found the experience. Wearing a disguise gave me a rare opportunity to spend hours with frontline personnel and really get to know them as individuals, without my status as the company's owner getting in the way. We connected deeply and honestly with one another as they opened up to me about their life struggles. I learned that many of them were facing any number of personal challenges, such as sick family members, subpar housing, unexpected financial hardships, or single parenthood.

As part of the format of *Undercover Boss*, bosses at the end of an episode reveal their true identities and offer gifts to employees to help them out in their lives. This was an especially meaningful part of the show for me—the part I loved the most. It gave me an opportunity to show our team members how grateful I was for their efforts: I made it financially possible for one team member to attend fashion school to pursue her dreams and helped another pay off his mortgage. I provided $100,000 in funding for a third team member to start his own business, and bought a fourth a house and a car while also arranging for her daughter to have a much-needed surgery.

After the first episode, the producers asked me back within the year to lead another episode—an unprecedented invitation. During my second experience, I realized that I had been holed up too much in corporate headquarters and really didn't know my team members as well as I wanted to. So, I changed up my routine and started to spend more time in our properties. In addition, I realized I needed to do more to support our global workforce, not just a few team members whom I'd happened to meet. I set up a

$2 million crisis fund that all of our team members could tap into at difficult times, chipping in $1 million of my own money with a matching grant from our company. From then on, team members at Diamond Resorts could feel sure that if they experienced an illness, a house fire, or some other tragedy, we'd lend a helping hand.

Few accomplishments are more satisfying than being of service to others and supporting them, both financially and otherwise. What are we on this earth for if not to take care of one another? I've understood this ever since my days working as a busboy—it's at the core of who I am and how I see the world. People often look down upon service personnel, but I see dignity, power, and grace in what they do. What I loved most about *Undercover Boss* is that it put the spotlight back on an ethic of serving others rather than yourself. The show depicted frontline folks who tried their best to listen to customers and attend to their needs. It showed leaders who, despite initially being detached or distracted, not only held workers accountable for providing service but realized their responsibility to serve their employees and take care of *them*.

At its best, business is a call to service on multiple levels that creates economic value for everyone. It inspires people to focus on the "we," not just on "me."

A Reign of Selfishness

Thinking back on that unique and benevolent TV show, and contrasting it with what I see around me in America today, I feel unsettled. Across our country, the selfish, unempathetic mentality captured in *The Apprentice* seems to be winning out over the spirit of service and generosity evident in *Undercover Boss*. For one thing, customer service in America is in serious decline. We pay more for products, services, and experiences yet seem to get less from the companies that are supposed to take care of us. It's no coincidence that customer satisfaction is down and that people are reporting more customer service issues than they once did.[5] This often isn't workers' fault—they *want* to treat customers better, but their managers are forcing them to do more with less, and they don't always get the training they need to treat others well.

Outside of the workplace, we see similar declines in willingness to serve. In 2022, charitable giving as a proportion of disposable income plunged to levels that hadn't been seen in almost thirty years.[6] Less than a quarter of Americans today volunteer their time in the community, reflecting continual declines since the turn of the twenty-first century.[7] Americans also are less likely to want to serve in the military.[8] Some of us might be too strained by our own personal circumstances to give back, but many simply seem content to ignore social problems in our communities, presuming that someone else will fix them. Overall, we just seem more likely to focus on our own well-being and forget about others.

Our reduced willingness to serve reflects a broader decline in public-spiritedness and connectedness. It's old news that Americans don't join civic organizations like the Lions Club or Rotary as much as we used to.[9] As sociologist Robert Putnam argued during the 1990s, we're content to "bowl alone" rather than join organized leagues that bring us into contact with others. Putnam's 2000 book *Bowling Alone* struck a nerve by documenting that Americans were becoming more atomized and isolated from one another—that "social capital" was declining and an important part of our social fabric was breaking down.[10]

Our retreat from communal life has since gone further than this.[11] We're thoroughly immersed in our private bubbles—more content to scroll Facebook than to enjoy real face time. Research suggests that most of us no longer socialize with our neighbors, and that a worrisome percentage of us don't know our neighbors at all: In one study, only about a quarter of people claimed to know most of the people living near them.[12] Changing daily routines mean that Americans also don't interact casually with neighbors as often as they used to—chatting while attending a PTA meeting, for instance.[13] We're in a "friendship recession," with many people—primarily men—saying they don't have as many close friends as folks once did.[14] And more of us also are living alone: As of 2022, nearly a third of all households were single-person.[15]

"What I wrote in *Bowling Alone* is even more relevant now," Putnam remarked in a 2024 podcast. "Why? Because what we've seen over the past twenty-five years since the book was published is a deepening and intensifying of that trend."[16]

A 2023 report from the US surgeon general proclaimed an "epidemic of loneliness and isolation," citing research that indicated about half of the adult population in the United States feels lonely.[17] As the report documented, the consequences of atomization are quite negative, both personally and socially. Loneliness is linked to an array of serious health maladies, to the point where "the mortality impact of being socially disconnected is similar to that caused by smoking up to 15 cigarettes a day, and even greater than that associated with obesity and physical inactivity."[18]

But more social fragmentation is also linked to increases in crime, making our communities more dangerous.[19] And as Putnam observes, it can lead to extremism. As young men become more isolated, they look to "some false community" to fulfill their social needs—a dynamic that played out in Nazi Germany and that seems to be repeating itself today. "It's not an accident that the people who are most attracted today to white nationalist violence are lonely young white men. Loneliness is bad for your health, but it's also bad for the health of the people around you."[20]

While violence fortunately is not the ultimate outcome in most cases, even the milder expressions of social fragmentation can be damaging. Simply put, we no longer seem to care much about one another or, frankly, even know how to behave compassionately. Academic researchers have spoken of "the decline of empathy" and "the rise of narcissism," to quote the title of one podcast.[21] If you've experienced road rage or a disturbing breach in civility on a commercial airplane, as more Americans these days have, you know what such phrases mean. On almost a weekly (if not daily) basis, we see video circulating on social media of Americans fighting, spitting on one another, or otherwise behaving rudely in a public space. In a 2023 survey by the American Bar Association, 85 percent of participants acknowledged a decline in civility compared with a decade earlier.[22]

We need to mend the social fabric in our country, and a great place to start is by rejecting the reign of selfishness and re-instilling an ethic of generosity and service. Here's the hard truth: We can't fix anything that's broken in our society unless we start focusing more on "we" and less on "me"—at work, in politics, and throughout our lives.

How to Practice More "We" and Less "Me"

Turning around our country requires a fundamental moral shift. We must reorient ourselves to serving others before ourselves— being helpful to them, attending to their needs, behaving more empathetically and compassionately. More broadly, we must think of ourselves as members of a *community*, not just as individuals with no crucial connections to those around us—and certainly not as interest groups who are either "the oppressed" or "the oppressor." We must regard one another as fellow human beings who deserve to be taken care of.

We all have the power to lead by example here. When we give a $5 bill to an unhoused person on the street, people around us notice and become more inclined to give in return. But don't take my word for it—this truism has been around for thousands of years. In the Bible, the Book of Mark reads, "Generosity begets generosity. Stinginess impoverishes."[23] Modern science also suggests that generosity and altruism generally are spread by example. When conducting experimental games, scientists have found that participants become more generous when they experience acts of generosity directed at them.[24]

But we don't just have the *power* to lead by example—we have the *duty* to do so. If we want to enjoy the fruits of living in a free society, we must be willing to shoulder the burden of citizenship, including the duty to step up and help solve problems in our communities.

Let's go back for a moment to that culture of grievance discussed in an earlier chapter. It's easy to bemoan how victimized we are, but we lose all credibility if we're not actively making at least some contribution to solving problems. The First Amendment to the Constitution guarantees us the legal right to gripe as much as we want. But if we fail to make any effort to effect change, we don't have the *moral* right.

Our elected leaders also must set an example here. Regardless of how high their position is, whether they serve on a town council or are on the national stage, their role is not to grandstand or mug for the cameras. It's not to enjoy the perks of high office or to play golf endlessly with their donor friends. And it's not to take stances on issues that seem smart, disruptive, or courageous but in fact allow problems to fester. Rather, it's to roll up their sleeves and improve our society.

Too many of our elected leaders are quick to serve their own financial and career interests over the public good whenever they find it convenient to do so. The examples occur on both sides of the aisle and are nauseatingly common. Former Democrat and now Independent Senator Kyrsten Sinema used to hold her nose at accepting corporate campaign money. Now she takes millions from big pharma and big finance, and opposes both raising taxes on corporations and cutting how much Medicare spends on prescription drugs. Republican Senator Susan Collins used to be against drilling in Alaska and for a cap on carbon emissions, but not anymore.[25] Was it a coincidence that in the interim she began raking in more money from big energy companies?

In recent years, as mentioned earlier, elected officials have profited from their positions and from the insider knowledge available to them, by trading in the stock market. Some make hundreds or even thousands of trades a year, and some even take positions on companies that they regulate as part of their official duties.[26] Note to elected officials: *You're not fooling anyone.* As surveys show, voters understand that special interests hold sway over lawmakers' decision-making, and they're not impressed.

They also believe that politicians aren't so concerned about what ordinary people think, and that leaders are primarily interested in their own welfare rather than the public's.[27] One 2023 study asked participants why they thought elected officials at all levels of government run for office. Almost two-thirds told researchers that they believe elected officials are in it to get rich. Careerism or a desire for fame also seemed like important motives to over half of respondents. And how many of those surveyed thought that all or most politicians run for office to serve the public good? Just 15 percent.[28]

We must get big money out of politics generally speaking, and individual leaders must get their act together. I can't help but remember that old TV ad where a child looks right at the camera and says, "When I grow up, I want to climb my way up to middle management."[29] Another child claims to dream of fulfilling the boring task of filing stuff all day long. Did any of our elected officials say to themselves as children, "I want to be a corporate lackey" or "I want to promise the public one thing and then do the exact opposite"? Is *that* why they got into politics?

I have to believe that most leaders join the race because they want to help people and build a better community, a better country. So my question to those who have gotten off track is: *At what point did you start to choose "me" over "we"?*

Elected officials aren't the only powerful people who behave irresponsibly and selfishly. Wealthy elites often do too. I believe in celebrating earned success, but I also strongly believe that wealth comes with social responsibility.

The wealthiest people in this country aren't nearly as generous philanthropically as they could be. We hear a lot about big donations that wealthy people give, but I'd argue that some of these often aren't as impressive as they might seem. Jeff Bezos's gift of $100 million to an organization called Feeding America was a nice gesture, but as a proportion of his wealth, it was miniscule. When you're worth nearly $150 billion, as Bezos was at the time, $100 million is chump change—the equivalent of about $75 as a proportion of income for a person making about $100,000.[30] Bezos isn't alone in his well-obscured miserliness. I won't name names, but I know lots of rich people who are stingy when it comes to giving to worthy causes or volunteering their time. They could be helping the poor or funding the next cure for cancer, but they'd rather buy another yacht or mega-mansion. It's all "me" and very little "we."

Of course, some wealthy people truly do go out of their way to support the "we." Bezos's ex-wife MacKenzie Scott seems like a good example. In 2019, she signed the Giving Pledge, acknowledging that she had a "disproportionate amount of money to share" and promising that she would keep giving it away "until the safe is empty."[31] As of December 2023, she'd given away more than $16 billion in five years to almost two thousand organizations—a considerable chunk of her net worth, which as of 2024 was about $34 billion.[32]

It's not just the amount Scott gives that speaks to her generosity, but *how* she gives it. You see, Scott doesn't stand over grantees' shoulders, micromanaging and telling them what to do with the money.[33] She just writes checks to deserving causes in areas such as education, equity and justice, economic security and opportunity, and health, taking her own ego out of the equation as much as possible.[34]

Let me tell you, this is utterly paradigm-shifting in the world of philanthropy. Imagine if more mega-billionaires started following this example of *swiftly* giving away wealth to today's most urgent causes. I'm no proponent of targeted redistributive policies, but can't we all agree that there is *some* cap to what luxuries any human being can possibly want or need? If the country's wealthiest gave away what they couldn't possibly use, by definition they wouldn't be denying themselves anything at all. But the social impact would be extraordinary.

Beyond merely setting an example, we need leaders in society—from politics, business, and other areas—to nudge *the rest of us* to orient ourselves toward serving others. The best, most successful leaders in the business world already do this, by placing great emphasis on customer service, and by training, inspiring, and empowering employees to care for customers. They know it's the right thing to do, but they also realize it's vital for their company's growth and sustainability.

Show me a successful and beloved business, like Trader Joe's, Chick-fil-A, or Costco, and I'll show you a workforce that is hell-bent on listening to customers and providing for their needs. In fact, all three of these companies ranked high on the *Forbes* list of Customer Experience All-Stars in 2024.[35] A weak or struggling business, on the other hand, is almost definitely one where the commitment to giving of oneself for others' benefit has flagged.

Emphasizing a service ethic can play a vital role in turning around a struggling company. When I bought Sunterra and began operating it as Diamond Resorts, I inherited an organization that lacked a strong commitment to service. Its culture was all about "me, me, me," and "we" didn't factor in all that much. Team members thought they could just focus on their established policies and procedures, and if those didn't allow them to serve customers' needs . . . well, that was just too bad. As I've suggested, team members said no a lot when customers made requests of us: "Sorry, that's not our policy." "No, we don't do it that way." Customers weren't very happy with their vacation experiences at Sunterra. Who enjoys hearing "no" when they've paid good money for a vacation? Team members, in turn, weren't able to enjoy the pleasure and fulfillment that comes with giving of themselves to others and making someone else's life a little bit better.

To put Diamond Resorts on a path to growth, we had to completely revamp our team members' orientation toward customers. I drew inspiration here from a saying of my father's: *Always give the customer more than you promised and more than they bargained for.* Providing this kind of exceptional value meant that our baseline answer to every reasonable customer request couldn't be "no" any longer. It had to be a resounding "yes."

The imperative of saying yes inspired and energized all of us to deliver for customers—to focus ourselves on truly understanding what customers cared about and providing for their needs as never before. What did this look like in practice?

It was the resort manager who, upon observing that a guest's cell phone wasn't working, without hesitation handed over her own personal phone to make calls.

It was the housekeeping team member who, upon hearing an international traveler making a comment that they missed their daily afternoon tea, went out of their way to complement their room's coffee machine with a brand new kettle.

It was the front desk agent who, upon learning that a couple was celebrating an anniversary, sent an arrangement of flowers and a bottle of bubbly to help mark the occasion.

The Meaning of Yes required that team members at all levels become "intrapreneurs" who thought of ways large and small that we could improve service—whether by increasing clarity and transparency around our sales process, overseeing physical improvements to our facilities, or incorporating new trends into our food and drink offerings to better keep up with guest preferences.[36] "A 'yes' doesn't mean you have to give away the whole company," our former chief experience officer Patrick Duffy clarifies. "A 'yes' just has to really be where you and the guest are really communicating so brilliantly and openly that when they leave, they feel victorious. They feel that they've been listened to."[37]

I helped to inculcate The Meaning of Yes by modeling it during my visits to our properties—efforts I stepped up after my *Undercover Boss* experience. I got right in there with our teams, showing them myself how we should best serve our customers. Because our team members at Diamond Resorts saw my determination to serve others, they felt inspired to provide exceptional service themselves. And they became more loyal to the company.

At one point, while having some differences of opinion with our union in Hawaii, I visited one of our properties there to speak personally with team members. But talking wasn't enough to communicate how much I valued them, so I *showed* them—by putting on my chef's hat and apron, stepping into the kitchen, and helping our culinary team cook a meal for hundreds of employees. I love to cook, especially dishes like shrimp ceviche, chili relleno, or prime rib. Preparing a meal for someone and serving it to them is one of the most simple, tangible, and meaningful ways I know of providing care. I can't speak for the quality of the food on this occasion, but the gesture generated goodwill, demonstrating to our team members that we were all in this together. As Steve Bell, our executive vice president of global human resources, remembers, "Team members were shocked" to learn that I had helped prepare the meal. "It was unbelievable," Bell says, "just a great time, great feeling."[38]

In addition to my own attempts to spread The Meaning of Yes, we made intensive, formal efforts to train team members around the world in our new, service-oriented way of operating. Duffy visited each of our properties and held seminars that dramatized the attitude toward service we required. Participants took part in role-playing, simulating what it meant to deliver superior service in actual situations.

"I did it face-to-face," Duffy remembered, "whether it was

three people or three hundred. We didn't do it over Zoom. We didn't do it via an email. We really wanted to make sure that they embraced it."[39] All these trips Duffy took weren't cheap, and it would take awhile before the improved service we provided led to a tangible boost to our business. But I was absolutely certain it would, and I was right. Within a few years, customer satisfaction jumped, and our business became more successful.

Leaders outside of business can nurture a spirit of generosity too, starting with efforts to make government agencies of all kinds more service-oriented. When I chaired Brand USA, our objective was to promote America around the world as an attractive and welcoming destination. But it wasn't long before I noticed something: The customer-facing government agents at our borders and in our airports weren't very welcoming. In fact, they were pretty *unwelcoming.* They did what customs officers at many countries often do—scowled, spoke harshly to you, gave you an unnecessarily hard time. This was a problem. We could advertise the United States and all of its exciting, breathtaking destinations as much as we wanted, but if the first thing tourists encountered at the airports was a scowling, unfriendly Department of Homeland Security officer, they might not come away with the most favorable impression.

To address this issue, we rolled out initiatives to persuade our Homeland Security officers to become more welcoming. Yes, it was vital that they check out the bad guys and prevent them from entering the country—that was priority number one. But while doing that job to the best of their abilities, did they have to treat everyone like a hardened criminal? Would it kill them to smile a little and say, "Welcome to the United States?" We made it part of the protocol for every customs officer to welcome every person seeking entry. It was a small gesture in the wide scheme of things, but that injection of a service mentality—that move to help someone, to brighten their day just a little—made a big difference.

Imagine if civil servants at all levels were trained and expected not only to serve a necessary administrative function, but to go beyond that and strive to be of genuine service. Maybe those trips to your state's Department of Motor Vehicles wouldn't be as oppressive as we're all accustomed to. And maybe that positive experience would improve our attitude toward government and make us a bit more civic-minded, proud of our country, and interested in service ourselves.

If it doesn't happen organically, perhaps we can spread an ethic of giving by instituting a mandatory period of service for all Americans. After all, we're used to contributing to society by paying taxes or performing jury duty. What if our society also asked us to spend some small amount of time each year serving meals in a shelter, mentoring young people, taking care of our public spaces, spending time with our seniors, or volunteering in some other way? Think of how healing it could be for our society to see Americans of all classes, ethnicities, genders, and so on come together to fill community needs. Supporting the public good by paying taxes is abstract. Seeing a smile of gratitude on a person's face when you give them a meal is tangible and immediate. This is how we can cement the bonds between us, one act of kindness at a time.

The idea of instituting national service isn't new. Countries like Israel require citizens to perform military service.[40] In France, young people now have to perform dozens of hours of service to help them "develop their role in society."[41] In the United States, we've had voluntary service programs like AmeriCorps, but a growing chorus of leaders and intellectuals are calling for mandatory public service, including Pete Buttigieg during his 2020 presidential run.[42]

Research suggests that the concept of mandatory service is popular among Americans. One survey found that 75 percent of people ages eighteen through twenty-four favor service, as do 80 percent of people ages twenty-five through thirty-seven.[43] At a time when it's hard to get Americans to agree that the sky is blue, let's pause for a moment to appreciate that a true supermajority wants to see our country get back to the practice of "we" before "me." In our fraught political and partisan times, that's a bright spot not just worth celebrating, but acting upon.

Rediscovering the Joys of Serving

Perhaps you're now feeling more inspired to give back and to elect leaders who take service seriously. If you need more prodding, remember that one of the best reasons of all to help others around you is because it *feels* good. Research shows that volunteering leads to a range of positive health outcomes, including a lower risk of death, psychological benefits like improved well-being, more satisfaction with life, less depression, and a greater sense of connection to others.[44] We become happier when we give—less stressed out and anxious.[45] Volunteering in particular also leads us to become more socially involved in other ways, such as by voting or joining groups in the community. One study found that people who volunteered were 12 percent more likely to vote than those who didn't donate their time.[46]

If you have disposable income, it might be fun to buy something for yourself, but that's nothing compared to the satisfaction of giving to a good cause. I've supported many organizations over the years, from local police associations to universities to arts institutions to religious organizations. I've also had the honor of sponsoring a popular enrichment program at West Point called "From Sea To Shining Sea." Designed to complement the rigorous educational program undertaken by young cadets with developmental extracurricular engagements in areas as diverse as government and politics, technology and innovation, and business and finance, this iniative teaches communication techniques that can help these future leaders serve as much-needed examples of integrity and decency for the rest of society. My partner on the project, Frank Luntz, brings in the most memorable speakers from the worlds of media, politics, and beyond to share their real-world experiences with cadets, so they might imagine how they'd confront the most pressing questions facing our country today.

Every donation I've made has been important and personally satisfying to me, whether or not I receive public recognition—in fact, especially if I don't. As gratifying as it can be, recognition injects an undertone of "me" into a gesture that's supposed to be about "we." The greatest pleasures I've gotten philanthropically have been gifts I've made anonymously. Want some examples? Sorry—I ain't telling!

In choosing where to channel philanthropic energy, I find it especially fulfilling to support causes related to long-standing interests of mine. Since childhood, I've been interested in medicine. While I ultimately chose a career in real estate, I've taken great pleasure over the years in supporting scientific and medical research. I've funded researchers at my alma mater, Brandeis University, to support advances in neuroscience. I've made grants to support the Prostate Cancer Foundation, St. Baldrick's Foundation (dedicated to curing childhood cancer), the Milken Institute's FasterCures center (aimed at bringing innovative treatments to patients), the Race to Erase MS (devoted to achieving advances in the treatment of muscular sclerosis), and more. I find it fascinating to learn about these organizations, to meet researchers on the front lines, and to become exposed to the research they're doing.

Thinking back to the times I spent working at Cedars-Sinai in Los Angeles and seeing hospital patients dealing with health challenges, I feel doubly good knowing that my gifts are helping in at least some small way to ease suffering. It's also nice to see my charitable donations potentially making a broader impact. An oncology center at the Veterans Administration Puget Sound Health Care System that I have funded contributed to research that has helped reduce the death rate of Black men from prostate cancer. Formerly, Black men were considerably more likely than their white counterparts to die of the disease; now their risk is about equal. During the pandemic, the center also helped determine the mechanism by which the Covid virus invades healthy cells. As researchers there found, and as others at UCLA and Johns Hopkins also confirmed, a protein called TMPRSS2 that is implicated in prostate cancer plays a role in allowing the Covid virus to enter uninfected cells.[47]

In some cases, I've been able to draw a direct link between resources I've allocated and lives that have been saved. In 2017, a gunman at a Las Vegas hotel brutally attacked attendees of a country music festival, killing fifty-eight that day and wounding hundreds more.[48] I was living in the city at the time, and I can tell you, the trauma that our local community experienced was horrible.

In the aftermath of the event, I wanted to do something to help us through it and to prevent future tragedies. Former Congresswoman Shelley Berkley, who at the time was CEO and senior provost at Touro University Nevada in Henderson, Nevada, came to me with an idea: To improve our community's resilience, she hoped to start a disaster training program at the school, aimed at first responders and members of the community. If more people knew how to provide on-the-spot emergency care to victims during a mass casualty situation, we could save lives. I decided to make an initial investment to get the project off the ground, spurring other donors to step up and give.

The disaster training center that we created, the only one of its kind in Nevada, was wildly successful. As Berkley notes, it wound up training all four thousand metropolitan police officers in Las Vegas—a big win for our community.[49] "If you're in the middle of an active shooting site," Berkley explains, "you can't have medical personnel on site, as they just become targets. Victims could be bleeding out, but if an officer had training, they could apply a tourniquet and stop the bleed, saving someone's life until medical personnel can safely arrive. Sometimes it's a matter of minutes, if not seconds, that can make a big difference in saving someone's life."[50] And now, any police officers you see in Las Vegas have the required training.

Fast-forward to December 2023. At the campus of the University of Nevada, Las Vegas, a former college professor went on a rampage with a 9-millimeter handgun, killing three faculty members at the school.[51] A fourth faculty member was critically wounded but survived.[52] As Berkley recounts, the police officer who found that fourth victim rendered aid, using techniques that they'd learned at Touro's disaster training center. "I didn't know this until I went to the memorial service at the university," Berkley says, "and the sheriff came over and told me, 'The disaster training that Touro does for the metro police—well, it saved another life.'" Wow. Hearing of that, amid the sorrow I feel for the other three people who died that day, brought some solace to my heart.

In some other situations, I've been able to help save the lives of people whom I already knew personally. In 2007, a man named Jacob Slavec came to work for Diamond Resorts at our Las Vegas offices. Jacob was only twenty-four—it was his first job out of college. A few years later, in 2010, I was saddened to learn that Slavec had received a devastating diagnosis. At the age of only twenty-seven, he learned that he had stage IV metastatic melanoma. It was a death sentence—doctors told him he had just months to live.

Fortunately, I was in a position to help. I was serving as chairman of the board at the Nevada Cancer Institute, a treatment facility in Las Vegas, which happened to be hosting a clinical trial for an experimental immunotherapy drug. I introduced Slavec to researchers, and he was able to join the clinical trial. I checked in regularly over the weeks and months that followed to make sure Slavec received the best possible care. Miraculously, this novel treatment worked. Within eighteen months, he was in complete remission. He remains cancer-free to this day, has a family and owns two successful businesses, and is loving life. I can't tell you how heartening it is to see him healthy, happy, and thriving.[53]

I don't want to make a big deal about my personal philanthropy, and certainly there are others who have given more than I have. My aim here is simply to evoke how satisfying it can be to provide service, in hopes of convincing you to do more of it.

All of us can make a difference, regardless of our station in life. I know this because I started giving back long before I became successful in business. My early efforts took the form of community activism, as I've already described: organizing efforts to beautify the Las Vegas Strip, oppose the storage of nuclear waste in Nevada, and prevent the University of Nevada, Las Vegas from overcharging students who were living in-state and qualified for lower tuition rates. Pushing for change didn't require much of a financial investment—only time and energy. Sometimes I ran into roadblocks, and that was frustrating. But the payoff was worth it. There's nothing like going around a local community and being able to see positive changes that you've helped bring about.

All of us can help raise money for our local library, or clean up a nearby river, or push to make our local schools better and more welcoming. Even just reaching out informally and helping neighbors is a valuable act. When my kids were small, I wasn't a perfect dad. Running and growing Diamond Resorts required long nights and weekends as well as frequent trips out of state and around the world. It was pretty all-encompassing, and in retrospect, I didn't get the balance right. My kids always knew that I loved them, and we treasured our time together, but I wasn't there for the daily schedule of sports practices and help with homework. But as my kids remind me, I did take the time to expose them to the joys of service.

My daughter, Tatiana, recalls our Christmas trips to Mexico each year, when we'd take the opportunity to buy a bunch of toys and treats at a local store and deliver them to local orphanages. She was in grade school when these trips began, and she'd play with children her age at the orphanages, painting their nails and braiding their hair. It was a small way to give back, but a meaningful one for everyone involved. Tatiana sees it as a formative part of her childhood, and it was an experience I am proud to have given her.

Sometimes when I'm scanning social media, I come across inspiring stories of people rendering service. On Instagram not long ago, I found a posting about a young man who faced the wrenching decision about his elderly grandmother, who required more care. Should he put her into a nursing home? He decided against it. Not content to see other people care for his grandmother, he opted to become her full-time caretaker and posted images from their times together to social media.

I haven't met this individual, and I don't know the specifics of his story, but this posting resonated with me, not least because of my experiences caring for my father during his battle with Alzheimer's disease. I could have put him into a nursing home, but I didn't feel right about it. My father had made me pinky-swear that he'd never go into a home. He was serious, and so was I. Where I come from, you *never* go back on a pinky-swear.

Caring for my father in my home was excruciating—his disease was a horrible, downward progression, beyond anything I ever could have imagined. But I did it, and now that he's gone, I wouldn't trade that time for anything. I learned so much about my dad as a person, and I'm glad that I had a chance to show him how much I loved him. Caring for my father made me stronger and more empathic as a family member, a leader, and a human being.

Legions of good people in our country are doing their best right now to serve others in a whole range of capacities. Americans have always been the most generous people on earth. We care about others. We help each other. This is who we are. We just need to rediscover that ethos, which seems to have been fading in recent decades. More of us need to step up, and those who are already giving—me included—need to intensify our efforts. My challenge to myself, and to you, is to do or give just a little more every day. Stay alert to the problems around you that afflict others. Find one more person around you to help. Find one more cause to dedicate your time to. Find one more dollar to donate.

Service might be a duty, but it isn't a burden—it's a privilege.

SOCIAL TRUST OR BUST

WHEN I WAS IN MY EARLY TEENS, I carried a few extra pounds. OK, it was more than a few. My dad didn't mince words: I wasn't chubby or big-boned. I was *fat*. Most parents today know that calling negative attention to a child's body or obsessing about calories isn't the healthiest approach. You don't want to damage their self-esteem or give them a complex. But my dad never got this memo. He drilled it into me that I was a "lard-ass."

My dad's harsh parenting technique did wind up working for me—a fact that my father, later in life, didn't hesitate to point out. But his call-it-as-you-see-it approach could have led to two very different outcomes: It could have damaged me for life, turning me into a serial killer whose first victim would have been my father, or it could have motivated me to get my butt off the couch and into the gym. Happily, it did the second. I would by no means advise that a parent call their kid a lard-ass, and I would never have dreamed of saying this to my own kids. But my dad's tough love led me to make a positive change in my life, and this decision opened up a new world for me—one full of new types of people and connections that I'd never expected to encounter.

By the time I was sixteen and could drive, I decided that I was going to change my body. I started eating right and going to my high school gym at 6 a.m. before classes. It was a turning point in my life. I discovered that I was good at lifting weights and that I liked how I looked and felt when I took care of myself. A new sense of agency emerged as I realized that with grit and discipline, I could change my circumstances. Fitness became a daily habit, boosting my confidence and convincing me that I could tackle anything.

By the time I arrived at Brandeis University, I was a committed bodybuilder and had packed on some serious muscle. I was one of the biggest, toughest-looking guys on campus and worked part time as a bouncer at a Boston nightclub. To maintain my physique, I ate six eggs every morning and trained for hours in the afternoons at P&P Gym, a hard-core muscle gym located in Waltham, Massachusetts.

If you've never been inside one of these places, let me paint a picture for you. This wasn't a clean and spiffy, high-end gym like Equinox; it wasn't even Planet Fitness. There was no ambient pop music in the background, no TVs for keeping you entertained while on cardio machines, no cheery staff members greeting you at the door. P&P Gym occupied a small, dingy warehouse space in a rough part of town on a street that bordered a cemetery.

The establishment had cement floors, old-school weight racks and benches, and Ozzy Osbourne and AC/DC blaring over the loudspeakers. A heavy smell of sweat hung in the air, and loud grunts and clanging weights rose above the music. It cost $25 a month to belong. You paid in cash, and owner Joe Rizzo noted it on a piece of paper affixed to his desk.[1]

P&P Gym was not fancy or corporate, but if you were serious about becoming a bodybuilder, this was the place to be. The gym was filled with big, tough guys wearing leather weightlifting belts and throwing up unbelievably large weights. Ted Arcidi, who bench-pressed over seven hundred pounds and once held the world record, worked out at P&P and was the biggest dude in the gym.

When I say these guys were tough, I'm not just talking about their hulk-like physiques. Some of these guys sold guns out of the trunks of their cars—totally illegal, and totally scary. Many were heavily tattooed, and (although I never asked) I'm betting some had been in prison. In short, this was a hard-knocks gym, and as a student at Brandeis University who hailed from Los Angeles, I could've been the odd man out.

And yet I wasn't. People didn't care at all about my social background. What they cared about was how hard I trained and how much weight I could lift. Since I was physically large and could bench-press over four hundred pounds, and since I worked myself so hard most days that I almost vomited, I quickly won these men's respect. In their eyes, I belonged there as much as anyone else did.

To be clear, my relationship with my weightlifting buddies didn't extend outside the gym—I had no wish to get involved in any questionable activities. But inside the gym, we found common ground and pursued a shared interest. I built up a nice, friendly rapport and was on a first-name basis with these guys. As we chatted between sets, I learned details about their lives. They would talk about their jobs, problems with girlfriends, challenges with parents or friends. I mostly stayed quiet, preferring to listen. One was tattooed from head to toe and would vanish mysteriously for periods of time. He happened to mention that he worked as a mercenary, and I had no idea what that meant—I had to look it up. To this day, I don't know how true this was, and I never pressed for details.

In the gym, our outside identities ceased to matter so much. We came together on a level playing field and respected one another. We worked hard toward a common goal, pushing our personal limits, spotting one another and keeping each other safe when four hundred pounds of iron was suspended above our heads, the steel bar bending and just our trembling arms keeping it up. In short, we earned each other's trust.

The hard truths explored in recent chapters focus primarily on public life and the external world of behaviors, policies, and discourse. But to truly turn around our country, we must go deeper and make an *internal* change too. We must change how we see one another, learning to set aside the various categories of race, class, gender, ethnicity, and so on, so we can connect more simply and directly as people and fellow citizens. We must learn to *trust* again.

It's easy to react defensively when confronted with people who are different from us—to be suspicious of them, to distance ourselves, to look away when we pass them in the street. But that won't allow us to repair the ruptures in our society and put us on a path toward safety and prosperity. As we do the hard work required to turn around our communities, we also must learn to feel a sense of brotherly or sisterly love. We must remember to respect one another as human beings, and believe that most of us are basically good people at heart. At the very least, we must learn to give one another the benefit of the doubt. That's the only way we'll trust one another again and move forward toward a better future.

A Growing Psychological Gulf

We've glimpsed how broken American community has become—how isolated and atomized many of us feel. An unfortunate part of this social unraveling, which in turn contributes to political polarization, is the decline of a basic sense of trust. It's not just that we don't trust institutions; we don't trust one another as individuals.

Some scholars have defined social trust as "a generalized belief about what 'most people' are like, including those whom one does not know and those different from oneself."[2] As *The New York Times* columnist David Brooks puts it, social trust is "the confidence that other people will do what they ought to do most of the time."[3] I think of trust as the baseline requirement for living together in society. It's the sense that others whom we don't know are in some fundamental sense just like us, and that they will behave in a reasonably upstanding way. Despite whatever differences might distinguish them, they are basically good people, which means that we can collaborate with them to achieve common goals.

Social trust of this kind existed back at P&P Gym. I might not have wanted to become business partners with these guys or to have them marry into my family, but I felt comfortable engaging freely with them in the context of the gym, even though I was different from them. Our shared focus on building muscle had the effect of blinding us to distractions like color, class, and so on. Yes, we registered these differences, but they faded to the background when we were pumping iron. In that gym, I knew I could count on these strangers to behave with decency toward me, as long as I did so in return. They would respect the rules, let me work out in peace, and give me help when I needed it.

Today, even this minimal level of trust and familiarity is greatly diminished in many American communities. We all feel it. Too often, our neighbors or colleagues at work are simply strangers to us; we also don't feel comfortable around them. Many times, we don't feel like we can talk openly with them or truly be ourselves. We don't feel an underlying sense of sharing something in common, and we may even doubt their motives and intentions.

If we express our opinion on an important subject, maybe they'll become offended and try to get us canceled. If we leave our door unlocked or our car unattended, maybe they'll steal something. If we show any kind of vulnerability, maybe they'll use it against us. According to data from 2019, almost three-quarters of people in their twenties reported believing that "most of the time, people just look out for themselves."[4] National surveys indicate that most people also feel that personal trust has been declining.[5] It's all pretty grim.

One indirect measure of how far social trust has declined might be the exponential rise in security cameras. When I was young, only high-security places like banks had cameras. These days, virtually every public space is continuously monitored. People also have security cameras in their doorbells and can keep tabs on their properties remotely. Americans spend $21 billion each year securing their homes: More than two out of three homes in the country are equipped with some device as a form of protection.[6]

Why is all this necessary? Because we don't trust our fellow Americans to do the right thing. We want to keep an eye on those around us, and we want a video record just in case anyone steals our property or harms us in some way. The notion that someone, somewhere is always watching helps us feel safe in a society that we perceive to be fundamentally threatening. Surveys in 2023 showed that fears of crime among Americans were the highest they'd been in decades.[7]

Closely related to a lack of trust is the increased tendency of many Americans to self-segregate or stay away from people who aren't like them—a trend that is probably both a cause and an effect of distrust. Think about it: How many of us today experience environments like P&P Gym, where we brush up against others who might be very different from us? The vast majority of metro areas—80 percent—have become more segregated.[8] As one report noted, "Everyone wants diversity. But not everyone wants it on their street."[9]

But segregation isn't just about race. Both online and in the real world, we tend to socialize with people who look like us, who have the same level of education, and who share our political beliefs. Most respondents in a 2022 poll affirmed that their friends tended to think the same way about politics that they did, to share a common ethnicity, and to subscribe to the same religious beliefs.[10] Other research has revealed that significant percentages of self-identifying Democrats wouldn't date partisans from the other side, that geographic resentments (urban versus rural) are running high, and that fewer Americans think it's important to be tolerant toward others.[11]

Cloistering among those who are like us makes us feel safe. But the more we do this, the more distanced we become from people who are unlike us, and the easier it becomes to mistrust them. Self-segregation also makes it harder for us to empathize with others and see their points of view on issues.[12] As we isolate more and more—socially, emotionally, and psychologically—the gaps betwccn us get bigger.

But perhaps we should stop and ask ourselves: Is this perceived gulf based on real and growing differences? Maybe not.

Some *Good* News for a Change

As I've found in my own life, Americans today have more in common than they think. It doesn't matter if they're Black or white, gay or straight, Christian or Muslim, successful financially or struggling: Most people I meet, even those who differ from me in demographical terms, ultimately turn out to be good, sane, decent people. They want to help you if they can, they exercise and respect basic common sense, and they're willing to collaborate with their neighbors to solve common problems. They love our country and want to succeed, just like we do.

I've always suspected that when you look at the issues and at the principles that Americans value most, a supermajority exists that straddles conventional partisan lines. Most people, I think, believe that everyone should get a fair shake under the law. Most believe that we should be able to live as we see fit, with government meddling kept to a minimum—and that the government should work for the public good, helping spread prosperity far and wide without squelching free enterprise. Most people think our streets should be safe and our borders secure. They also think America should do the right thing on the world stage, supporting our alliances and standing up to dictators when necessary. Oh, and while they might harbor different religious views, most tend to think that government should stay out of people's bedrooms and keep their hands off individuals' bodies.

Research suggests that Americans do indeed agree with one another a surprising amount of the time. It's true that one 2024 survey confirmed that Republicans valued the right to bear arms more than Democrats do, while Democrats saw freedom of the press as more important. Still, as a news report noted, large majorities of Americans from across the two political parties agreed on "most of the country's core values including the right to vote and freedom of religion."[13] That's a pretty big deal.

When it comes to the basic concepts that define our democracy and social life, the vast majority of us are still very much on board. And we're even coming together more than we think on specific issues, like whether states should protect access to abortion (most people think they should) or whether colleges should pursue affirmative action policies in making admission decisions (most people think they shouldn't).[14] As political scientist Michael Albertus said, "If you get a bunch of normal people at random and put them in a room together and chat about issues, there's a lot more convergence than you might imagine."[15]

If most people tend to see eye to eye, why do we see so much friction unfolding all around us? As I suggested in an earlier chapter, certain forces in our society—namely, the political elite and the media—are artificially dividing us *for their own benefit*.

Let's start with the political elite: elected officials, pundits, party officials, donors, consultants, and so on. These people eat, sleep, and breathe politics, and they tend to hold more extreme views than the average American does. Meanwhile, most Americans don't follow the ups and downs of every political race, and they don't care about it *that* much. Who has the time? We all have other things on our minds, like running businesses, raising kids, pursuing hobbies, and frankly just enjoying life. But that doesn't stop elected officials and operatives on both sides of the aisle from ginning up conflict, demonizing the other side and heightening underlying racial, class, and geographic fault lines. They intentionally rile us up and get us angry, whether to garner votes, rake in dollars, or consolidate power in some way—and as surveys show, we are indeed mad as hell.[16]

I'm not the only one to pin blame on the political elite. Rachel Kleinfeld of the Carnegie Endowment for International Peace has come to similar conclusions after reviewing the research on polarization. "Most people think Americans of different parties hold radically different views, and that's not true," she has argued. "There's a lot of overlap in what Americans from both parties think, although they differ in intensity."

What's happening is that the leaders of our two big political parties have been throwing candidates at us who are more
extreme than we are. "Voters are not getting the choices they
deserve, when we look at the difference between their beliefs and
the beliefs of elected leaders," Kleinfeld explains.[17] In this regard,
polarization is more of a strategy for winning votes than a fact of
American life. It's artificial, and the rest of us are being pushed
into buying it—a phenomenon that some scholars are calling
"learned divisiveness."[18] This is one reason so many Americans
are disillusioned with politics, feeling angry and exhausted by it.[19]
"People don't want to be hateful and divisive and untrusting,"
Kleinfeld says. "They're that way because they're being told that
nothing works, and they're getting frustrated with the systems."[20]

Online platforms are just fueling the learned divisiveness in
our real-world society. Social media is rife with misinformation
and people spouting extreme views.[21] The algorithms social media
companies use, making it easier for lies and extreme ideas to spread
and drown out the truth, are a big part of the problem.[22] But so
is the overall social media environment, which makes it easier for
emotional, sensationalist, extreme content to spread. As Tristan
Harris, who helped found a group called the Center for Humane
Technology, observes, "The more . . . outrageous language you
use, the more inflammatory language, contemptuous language,
the more indignation you use, the more it will get shared. So we
are being rewarded for being division entrepreneurs."[23]

Kleinfeld suggests that many traditional media outlets foster
divisiveness by offering more simplistic, sensational, polarizing
content. Leaders at these companies think this approach will snare
people's attention, but that's not necessarily true. Kleinfeld points

to research suggesting that people actually crave more positive, nuanced, solutions-oriented news coverage—and that they're not getting it.

When I was a kid, Walter Cronkite and his generation of news anchors often managed to find a positive story to tell at the end of their broadcasts. But these days, we seldom get even that. How many times have you avoided or turned off the news because the constant negativity is getting to you and dragging you down? People might actually trust and like the news media more if they were to change up their formula and stop with all the negativity and click-baiting.[24] If everyone's news feed balanced important current events with hopeful stories instead of alarming ones, our society might begin to become more trusting and less divisive.

Time and again, the media seems to perpetuate distortions of truth, delivering a constant drumbeat of warning and distress that fosters divisiveness and a breakdown of social trust. Remember that 2023 survey I mentioned earlier about how fearful Americans have become of crime? The year of that survey, crime was actually down.[25] Yet *that* piece of good news didn't seem to penetrate our collective psyche.

Likewise, many of us believe that the economy is a lot worse than it is. I know that inflation has been devastating for American families, and that high prices on homes make it extraordinarily difficult these days to pursue the American dream. I also understand that economic sentiment—how people feel about the market, jobs, and the cost of living—matters a great deal. But was the American economy in a recession during the spring of 2024, as many Americans thought?[26] Actually, no. Would knowing this information and being aware that inflation has been on a steady retreat make people feel more optimistic about their lives and our collective future? Since perception often shapes our reality, who's to say?

What we're witnessing today is nothing other than a massive and pernicious mind warp being inflicted on the American people. This situation has arisen not primarily as a result of some conspiracy or master plan—although plenty of devious people in Moscow and Beijing are plotting as we speak to divide our country by stuffing us full of disinformation. Rather, we're muddled and confused about our relationship with our fellow Americans thanks to a confluence of broad political, technological, and social trends.

The real question is: What can we do about it?

Combatting Disrespect and Distrust

In our personal lives, we can choose to fight self-segregation and welcome others in. We shouldn't content ourselves with living inside our comfortable little bubbles of self-reinforcing ideas and information. Let's look for opportunities to connect with others. What version of P&P Gym might still exist in your area? Work up the courage to stop by and participate.

We can decide to be joiners rather than avoiders. Running clubs, bird-watching clubs, knitting clubs, skateboarding clubs, book clubs, investing clubs—there's something for everyone. It might feel awkward at first, maybe even a bit scary. But if we keep an open mind, and focus on listening and learning rather than talking, we might be surprised at the connections we can make. Over time, our whole view of community and our fellow Americans might shift. Instead of letting outside forces cast people different from us as suspicious "others," we might be better able to focus on our shared humanity.

To save our political system and rejuvenate our communities, all of us need to put our personal politics on the back burner a little bit. We aren't simply a divided society of Democrats versus Republicans. We're a fascinating collection of individuals with complex, layered identities who are worth getting to know. Let's nurture and rediscover other parts of ourselves, beyond our partisan affiliations. Let's experience the joys of finding unexpected connections with others who might not share our superficial identity markers but who *do* share some of our innate interests.

We can start to rediscover these parts of ourselves and others even without places like P&P. You can even expand your social life from the comfort of your own home. I love to entertain frequently, and believe me, nothing makes for a more boring gathering than inviting people who all share the same views, live in the same neighborhood, and like the same things. Snoozefest!

I've mentioned elsewhere that I maintain friendships with both Democrats and Republicans, but my desire to reach out and connect doesn't end there. I hang out with many others whose outward identities differ from mine: members of the LGBTQIA community, religious Christians, Hispanics, Blacks, Asians, Muslims, Buddhists, atheists. Not everyone is necessarily a close friend, and I know some people in my circle disagree with me fervently on specific issues. But I truly value the opportunity to gain exposure to new ideas, learn about unfamiliar customs, and bond over those values and beliefs that we do share in common. This diversity in my social life is both fun and fulfilling.

If we stay alert, we can often find unexpected opportunities to engage with others outside of our usual social networks. I'm constantly trying to do this, chatting up people wherever I go, from the coffee shop to the gas station to waiting in elevators. What if, instead of enduring awkward silences, we made it a point to strike up a polite or silly conversation? Take out the earphones, dang it! Talk to someone—they won't bite!

I recently wanted to acquire a particular phone number that had some personal meaning to me, so on a lark I called up the person who owned it—a total stranger—to ask if they'd let me have it. The man turned out to be a very conservative Republican and a religious Christian. We chatted for a while on the phone, and each of us was struck by how much we were enjoying each other's company. I decided to invite him to my home, and he accepted. A few days later, he showed up!

He stayed for hours, engaging with me in a twisting and turning conversation that took us to all sorts of surprising subjects: his love of the outdoors, our shared appreciation for communities of faith, how neither of us could imagine calling anywhere else home but Southern California. Would I call this gentleman a close friend? No. But we *did* become friends that day, and we are still in touch. He now knows, if he didn't before, that he has some things in common with someone who is both Jewish and a Democrat. And I had it reaffirmed for me once again that strangers aren't really that strange at all. We're Americans, with much to teach one another.

I've been doing this kind of thing for years in small, quirky ways, and it has led to the deepening of relationships that otherwise might have stayed at the surface. When living in Las Vegas and building my company, I was on the road all the time, so my family hired a nanny, Alma Matos, to help with our three young kids. As a Mexican American woman, Alma might not have seemed to have much in common with me or my family, and we could have kept the relationship strictly business. But instead we made a point of welcoming Alma with open arms, both on the clock and off. Frequently, that meant sharing meals with her. That's my attitude: If you're in my house, you sit and eat. Food is for sharing.

Breaking bread with Alma allowed us to set aside the employer-employee dynamic temporarily. As we sat around the table chatting, we were simply friends and fellow human beings. Because of that human contact, which occurred regularly over a period of years, Alma became more than just an employee—she became family to us and remains so to this day.

If you're looking for more formal ways to connect with others, philanthropy and community service can be a great opportunity to build social trust by interacting with others who might be different from you in some ways. I've mentioned my work with the Dream Center in Los Angeles. One reason I love to engage with this faith-based Christian organization, aside from the fact that they do incredible work and help thousands of people in my community, is that I get a chance to spend time with these individuals, hear about their experiences, and share my own. We come together in a place of mutual respect, setting aside our differences to learn and enjoy a few laughs. We focus on what we have in common—and believe me, there's plenty. Ultimately, all of us want the same thing: a chance to live the American dream and to see our kids do better than we did. If you have the resources—whether it's extra time, attention, or money—to share, I really hope you'll consider doing so in a way that allows you to reach across the social divide.

If you lead a company, you can build social trust by welcoming in diverse people as employees, vendors, and customers. This isn't about slavishly applying some DEI ideology, but rather about trying to run the best, most relevant, most appealing, and most successful company you can. Allow me to cite a few examples of folks who helped bring different perspectives to leadership at Diamond Resorts: We had Steve Bell, a gregarious, larger-than-life figure serving as our successful, longtime global head of human resources. A Black man who hailed from the Northeast but came to call Las Vegas home, he had a laugh so hearty that it shook the items on his office desk. I also hired Mike Flaskey, a Southern conservative Christian who was more comfortable hunting and fishing in rural Florida than walking city streets, to work alongside us as our CEO. Did cultivating such differences on our team create unmanageable personal tensions? Not at all. We had the sorts of healthy disagreements about business matters that make good leadership teams great. But we all got along—Flaskey, Bell, me, and others from diverse backgrounds—because we focused on our common mission of building a great company. We operated from a baseline level of social trust.

As the years passed, and as trust built up among us, many of us did more than just get along. We became good friends, even brothers and sisters in arms. Flaskey, who in 2010 was CEO of a company that developed second homes, remembers that at first he wasn't interested in working for us at Diamond. I persisted because I saw his talent and knew he'd be able to contribute in crucial ways, and I was right. I probably disagreed with Flaskey at least 50 percent of the time when it came to politics and hot-button issues. But I grew to love that guy as a friend and was thrilled to have him on my team—and I'm grateful that he feels the same about me.

"I'm a deer hunter," Flaskey told a member of my research team. "I'm a bow hunter. I'm a fricking Southern Republican dude, and I love this man who's a fricking left liberal."[27] In his mind, maybe I'm a "left liberal," but after reading this book you know that I'm actually a pragmatic problem-solver—a moderate through and through, even if my tactics might err on the side of disruptive and unconventional. Still, Flaskey is right in noting how a personal relationship can flourish if you put politics in a box and agree to disagree. In his words, our business relationship, which was extremely successful, "is just another example of how two people from completely different backgrounds not only work together but love each other."

Whether leaders say they're taking a color-blind approach to doing business or subscribe to the idea of measuring and monitoring diversity levels, one thing is true: If you really want to build a culture where inclusion is real and not just a slogan, you must stand up aggressively to prevent mistrust from seeping in. Left unchecked over time, suspicion and emotional distance can lead to something far more malignant: outright bigotry.

I made it absolutely clear to everyone that in my company, you didn't disrespect people over their identity or their politics. You just didn't. You showed up every day, worked hard for the good of the company, and showed kindness and love. Most of the time, people got the memo and behaved well. When they didn't, I laid down the law.

I'll never forget the time we uncovered a sales representative who was proud about having developed various sales presentations for prospective customers based on identity. He had a presentation for Blacks, one for Jews, one for Asians, one for Caucasians, and who knew if there were others. As you might expect, these presentations were riddled with hurtful and ignorant stereotypes. This was the *opposite* of how I wanted to market our company to customers.

I asked this salesperson to come to my office and walk me through his presentations. I wanted to see for myself what he was doing. Although I was furious, I listened and didn't speak. But when he finished, I told him that what he had presented violated Diamond Resorts' core principle of caring for guests and for each other: We see people for who they are as individuals, not through some lens that reduces them to something less. And then I told him to go see Steve Bell, our head of HR, who had no qualms about seeing to this salesperson's swift termination. We had a zero-tolerance policy for disrespecting others, and on this rule in particular there was absolutely no room for second chances. Our stance was a strong one, and I'm proud of it. The total lack of ambiguity helped to create the conditions for social trust to flourish.

Take That First Step

You might wonder whether one individual's small personal acts can really help change the overall atmosphere of divisiveness and distrust in America. Well, what else are we going to do? Should we instead retreat to our respective corners, hoping that the outside world will somehow change on its own? News flash: It won't.

But I sincerely do believe that yes, personal outreach is the *only* way to make a difference. And better yet, there's science behind it. When interacting with strangers, we tend to trust people who resemble others in the past whom we've known to be trust-worthy, and we mistrust people whom we judge as resembling the liars, cheats, and connivers we've known. As one researcher has observed, "Our brains deploy a learning mechanism in which moral information encoded from past experiences guides future choices."[28]

While this cognitive process may not be totally fair, it does provide us with an opportunity to take that first step toward build-ing social trust. Once we've engaged with someone whose identity differs from ours and found them to be basically good and decent, we're more likely to presume goodness in others who belong to the same identity group. We give strangers and new acquaintances the benefit of the doubt. We don't shrink back in mistrust. Over time, we become even more accepting and open-minded.

We actually see this borne out all the time. Research has found that Americans are more likely to say that they'd be comfortable learning that a friend is gay if they already were close friends with a gay person, or even merely acquainted with a gay person.[29] Even just a few connections with people from other walks of life can prove transformational, opening us up to still more social trust and diverse encounters in the future. But to reap all the benefits, we must make that first effort to meet and connect with others who are unlike us.

Imagine if each of us resolved to undergo a bit of discomfort in order to welcome in someone different from us. It would transform our society. Sure, we might have some unpleasant experiences—but that's the point, isn't it? To have real, authentic experiences that push us past our self-imposed enclaves and comfort zones. To decide for ourselves who is worthy of our trust and time, rather than letting the media and "influencers" dictate these important decisions.

Unpleasant experiences or not, I bet the majority of us would come away transformed, newly aware that our differences aren't nearly as important as what we share in common. We would feel more affection, more social trust, a greater sense of belonging to a community. This perception would make us more willing and even excited to set aside the rancor and come together around common projects. We would feel a rekindling of love for our fellow humans, motivating us to sacrifice more often for the common good.

Love might not be all you need to get by in politics and life. Social trust might not be entirely enough either. But we can't get by without them. To truly turn our country around, we must rebuild trust in ourselves, each other, and our shared American project.

That, my friends, might well be the hardest truth of all.

IT'S UP TO US

IN WORKING ON THIS BOOK, I've been inspired by my children and others in the rising generations of Americans. I want *all* young people in our country to have the bright, prosperous future they deserve. Growing up I was fortunate enough to experience a particularly idyllic side of California, especially during my summers at Brooktrails. The California I knew had serious flaws, including racial inequality, drugs, and air pollution, but it was on balance a beautiful place with abundant nature, safe neighborhoods, strong communities, and widespread economic opportunity. Much of America was like that too. A sense of optimism and dynamism reigned—the idea that you could accomplish anything so long as you worked hard enough.

That optimism and dynamism has waned. We're stuck and stagnant, and we know it. The solution isn't to try to realize some nostalgic view of the past, adopting a set of retrograde and ineffective policies in some misguided attempt to "make America great again." Nor, as we've seen in California and elsewhere, is it to indulge in a set of idealistic, but not realistic, social and cultural experiments, spending untold billions in ways that do more virtue-signaling than problem-solving. We must find a new way forward, adopting pragmatic policies and approaches that reflect the commonsense, enduring principles described in this book.

Most Americans aren't idealogues. What we want from leaders are solutions that might not deliver perfection but that undeniably help to move the ball forward. We want real leadership grounded in hard truths. But we can't wait for leadership like this to materialize. We must deliver it ourselves.

We must all show integrity, standing up for what is right even when doing so exposes us to discomfort and risk.

We must all collaborate better across political divides, and open ourselves to difficult but honest conversations in which we hear each other out and work through disagreements.

We must all uphold the basic rules, laws, and conventions that allow for the healthy, stable society we too often take for granted.

We must all fight hard for economic inclusivity, knowing that we do well when our neighbors are also prospering.

We must all bypass complacent leaders who tolerate government inefficiency and unaccountability, and champion those with the audacity to disrupt for the collective good.

We must all rededicate ourselves to service, unleashing the magic of "we" over the complacency of "me."

And in ways big and small, we must all seek to rediscover

common ground with others who might not look, think, worship, or vote as we do, especially in the aftermath of the 2024 election.

In short, we must try to cultivate the kind of seriousness we want to see in our elected officials. It's easy to offer superficial, Band-Aid solutions. Politicians do it all the time. But if you never try to solve complex problems at their root, then sooner or later you wind up asking yourself the question I posed at the beginning of this book: *How the* hell *did we get here?*

An approach known as the social determinants of health considers the many factors that make for healthy living, including a good diet, proper housing, access to clean air and water, access to job opportunities, and so on.[1] To make a population healthier, we can't just focus on one or two of these factors—we need to address as many as possible. I'd argue that something similar holds when addressing economic and social issues. We must go deep and broad, looking at the many reasons why challenges in our communities arise and putting a variety of bold, creative remedies in place. But that requires both elected leaders and citizens who are committed, diligent, pragmatic, public-minded, ethical, and courageous—in other words, serious.

Serious people come from all backgrounds, and we must celebrate them when we find them. I've said a few words about my mentor, the late Senator Harry Reid of Nevada, who rose from humble origins to become, against the odds, one of the most effective leaders our country has ever seen. When he stepped down in 2017, having served eight years as Senate majority leader, he left a proud legacy of pragmatism and accomplishment that made millions of lives materially better.

I was so moved by Harry's example and so grateful for his contributions to the nation that in 2021 I helped advance a project I hoped would make him smile: leading an effort to rename the airport in Las Vegas the Harry Reid International Airport. This wasn't easy, but I mobilized the political skills Harry had taught me to resolve an intractable stalemate and get it done. Harry's friends and supporters had been trying for seven years to honor him in this way but lacked the connections or relationships with the community to make it happen. Their plan to use taxpayer dollars to change the name aroused opposition from the county commissioners charged with making a decision on the matter.

When I got involved, we managed to resolve this issue in just a few months. To get around the opposition to using public funds, I proposed paying for the name change via a public-private partnership. When several commissioners reacted positively, I asked them to spread word of the idea and told them I'd be happy if all of us collectively took credit for it. I wanted this to be a shared success.

In the end, I managed to convince five out of the seven commissioners in advance of a four-hour public hearing that would take up the question. At the hearing itself, we convinced the other two commissioners, resulting in a 7–0 vote in favor of the name change. This was a dramatic turnaround, considering how lengthy the logjam had been. The plan to honor Harry went forward and was finalized just weeks before his passing. Today, Senator Reid's legacy spans from Searchlight to the skies.

I hope we'll all draw inspiration from Harry and other exemplary leaders like him. Benjamin Franklin might be right— that democratic republics like the United States aren't easy to maintain, and that our greatest challenge may be to keep ours intact. But I firmly believe that if we set aside our differences and work together, we can succeed. More than that: I believe that America's best days can be ahead of us—that our children can be safer, healthier, and more prosperous than we are.

It's up to us to make it happen. We can't do the same old thing and expect different results; as the saying goes, that is the very definition of insanity. So, let's get out the broom, sweep out the ideologues who try to divide us, and elect a new generation of pragmatic problem-solvers who can bring us back together again. Let's roll up our sleeves and embark on the greatest turnaround project our country—and the world—has ever seen.

HARRY REID

Senate Majority Leader, 2007-2015
Senate Democratic Leader, 2005-2017

United States Senate, 1987-2017
United States House of Representatives, 1983-1987

November 19, 2021

Dear Stephen,

Thank you for everything you have done to support the renaming of the airport in my honor. From your testimony to your behind-the-scenes efforts to your incredibly generous donation, my heart is full of appreciation.

I have called for the removal of Senator Pat McCarran's name from our airport for many years – long before anyone suggested his name be replaced with mine. I am humbled by your role in making this change possible. But above all, I am proud to call you my son. My admiration and love for you is unending.

As we approach the holidays, please know that Landra and I wish you and yours all the joys of the season and happiness throughout the coming year.

Sincerely,

Harry

Harry Reid

ACKNOWLEDGMENTS

ONE OF THE MOST TERRIFYING SIGHTS for any author is a blank page. Finding the right words—especially if you are dyslexic like me—and putting down on paper one's forty-plus years of professional life lessons, observations, and hard truths can be a joyous but beastly task.

A book of this magnitude doesn't just happen by itself. For giving heartfelt support, for offering enthusiastic encouragement, for helping me find that inner voice, for making me dig deeper, for getting into countless hours of debate, for embodying unwavering work ethic, I want to thank my incredible sparring partners Seth Schulman, Kelly Royal, Kris Pauls, and everyone at Disruption Books. I will never forget your inspiration, optimism, and reassurance.

To all my professional friends and colleagues along the way, thank you for joining me on my journey.

To all my friends who are now family—you know who you are—thanks for always taking my calls no matter what time, no matter what day.

To my daily lifelines, Mabel and Brandon, thanks for always pointing me in the right direction.

And to my greatest loves of all, my children, and all my adopted children, thank you for being my driving force, my fire, my life's purpose, and for letting Pappa Bear be Pappa Bear. You're the reason I take breath.

I'm a lucky man.

NOTES

EPIGRAPH

1   "September 17, 1787: A Republic, If You Can Keep It," National Park Service, accessed October 9, 2024, https://www.nps.gov/articles/000/constitutionalconvention-september17.htm#:~:text=%2D%2DBenjamin%20Franklin's%20response%20to,a%20republic%20or%20a%20monarchy%3F%22.

INTRODUCTION

1   "California Is Gripped by Economic Problems, with No Easy Fix," *The Economist*, March 31, 2024, https://www.economist.com/united-states/2024/03/31/california-is-gripped-by-interlocking-economic-problems-with-no-easy-solution.

2   Kira Billman, "If You're Not a Teacher, You Have No Idea How Bad It Is Right Now," *EdSource*, January 21, 2024, https://edsource.org/2024/if-youre-not-a-teacher-you-have-no-idea-how-bad-it-is-right-now/704128.

3   Amy Graff, "SF Police Shoplifting Crackdown Leads to 17 Arrests in One Day at Single Store," *SFGATE*, November 30, 2023, https://www.sfgate.com/bayarea/article/san-francisco-police-arrest-17-shoplifting-18525425.php.

4   Dan Walters, "California Keeps Its Title as Having the Nation's Highest Poverty Rate," *Cal Matters*, September 13, 2023, https://calmatters.org/commentary/2023/09/california-poverty-rate/.

5   Kate Wolffe, "As Health Care Gets More Expensive, California Looks to Limit Cost Increases," *Capradio*, April 29, 2024, https://www.capradio.org/articles/2024/04/29/as-health-care-gets-more-expensive-california-looks-to-limit-cost-increases/.

6   Adam Beam, "Gov. Gavin Newsom Proposes Painful Cuts to Close California's Growing Budget Deficit," *AP News*, May 10, 2024, https://apnews.com/article/california-budget-deficit-gov-gavin-newsom-8f502d57d00d551c0b6b6331367f7a25.

7   George Skelton, "Why Californians Are Fleeing This Once-Golden State," *Los Angeles Times*, April 8, 2024, https://www.latimes.com/california/story/2024-04-08/why-californians-are-fleeing-this-once-golden-state.

8   Andrew Daniller, "Americans Take a Dim View of the Nation's Future, Look More Positively at the Past," Pew Research Center, April 24, 2023, https://www.pewresearch.org/short-reads/2023/04/24/americans-take-a-dim-view-of-the-nations-future-look-more-positively-at-the-past/.

9   Lydia Saad, "Historically Low Faith in US Institutions Continues," *Gallup News*, July 6, 2023, https://news.gallup.com/poll/508169/historically-low-faith-institutions-continues.aspx#:~:text=Last%20year%2C%20Gallup%20recorded%20significant,and%2011%20percentage%20points%2C%20respectively.

10   Suzanne Blake, "All Types of Crime Are Falling Except One," *Newsweek*, July 25, 2024, https://www.newsweek.com/all-types-crime-falling-except-shoplifting-1930401.

11   "Revenue of Diamond Resorts International Worldwide 2010–2015," Statista, February 29, 2016, https://www.statista.com/statistics/509688/diamond-resorts-international-revenue/.

12   *Diamond Resorts International, Inc. Fiscal 2013 Annual Report* (Diamond Resorts International, Inc., Form 10-K 2013), https://www.annualreports.com/HostedData/AnnualReportArchive/d/NYSE_DRII_2013.pdf.

13   For the details on this turnaround story, see Stephen J. Cloobeck, *Checking In: Hospitality-Driven Thinking, Business, and You* (Greenleaf, 2018).

HARD TRUTH #1

1   Gary Toyn, "In Memoriam: Harry Reid and his 'Mother of Faith,'" LinkedIn, December 29, 2021, https://www.linkedin.com/pulse/memoriam-harry-reid-his-mother-faith-gary-toyn/.

2   Nolan D. McCaskill, "Harry Reid: 'I Learned a Lot in Honesty from a Man who Ran a Whorehouse,'" *Politico*, April 14, 2016, https://www.politico.com/story/2016/04/harry-reid-whorehouse-childhood-221962.

3   "Harry Reid," *Encyclopedia Britannica*, updated September 13, 2024, https://www.britannica.com/biography/Harry-Reid.

4   Senator Harry Reid, *The Good Fight: Hard Lessons from Searchlight to Washington* (Berkley, 2008), chap. 8, Kindle.

5   Reid, *The Good Fight*, chap. 8.

6   Reid, *The Good Fight*, chap. 8.

7   Reid, *The Good Fight*, chap. 8.

8   Reid, *The Good Fight*, chap. 8.

9   Eoin Higgins, "Harry Reid Understood Power," *The Nation*, December 31, 2021, https://www.thenation.com/article/politics/harry-reid-obit/.

10   Paul Kane, "Searchlight, Las Vegas and the Two Identities of Harry Reid," *Washington Post*, December 29, 2021, https://www.washingtonpost.com/powerpost/searchlight-las-vegas-and-the-two-identities-of-harry-reid/2021/12/29/46a7887e-6855-11ec-96f3-b8d3be309b6e_story.html.

11   Higgins, "Harry Reid Understood Power."

12   Tom Daschle, "Remembering a Man Who Wouldn't Stay Down," *The Hill*, January 8, 2022, https://thehill.com/blogs/congress-blog/politics/588831-tom-daschle-remembering-a-man -who-wouldnt-stay-down/.

13   "Boston Tea Party," *Encyclopaedia Britannica*, updated July 31, 2024, https://www.britannica.com/event/Boston-Tea-Party.

14   "Declaration of Independence: A Transcription," National Archives, last reviewed July 3, 2024, https://www.archives.gov/founding-docs/declaration-transcript.

15   Richard Weissbourd and Chris Murphy, "We Have Put Individualism Ahead of the Common Good for Too Long," *Time*, April 11, 2023, https://time.com/6269091/individualism-ahead-of -the-common-good-for-too-long/.

16   Aleks Phillips, "Americans Don't Want to Fight for Their Country Anymore," *Newsweek*, November 10, 2023, https://www.newsweek.com/american-military-recruitment-problems -public-apathy-1842449.

17   Lydia Saad, "Personal Safety Fears at Three-Decade High in US," *Gallup News*, November 16, 2023, https://news.gallup.com/poll/544415/personal-safety-fears-three-decade-high.aspx; "American Volunteerism Continues to Decline, Studies Find," *Philanthropy News Digest*, December 12, 2023, https://philanthropynewsdigest.org/news/american-volunteerism-continues-to-decline-studies -find; Laurie Santos, "Why Americans Are Lonelier and Its Effects on Our Health," interview by John Yang, *PBS NewsHour*, January 8, 2023, https://www.pbs.org/newshour/show/why-americans -are-lonelier-and-its-effects-on-our-health; Emily Peck, "Americans Are Increasingly Disgruntled at Work," *Axios*, January 25, 2023, https://www.axios.com/2023/01/25/americans-increasingly -disgruntled-at-work.

18   Robert Reich, "Why So Many Americans Feel So Powerless," Substack, April 26, 2015, http://robertreich.org/post/117461327725.

19   "Stress in America 2022: Concerned for the Future, Beset by Inflation," American Psychological Association, accessed August 7, 2024, https://www.apa.org/news/press/releases/stress/2022/ concerned-future-inflation.

20   Arthur Zaczkiewicz, "Global Consumer Stress Levels Surge Amid Political Uncertainty, Kearney Report Finds," *WWD*, July 24, 2024, https://wwd.com/business-news/business-features/ consumer-stress-levels-surge-amid-political-uncertainty-kearney-report-finds-1236503141/.

21   Jared Sousa, "American Dream Far from Reality for Most People: Poll," *ABC News*, January 15, 2024, https://abcnews.go.com/Politics/american-dream-reality-people-poll/story?id=106339566.

22   Tim Daly, "Grade Inflation Is Locking in Learning Loss, Part 1," Fordham Institute, November 14, 2023, https://fordhaminstitute.org/national/commentary/grade-inflation-locking -learning-loss-part-1.

23   Wellesley Public Media, "You Are Not Special Commencement Speech from Wellesley High School," YouTube video, 12:45, June 7, 2012, https://www.youtube.com/watch?v=_lfxYhtf8o4.

24   "Entrepreneurship and the Decline of American Growth," Joint Economic Committee Republicans, December 14, 2022, https://www.jec.senate.gov/public/index.cfm/republicans/2022/12/ entrepreneurship-and-the-decline-of-american-growth; Stephen Marche, "Today's Teenagers Have Invented a Language That Captures the World Perfectly," *The New York Times*, June 25, 2024, https://www.nytimes.com/2024/06/25/opinion/gen-z-slang-language.html.

25   Frank Bruni, *The Age of Grievance* (Avid Reader Press, 2024), 5.

26   Bruni, *The Age of Grievance*, 23.

27   Curt Rice, "How Blind Auditions Help Orchestras to Eliminate Gender Bias," *The Guardian*,
     October 14, 2013, https://www.theguardian.com/women-in-leadership/2013/oct/14/
     blind-auditions-orchestras-gender-bias.

28   Conor Friedersdorf, "A Uniquely Terrible New DEI Policy," *The Atlantic*, October 13, 2023, https://
     www.theatlantic.com/ideas/archive/2023/10/dei-policy-california-community-college/675629/.

29   Cora Lewis and Linley Sanders, "Most Americans Say They Pay 'Too Much' and See Poor Value in
     Taxes, AP-NORC Poll Shows," *PBS NewsHour*, January 28, 2024. https://www.pbs.org/newshour/
     politics/most-americans-say-they-pay-too-much-and-see-poor-value-in-taxes-ap-norc-poll-shows.

30   Juhohn Lee, "The Federal Government Wastes at Least $247 Billion in Taxpayer Money Each
     Year. Here's How," CNBC, updated May 24, 2023, https://www.cnbc.com/2023/04/18/heres-how
     -the-federal-government-wastes-tax-money.html.

31   Lindsay Koshgarian, "The Pentagon Just Can't Pass an Audit," *Colorado Newsline*, December 6, 2023,
     https://coloradonewsline.com/2023/12/06/pentagon-cant-pass-audit/.

32   "How Lower-Income Americans Get Cheated on Property Taxes," *The New York Times*, April 3, 2021,
     https://www.nytimes.com/2021/04/03/opinion/sunday/property-taxes-housing-assessment
     -inequality.html.

33   Sara Morrison, "Section 230, the Internet Law That's Under Threat, Explained," *Vox*,
     updated February 23, 2023, https://www.vox.com/recode/2020/5/28/21273241/section-230
     -explained-supreme-court-social-media.

34   Leo Stallworth, "Parents Blame Snapchat for Role in Children's Deaths, Urge Action by Congress,"
     ABC7 News, May 22, 2024, https://abc7.com/post/parents-blame-snapchat-role-childrens
     -fentanyl-deaths-demand/14855927/.

35   Angela Yang, "Mark Zuckerberg Apologizes to Parents at Online Child Safety Hearing," NBC News,
     January 31, 2024, https://www.nbcnews.com/tech/social-media/mark-zuckerberg-apologizes
     -parents-online-child-safety-hearing-rcna136578; Abigail Adams, "Mark Zuckerberg and Snapchat
     CEO Evan Spiegel Apologize to Parents at Congressional Social Media Hearing," *People*,
     January 31, 2024, https://people.com/meta-snapchat-ceos-apologize-to-parents-at-congressional
     -hearing-8557010.

36   For a local example, please see Eric Umansky, "How the N.Y.P.D. Quietly Shuts Down Discipline
     Cases Against Officers," *The New York Times*, June 27, 2024, https://www.nytimes.com/2024/06/27/
     nyregion/how-the-nypd-quietly-shuts-down-discipline-cases-against-officers.html.

37   Devon Ombres, "With Its Release of a New Nonbinding Code of Conduct, the Supreme
     Court Fails on Ethics Again," Center for American Progress, November 15, 2023,
     https://www.americanprogress.org/article/with-its-release-of-a-new-nonbinding-code-of
     -conduct-the-supreme-court-fails-on-ethics-again/.

38   Lindsay Whitehurst, "Justice Alito's Home Flew a US Flag Upside Down after Trump's
     'Stop the Steal' Claims, a Report Says," *AP News*, May 17, 2024, https://apnews.com/article/
     supreme-court-flag-stop-steal-alito-trump-9a32d658f5c5baa2bacba25bce7c48cd.

39   Ombres, "New Nonbinding Code of Conduct."

40   "America's Supreme Court Should Adopt New Ethics Standards," *The Economist*, September 6, 2023, https://www.economist.com/leaders/2023/09/06/americas-supreme-court-should-adopt -new-ethics-standards.

41   "Hilton Grand Vacations: Diamond Resorts Wins Critical Ruling to Protect Customers From Nationwide Consumer Scam," Hilton Grand Vacations, March 24, 2023, https://corporate.hgv .com/news/news-details/2023/Diamond-Resorts-Wins-Critical-Ruling-to-Protect-Customers- From-Nationwide-Consumer-Scam/default.aspx#:~:text=In%20the%20lawsuit%2C%20 Diamond%20alleges,supposed%20timeshare%20%22exit%22%20services; "Diamond Resorts Marks Win Against Timeshare Exit Company," Wyndham Destinations, November 19, 2019, https://www.timeshare.com/us/en/resources/timeshare-exit-scams/2019/diamond-resorts -marks-win-against-timeshare-exit-company; "Diamond Resorts' Legal Victory Shuts Down Fraudulent Timeshare Exit Companies," *AP News*, July 24, 2020, https://apnews.com/article/ de1c80cd4431c189957549989994b311.

42   Mike Flaskey (former CEO of Diamond Resorts), interview with the author, April 12, 2024.

43   *Extended Mass Layoffs in 2008*, Report 1024, US Bureau of Labor Statistics, June 2010, https://www.bls.gov/opub/reports/mass-layoffs/archive/extended_mass_layoffs2008.pdf.

44   Tony Case, "WTF Is the Great Betrayal?" *WorkLife*, February 14, 2023, https://www.worklife.news/talent/wtf-is-the-great-betrayal/.

45   Benjy Hansen-Bundy, "The Unrelenting 'Great Betrayal' Has Killed the Dream of the Cushy Tech Job," *Fast Company*, January 28, 2024, https://www.fastcompany.com/91017704/ the-unrelenting-great-betrayal-has-killed-the-dream-of-the-cushy-tech-job.

46   Jennifer Dulski, "3 Blatant Ways the Great Betrayal Is Damaging Workplace Culture and How Leaders Can Rebuild Trust," *Fast Company*, March 15, 2024, https://www.fastcompany .com/91058165/3-blatant-ways-the-great-betrayal-is-damaging-workplace-culture-and-how -leaders-can-rebuild-trust.

47   Steve Sisolak (former governor of Nevada and former member of the Nevada Board of Regents), interview with the author, May 13, 2024.

48   Kane, "Searchlight, Las Vegas and the Two Identities of Harry Reid."

HARD TRUTH #2

1   Liz Elting, "The US Women's National Soccer Team—A Case Study in the Collective Power of Women and Doing the Impossible," *Forbes*, March 4, 2022, https://www.forbes.com/sites/ lizelting/2022/03/04/the-us-womens-national-soccer-team-a-case-study-in-the-collective -power-of-women-and-doing-the-impossible/.

2   "Lilly: USA's 99ers Created Societal Change," Inside FIFA, March 18, 2019, https://inside.fifa.com/tournaments/womens/womensworldcup/france2019/news/ lilly-usa-s-99ers-created-societal-change.

3   Erik Spanberg, "World Cup: Summer of '99," *Sports Business Journal*, June 3, 2019, https:// www.sportsbusinessjournal.com/Journal/Issues/2019/06/03/In-Depth/Summer-of-99.aspx.

4   Elting, "US Women's National Soccer Team."

5   Jaide Timm-Garcia, "Women's World Cup: The Match That Changed Women's Football," CNN, July 23, 2019, https://www.cnn.com/2019/05/31/football/usa-1999-womens-world-cup-victory-brandi-chastain-mia-hamm-wwc-spt-intl/index.html.

6   Timm-Garcia, "Women's World Cup."

7   Spanberg, "World Cup: Summer of '99."

8   "Lilly: USA's 99ers Created Societal Change," Inside FIFA.

9   Elting, "US Women's National Soccer Team."

10   General Stanley A. McChrystal, *Team of Teams: New Rules of Engagement for a Complex World* (Portfolio, 2015), 94.

11   McChrystal, *Team of Teams*, 98.

12   Patrick Duffy (former chief experience officer at Diamond Resorts), interview with the author, June 6, 2024.

13   Abbi Stanley, "Poll: 47% of Americans Think a Civil War Is Likely," ABC 10 News, May 21, 2024, https://www.news10.com/news/national/poll-47-of-americans-think-a-civil-war-is-likely/.

14   Barbara F. Walter, *How Civil Wars Start: And How to Stop Them* (Crown, 2022), 135, 156, 160.

15   Hannah Knowles, "Vulgarities, Insults, Baseless Attacks: Trump Backers Follow His Lead," *Washington Post*, November 19, 2023, https://www.washingtonpost.com/elections/2023/11/19/donald-trump-insults-vulgarities-republicans/.

16   Zachary Jonathan Jacobson, "Many Are Worried about the Return of the 'Big Lie.' They're Worried about the Wrong Thing," *Washington Post*, May 21, 2018, https://www.washingtonpost.com/news/made-by-history/wp/2018/05/21/many-are-worried-about-the-return-of-the-big-lie-theyre-worried-about-the-wrong-thing/. To be precise, Jacobson defines the big lie as "a strategy of propaganda that focused on the mass dissemination of a single or a few chief falsehoods to a target population"—the apex of a "pyramid" of deceptions trickling down into society.

17   Philip Bump, "Why Do Republicans Disproportionately Believe Health Misinformation?" *Washington Post*, August 22, 2023, https://www.washingtonpost.com/politics/2023/08/22/republicans-vaccines-polls/; Martha McHardy, "Fox News Pushes Conspiracy Theory That Taylor Swift Is a Psy-Op," *Yahoo News*, January 10, 2024, https://au.news.yahoo.com/lifestyle/fox-news-pushes-conspiracy-theory-204441880.html; Bill Barrow and Jill Colvin, "Trump Escalates His Immigration Rhetoric with Baseless Claim About Biden Trying to Overthrow the US," *AP News*, March 2, 2024, https://apnews.com/article/trump-immigration-biden-gop-voters-border-migrants-1fc6624188f540f495e1087bee64318e.

18   John McWhorter, "Let's Have Fewer Cancellations. Let People Take Their Lumps, Then Move On," *The New York Times*, August 12, 2022, https://www.nytimes.com/2022/08/12/opinion/woke-cancellations.html.

19   "Inflation, Health Costs, Partisan Cooperation Among the Nation's Top Problems," Pew Research Center, June 21, 2023, https://www.pewresearch.org/politics/2023/06/21/inflation-health-costs-partisan-cooperation-among-the-nations-top-problems/.

20   Pamela Paul, "You've Been Wronged. That Doesn't Make You Right," *The New York Times*, April 25, 2024, https://www.nytimes.com/2024/04/25/opinion/oppression-victim-offensive.html.

21   Zaid Jilani and Jeremy Adam Smith, "What Is the True Cost of Polarization in America?" *Greater Good Magazine*, March 4, 2019, https://greatergood.berkeley.edu/article/item/what_is_the_true_cost_of_polarization_in_america.

22   Moira Warburton, "Why Congress Is Becoming Less Productive," *Reuters*, March 12, 2024, https://www.reuters.com/graphics/USA-CONGRESS/PRODUCTIVITY/egpbabmkwvq/.

23   Jay J. Van Bavel et al., "The Costs of Polarizing a Pandemic: Antecedents, Consequences, and Lessons," *Perspectives on Psychological Science* 19, no. 4 (2023), https://doi.org/10.1177/17456916231190395.

24   Jessie O'Brien, "Overcoming Polarization in Local Government through Strategic Community Engagement," *PM Magazine*, December 1, 2022, https://icma.org/articles/pm-magazine/overcoming-polarization-local-government-through-strategic-community-engagement.

25   Zhiwei Chen et al., "The Price of Political Polarization: Evidence from Municipal Issuers during the Coronavirus Pandemic," *Financial Research Letters* 47, part B (2022), 102781, https://doi.org/10.1016/j.frl.2022.102781.

26   Nicholas Riccardi, "Conservatives Go to Red States and Liberals Go to Blue as the Country Grows More Polarized," *AP News*, July 5, 2023, https://apnews.com/article/polarization-republicans-democrats-abortion-gender-colorado-idaho-406b5a841d4d47c8a08cf054c38bb2a0; Yascha Mounk, "The Doom Spiral of Pernicious Polarization," *The Atlantic*, May 21, 2022, https://www.theatlantic.com/ideas/archive/2022/05/us-democrat-republican-partisan-polarization/629925/.

27   Paul Barrett et al., "How Tech Platforms Fuel US Political Polarization and What Government Can Do About It," Brookings Institution, September 27, 2021, https://www.brookings.edu/articles/how-tech-platforms-fuel-u-s-political-polarization-and-what-government-can-do-about-it/.

28   Katherine Fung, "What Is Split-Ticket Voting and How Did It Impact 2024 Election?," *Newsweek*, November 6, 2024, https://www.newsweek.com/what-split-ticket-voting-how-did-it-impact-2024-election-1981760.

29   Rachel Kleinfeld, "Polarization, Democracy, and Political Violence in the United States: What the Research Says," Carnegie Endowment for International Peace, September 5, 2023, https://carnegieendowment.org/research/2023/09/polarization-democracy-and-political-violence-in-the-united-states-what-the-research-says?lang=en.

30   "Preamble Overview," Constitution Annotated, accessed July 22, 2024, https://constitution.congress.gov/browse/essay/pre-1/ALDE_00001231/.

31   United States Congress, Senate, "Washington's Farewell Address to the People of the United States," 106th Cong., 2d sess., 2000, S. Doc. 106-21, 11, https://www.govinfo.gov/content/pkg/GPO-CDOC-106sdoc21/pdf/GPO-CDOC-106sdoc21.pdf.

32   "Kenny Guinn On the Issues," OnTheIssues, accessed July 22, 2024, https://www.ontheissues.org/Kenny_Guinn.htm.

33   Jannelle Calderon, "Is the Las Vegas Strip Located in Las Vegas?" *Nevada Independent*, December 4, 2023, https://thenevadaindependent.com/article/fact-brief-is-the-las-vegas-strip-located-in-las-vegas.

34   Shelley Berkley (former US congresswoman from Nevada), interview with the author, April 29, 2024.

35   "Las Vegas Blvd Beautification Project," *Lifescapes International*, accessed July 22, 2024,
      https://lifescapesintl.com/project/las-vegas-strip/.

36   James Murren (former CEO of MGM Resorts International), interview with the author,
      May 29, 2024.

37   Murren, interview.

38   Greg Schneider and Eric Pianin, "Nuclear Dump's Foes Hopeful: Reid, Now No. 2 Senate Leader,
      Organizes Against Yucca Mountain," *Washington Post*, June 12, 2001, https://www.washingtonpost.com
      /archive/business/2001/06/13/nuclear-dumps-foes-hopeful/0cd4f3f0-203f-44c3-b31d-788474b09527/.

39   Stephen J. Cloobeck, "Guest Columnist Stephen J. Cloobeck: Tour Yields Only a Mountain
      of Rhetoric," *Las Vegas Sun*, March 23, 2001, https://lasvegassun.com/news/2001/mar/23/
      guest-columnist-stephen-j-cloobeck-tour-yields-onl/.

40   Jeff German, "Columnist Jeff German: Casinos Finally Heed Call on Dump," *Las Vegas Sun*,
      January 11, 2002, https://lasvegassun.com/news/2002/jan/11/columnist-jeff-german-casinos
      -finally-heed-call-on/; "Exec Enters Yucca Battle," *Las Vegas Sun*, January 5, 2001, https://
      lasvegassun.com/news/2001/jan/05/exec-enters-yucca-battle/.

41   Murren, interview.

42   "Governor Sisolak, Nevada Covid-19 Private Sector Task Force provide update on," Office of the
      Governor of Nevada, June 23, 2021, https://gov.nv.gov/layouts/full_page.aspx?id=332971.

HARD TRUTH #3

1   My account of this incident draws on Jeff McDonald, "One San Diego Teen's Fender-Bender
     Is a Lesson in Government Accountability—and the Lack of It," *San Diego Union-Tribune*,
     updated June 17, 2024, https://www.sandiegouniontribune.com/2024/06/15/one-san-diego
     -teens-fender-bender-is-a-lesson-in-government-accountability-and-the-lack-of-it/.

2   Richard Haass, *The Bill of Obligations: The Ten Habits of Good Citizens* (New York: Penguin, 2023).

3   "History of Law Day," American Bar Association, accessed July 22, 2024, https://www.americanbar
     .org/groups/public_education/law-day/history-of-law-day/.

4   "A Proclamation on Law Day, USA, 2023," White House, April 28, 2023, https://www.whitehouse
     .gov/briefing-room/presidential-actions/2023/04/28/a-proclamation-on-law-day-u-s-a-2023/.

5   "A Proclamation on Law Day," White House.

6   Adams wrote this phrase in the constitution for the State of Massachusetts. Matthew Spalding,
     "Rule of Law: The Great Foundation of Our Constitution," *Intercollegiate Review*, January 19, 2016,
     https://isi.org/intercollegiate-review/rule-of-law-the-great-foundation-of-our-constitution/.

7   Joedy McCreary, "No, California Proposition 47 Doesn't Allow You to Steal $950 in Store
     Items | Fact Check," *USA Today*, September 13, 2023, https://www.usatoday.com/story/news/
     factcheck/2023/09/13/post-falsely-claims-shoplifting-is-allowed-in-california-fact-check-theft
     -prop-47-950-stealing/70827188007/.

8   "Felony Theft Amount by State 2024," World Population Review, accessed October 9, 2024, https://worldpopulationreview.com/state-rankings/felony-theft-amount-by-state; "No on Prop 36: Keep California's Communities Safe and Stable," Vera, updated September 19, 2024, https://www.vera.org/explainers/prop-36-californias-ballot-proposition-to-recall-prop-47-explained.

9   Jake Horowitz and Monica Fuhrmann, "States Can Safely Raise Their Felony Theft Thresholds, Research Shows," Pew Trusts, May 22, 2018, https://www.pewtrusts.org/en/research-and-analysis/articles/2018/05/22/states-can-safely-raise-their-felony-theft-thresholds-research-shows#:~:text=Research%20shows%20that%20addiction%20interventions,effective%20alternative%20to%20increased%20incarceration.

10   "No on Prop 36," Vera.

11   Magnus Lofstrom, "Testimony: Crime Data on Retail Theft and Robberies in California," Public Policy Institute of California, January 4, 2024, https://www.ppic.org/blog/testimony-crime-data-on-retail-theft-and-robberies-in-california/.

12   Marc Sternfield, "Shoplifting Reports Soared in L.A. Last Year," KTLA 5, February 12, 2024, https://ktla.com/news/local-news/shoplifting-cases-soar-in-los-angeles/.

13   Bridgette Bjorlo, "Sacramento Ranks 7th Worst for Organized Retail Theft," ABC 10 News, October 24, 2023, https://www.abc10.com/article/news/local/sacramento-ranks-organized-retail-theft/103-3e80f766-72ca-4682-8d9c-61ba6ac97702; "Organized Retail Crime," National Retail Federation, accessed July 23, 2024, https://nrf.com/advocacy/policy-issues/organized-retail-crime.

14   Josh DuBose, "Retail Company in California Using Body-Worn Cameras to Deter Shoplifters," KTLA 5, June 5, 2024, https://ktla.com/news/california/retail-company-in-california-using-body-worn-cameras-to-deter-shoplifters/.

15   "Progressive California Democrats Look to Combat Retail Theft While Maintaining Liberal Stance," CBS News Bay Area, March 22, 2024, https://www.cbsnews.com/sanfrancisco/news/progressive-california-democrats-look-to-combat-retail-theft-while-maintaining-liberal-policies/.

16   "Governor Newsom Signs Legislative Package," *West Sacramento News Ledger*, August 19, 2024, https://www.westsacramentonewsledger.com/2024/08/19/502013/governor-newsom-signs-legislative-package.

17   "Proposition 36," Legislative Analyst's Office, propositions on the November 5, 2024, ballot, accessed October 9, 2024, https://lao.ca.gov/BallotAnalysis/Proposition?number=36&year=2024.

18   Justin Fox, "Illegal US Border Crossings Aren't Really Breaking Records," *Bloomberg*, March 20, 2024, https://www.bloomberg.com/opinion/articles/2024-03-20/illegal-us-border-crossings-aren-t-really-breaking-records.

19   Gaby Del Valle, "The Number of Migrants Is Not the Problem—Our Asylum System Is," *The Nation*, November 2, 2023, https://www.thenation.com/article/politics/immigration-migrants-democrats/; "To Resolve the Humanitarian and Administrative Border Crisis, the US Must Fix the Broken Asylum System, Help Stabilize the Western Hemisphere, and Provide Robust, Orderly Migration Pathways," Center for American Progress, February 5, 2024, https://www.americanprogress.org/article/to-resolve-the-humanitarian-and-administrative-border-crisis-the-u-s-must-fix-the-broken-asylum-system-help-stabilize-the-western-hemisphere-and-provide-robust-orderly-migration-pathways/; Will Freeman, "Why New York Is Experiencing a Migrant Crisis," Council on Foreign Relations, October 5, 2023, https://www.cfr.org/article/why-new-york-experiencing-migrant-crisis.

20   Jeffrey S. Passel and Jens Manuel Krogstad, "What We Know About Unauthorized Immigrants Living in the US," Pew Research Center, July 22, 2024, https://www.pewresearch.org/short-reads/2024/07/22/what-we-know-about-unauthorized-immigrants-living-in-the-us/.

21   Mark Powell, "California Property Owners Need More Protections Against Squatters Now," *San Diego Union-Tribune*, updated April 10, 2024, https://www.sandiegouniontribune.com/california-property-owners-need-more-protections-against-squatters-now.

22   Suzanne Blake, "Squatter Bars Landlord From His Own $2 Million Home," *Newsweek*, March 22, 2024, https://www.newsweek.com/squatter-forces-landlord-out-home-washington-1882028.

23   "California Landlords Are Buying Out-of-State Due to Squatter Fears," CBS4 News, February 8, 2024, https://cbs4indy.com/business/press-releases/ein-presswire/687146178/california-landlords-are-buying-out-of-state-due-to-squatter-fears/.

24   Jesse Bedayn, "Jewish Students Grapple with How to Respond to Pro-Palestinian Campus Protests," *AP News*, May 3, 2024, https://apnews.com/article/israel-palestinian-campus-protest-jewish-student-2e904dac59c6fda38b0c13831ba89ead; Chris McGreal, "How Pervasive Is Antisemitism on US Campuses? A Look at the Language of the Protests," *The Guardian*, May 3, 2024, https://www.theguardian.com/us-news/article/2024/may/03/college-gaza-protests-antisemitism; Katelyn Cordero et al., "Anti-Israel Protests on College Campuses Drive Calls for Increased Safety," *Politico*, October 26, 2023, https://www.politico.com/news/2023/10/26/anti-israel-protests-college-campuses-00123875.

25   McGreal, "How Pervasive Is Antisemitism on US Campuses?"

26   Shawn Hubler, "Crosstown Rivals Publicly Criticized Over Campus Protests," *The New York Times*, May 3, 2024, https://www.nytimes.com/2024/05/03/us/usc-ucla-criticism-campus-protests.html.

27   Miles J. Herszenhorn and Claire Yuan, "'I Am Sorry': Harvard President Gay Addresses Backlash Over Congressional Testimony on Antisemitism," *Harvard Crimson*, December 8, 2023, https://www.thecrimson.com/article/2023/12/8/gay-apology-congressional-remarks/.

28   Alanna Durkin Richer, Eric Tucker, and Michael Kunzelman, "What to Know about the Supreme Court Immunity Ruling in Trump's 2020 Election Interference Case," *AP News*, July 1, 2024, https://apnews.com/article/trump-immunity-supreme-court-capitol-riot-trial-72ec35de776315183e1db561257cb108.

29   Lindsay Whitehurst, "Sotomayor's Dissent: A President Should Not Be a 'King Above the Law,'" *AP News*, July 1, 2024, https://apnews.com/article/supreme-court-immunity-trump-president-jan-6-2350bee785c85282a97af9485b94b982.

30   Bill Melugin and Shelly Insheiwat, "FOX 11 Obtains Exclusive Photos of Gov. Newsom at French Restaurant Allegedly Not Following Covid-19 Protocols," FOX 11, updated November 18, 2020, https://www.foxla.com/news/fox-11-obtains-exclusive-photos-of-gov-newsom-at-french-restaurant-allegedly-not-following-covid-19-protocols.

31   Thomas Fuller, "For California Governor the Coronavirus Message Is Do as I Say, Not as I Dine," *The New York Times*, updated September 14, 2021, https://www.nytimes.com/2020/11/18/us/newsom-california-covid-french-laundry.html.

32   Tom Philp, "Like the French Laundry Scandal, Gov. Gavin Newsom Has to Eat It on 'Panera-Gate': Opinion," *Sacramento Bee*, March 1, 2024, https://ca.news.yahoo.com/french-laundry-scandal-gov-gavin-194100874.html.

33   Ariel Zilber, "Panera Bread Exempt from California's $20 Minimum Wage Law after Owner Donated to Gov. Newsom: Report," *New York Post*, updated February 29, 2024, https://nypost.com /2024/02/28/business/panera-bread-exempt-from-california-wage-law-after-newsom-donation/; David Mendoza, "The Newsom Panera Bread Scandal Is an Admission That Minimum Wage Laws Are Harmful," *Orange County Register*, updated March 28, 2024, https://www.ocregister .com/2024/03/23/the-newsom-panera-bread-scandal-is-an-admission-that-minimum-wage-laws -are-harmful/; Jeremy B. White, "Facing Backlash, Newsom Says Fast Food Carveout Doesn't Apply to Donor's Company," *Politico*, updated February 29, 2024, https://www.politico.com/ news/2024/02/29/gavin-newsom-fast-food-panera-00144282.

34   See, for example, "Panera Bread and the California Circuses," *Wall Street Journal*, March 1, 2024, https://www.wsj.com/articles/panera-bread-gavin-newsom-greg-flynn-california-restaurants-seiu -d3671d82; "Editorial: Californians Knead Answers. Did Panera Bread Get an Exemption from $20 Minimum Wage Law?" *Los Angeles Times*, February 29, 2024, https://www.latimes.com/opinion /story/2024-02-29/editorial-californians-knead-the-truth-about-panera-bread-exemption-from-20 -minimum-wage-law#:~:text=The%20exemption%20applies%20only%20to,pays%20the%20new %20minimum%20wage.

35   Adam Beam, "Confidentiality Pact Deepens Mystery of How Bakery Clause Got into California Minimum Wage Law," *AP News*, March 11, 2024, https://apnews.com/article/california-newsom -panera-fast-food-minimum-wage-065e18510570481cf69eefc84b8359e0.

36   Michael R. Sisak et al., "Guilty: Trump Becomes First Former US President Convicted of Felony Crimes," *AP News*, May 31, 2024, https://apnews.com/article/trump-trial-deliberations-jury -testimony-verdict-85558c6d08efb434d05b694364470aa0; Stefan Becket, "What Was Trump Convicted Of? Details on the 34 Counts and His Guilty Verdict," CBS News, June 3, 2024, https://www.cbsnews.com/news/trump-charges-conviction-guilty-verdict/.

37   Sarah Fortinsky, "Indicted While in Office: Menendez Among 7 Members of Congress Charged in Recent Years," *The Hill*, October 1, 2023, https://thehill.com/homenews/4230828-indicted -while-in-office-menendez-among-7-members-of-congress-charged-in-recent-years/.

38   "Modest Increase in Official Corruption Convictions in 2023," TRAC Reports (Syracuse University), January 31, 2024, https://trac.syr.edu/reports/737/#:~:text=According%20to%20 these%20government%20records,convictions%20or%2080%20in%20total.

39   Karen J. Greenberg, "Government Accountability Has Been Long Gone in the US," *The Nation*, August 4, 2020, https://www.thenation.com/article/politics/trump-coronavirus-accountability/.

40   Cailey Griffin and Amy Mackinnon, "Report: Corruption in US at Worst Levels in Almost a Decade," *Foreign Policy*, January 28, 2021, https://foreignpolicy.com/2021/01/28/report -transparency-international-corruption-worst-decade-united-states/; "Corruption Perceptions Index 2023," Transparency International, 2024, accessed October 9, 2024, https://www .transparency.org/en/cpi/2023.

41   "Modest Increase in Official Corruption Convictions," TRAC Reports.

42   Michael Berens and John Shiffman, "Thousands of US Judges Who Broke Laws or Oaths Remained on the Bench," *Reuters*, June 30, 2020, https://www.reuters.com/investigates/special -report/usa-judges-misconduct/; Erik Ortiz, "Robed in Secrecy: How Judges Accused of Misconduct Can Dodge Public Scrutiny," *NBC News*, December 26, 2021, https://www.nbcnews.com/news/ us-news/robed-secrecy-judges-accused-misconduct-can-dodge-public-scrutiny-rcna7638.

43   Berens and Shiffman, "Thousands of US Judges."

44   Jeffrey M. Jones, "Supreme Court Trust, Job Approval at Historical Lows," *Gallup News*, updated
     October 6, 2022, https://news.gallup.com/poll/402044/supreme-court-trust-job-approval-historical
     -lows.aspx#:~:text=A%20new%20low%20of%2047,expressed%20this%20level%20of%20trust.

45   "2023 State of the State Courts—National Survey Analysis," National Center for State Courts,
     December 18, 2023, https://www.ncsc.org/__data/assets/pdf_file/0039/96879/2023-SoSC-Analysis
     -2023.pdf. This poll showed a possible small uptick in 2023, although the significance of that
     remains unclear.

46   Emily Washburn, "America Less Confident in Police Than Ever Before: A Look at the Numbers,"
     Forbes, February 3, 2023, https://www.forbes.com/sites/emilywashburn/2023/02/03/america-less
     -confident-in-police-than-ever-before-a-look-at-the-numbers/.

47   Jacob Bogage and Jacqueline Alemany, "Bipartisan Senate Group Proposes Ban on Congressional
     Stock Trading," *Washington Post*, July 10, 2024, https://www.washingtonpost.com/business/2024
     /07/10/senate-ban-congressional-stock-trading; Rebecca Picciotto, "Senators Strike Bipartisan
     Deal for a Ban on Stock Trading by Members of Congress," CNBC, Wednesday, July 10, 2024,
     https://www.cnbc.com/2024/07/10/senators-strike-bipartisan-deal-for-a-ban-on-stock-trading
     -by-members-of-congress.html?os=__.

48   Bruce K. Chapman, "Caesar's Wife and the Politics of Destruction," *Wall Street Journal*, September
     27, 2018, https://www.wsj.com/articles/caesars-wife-and-the-politics-of-destruction-1538088258.

49   Roger Dow (former president and CEO of US Travel Association), interview with the author,
     May 1, 2024.

50   Ken Ritter, "Report on UNLV Student Boxing Death Draws Anger, Not Action," *AP News*,
     August 23, 2022, https://apnews.com/article/sports-crime-las-vegas-nevada-university-of
     -6ae94a495ce7ad792ff435c30842546e.

51   Kirsten Joyce, "Nevada Athletic Commission Chairman Threatens Sheriff Lombardo with
     Charges Following UNLV Student's Death," 8 News, October 18, 2022, https://www.8newsnow
     .com/news/nevada-athletic-commission-chairman-threatens-sheriff-lombardo-with-charges
     -following-unlv-students-death/; Casey Harrison, "Nevada Athletic Commission Chairman Blasts
     Metro for Probe of Fatal Boxing Event," *Las Vegas Sun*, August 24, 2022, https://lasvegassun.com/
     news/2022/aug/24/nevada-athletic-commission-chairman-citing-ags-rep/; *Investigative Report:
     2021 Kappa Sigma Fight Night*, Office of the Attorney General (Case No. 11801-3352), August
     2022, https://boxing.nv.gov/uploadedFiles/boxingnvgov/content/schedule/22_Agendas/Kappa_
     Sigma_Fight_Night_Final_Investigation_Report.pdf.

52   Jesse Holland, "Former NSAC Chairman Admits 'Mistake' in Sanctioning Power Slap Fighting—
     'I Regret It,'" *MMA Mania*, March 9, 2023, https://www.mmamania.com/2023/3/9/23632175/
     former-nsac-chairman-admits-mistake-sanctioning-power-slap-fighting-i-regret-it-dana-white;
     Paulina Dedaj, "Ex-Nevada State Athletic Commission Chair Expresses Regret Over Dana White's
     Slap League: 'I Made a Mistake,'" *Fox News*, March 9, 2023, https://www.foxnews.com/sports/ex
     -nevada-state-athletic-commission-chair-expresses-regret-over-dana-whites-slap-league-made-mistake.

53   Annie Ma and Ben Finley, "Schools Face Pressure to Take Harder Line on Discipline," *AP News*,
     January 21, 2023, https://apnews.com/article/teaching-school-boards-district-of-columbia
     -newport-news-education-124a978f3f76f53f1cb90ae4da21da4a.

54   Kristina Watrobski, "Virginia School Cancels Classes Due to Teacher Protest over Classroom Violence: 'No One Listens,'" ABC News 7, November 20, 2023, https://wjla.com/news/local/dozens -of-virginia-high-school-teachers-call-out-sick-to-protest-violence-disheartening-charlottesville -city-schools-virginia-education-bullying-discipline-crisis-in-the-classroom; Luona Lin et al., "What's It Like to Be a Teacher in America Today?" Pew Research Center, April 4, 2024, https://www.pewresearch .org/social-trends/2024/04/04/whats-it-like-to-be-a-teacher-in-america-today/; Jessica Grose, "Teachers Can't Hold Students Accountable. It's Making the Job Miserable," *The New York Times*, October 4, 2023, https://www.nytimes.com/2023/10/04/opinion/teachers-grades-students-parents.html.

55   Daniel Buck, "Teachers Are Fed Up with No-Consequence Discipline," Fordham Institute, January 18, 2024, https://fordhaminstitute.org/national/commentary/teachers-are-fed-no -consequence-discipline.

56   "National Survey Finds Just 1 in 3 Americans Would Pass Citizenship Test," Institute for Citizens and Scholars, October 3, 2018, https://citizensandscholars.org/resource/national-survey-finds -just-1-in-3-americans-would-pass-citizenship-test/.

57   Tim Donahue, "If Everyone Gets an A, No One Gets an A," *The New York Times*, October 23, 2023, https://www.nytimes.com/2023/10/23/opinion/grade-inflation-high-school.html.

58   Tom Fleischman, "Flexible Due Dates Lower Student Stress Without Loss of Rigor," *Cornell Chronicle*, March 22, 2024, https://news.cornell.edu/stories/2024/03/flexible -due-dates-lower-student-stress-without-loss-rigor.

59   Rates were increasing even before the pandemic. See, for example, *2022 National Healthcare Quality and Disparities Report* (Rockville, MD: Agency for Healthcare Research and Quality, 2022), "Child and Adolescent Mental Health," Report No.: 22(23)-0030, https://www.ncbi.nlm.nih.gov/books/ NBK587174/#:~:text=Nearly%2020%25%20of%20children%20and,in%20the%20decade%20 before%202019.

60   "Moral Issues," *Gallup News*, accessed July 25, 2024, https://news.gallup.com/poll/1681/moral-issues.aspx.

61   Kelsey Ables, "Think We're Losing Our Morals? That's a Common Illusion, Research Says," *Washington Post*, June 15, 2023, https://www.washingtonpost.com/wellness/2023/06/15/ humanity-morality-decline-illusion/.

62   Megan Brenan and Jeffrey M. Jones, "Ethics Ratings of Nearly All Professions Down in US," *Gallup News*, January 22, 2024, https://news.gallup.com/poll/608903/ethics-ratings-nearly -professions-down.aspx.

63   Judy Siegel-Itzkovich, "US Study Shows Voters Willing to Be Morally Flexible When It Comes to Politicians," *Jerusalem Post*, updated August 23, 2024, https://www.jpost.com/international/ article-799366.

64   "Survey: 77% of Employers See Increase in Job Ghosting," *HRO Today*, December 21, 2023, https://www.hrotoday.com/news/survey-77-of-employers-see-increase-in-job-ghosting/; "Report: Top 6 Reasons Gen Z and Millennials Ghost," Thriving Center of Psychology (blog), September 21, 2023, https://thrivingcenterofpsych.com/blog/gen-z-millennial-ghosting -statistics/; "80+ Shocking Employee Theft Statistics (2024)," Current Ware, accessed July 25, 2024, https://www.currentware.com/blog/employee-theft-statistics/; "Over Half of Employees Report Lying on Resumes," *HRO Today*, February 20, 2024, https://www.hrotoday.com/news/ over-half-of-employees-report-lying-on-resumes/; "The Most Common Lies People Use on Dating Apps Revealed by Experts," *Newsweek*, April 26, 2023, https://www.newsweek.com/ dating-experts-most-common-lies-dating-apps-1781178.

65   "What Is the Rule of Law," American Bar Association, accessed July 25, 2024, https://www.americanbar.org/advocacy/rule_of_law/what-is-the-rule-of-law/.

HARD TRUTH #4

1   "Louis Ruiz, 88, Founder of Mexican Food Line, Is Dead," *The New York Times*, April 10, 2007, https://www.nytimes.com/2007/04/10/business/worldbusiness/10ruiz.html.

2   Esra Hashem, "Great Examples of Giving Back," *Campus News*, Fresno State, November 27, 2017, https://campusnews.fresnostate.edu/november-27-2017/article-oagxqa.

3   Fred Ruiz, "Fred Ruiz Credits Mexican Immigrants for Making Ruiz Foods a $1 Billion Company," *Fresno Bee*, May 17, 2022, https://www.fresnobee.com/vida-en-el-valle/opinion-es/article 261542537.html.

4   Ruiz, "Fred Ruiz Credits Mexican Immigrants."

5   "Family Owned Since 1964," Ruiz Foods, accessed August 15, 2024, https://ruizfoods.com/ company/our-history/.

6   Lisa Morehouse, "Burrito Royalty: How the Ruiz Family Built a Frozen Mexican Food Empire," *Splendid Table*, April 5, 2019, podcast transcript, https://www.splendidtable.org/story/2019/04/05/ burrito-royalty-how-the-ruiz-family-built-a-frozen-mexican-food-empire.

7   Please see the company website, ruizfoods.com, as well as Melissa Montalvo, "These Corporate Food Industry Jobs Are Leaving California's Central Valley for Texas," *Fresnoland*, May 25, 2023, https://fresnoland.org/2023/05/25/ruiz-foods-frozen-food-business-moving-jobs-to-texas/; Ruiz, "Fred Ruiz Credits Mexican Immigrants."

8   Noor Adatia, "Frozen Mexican Food Behemoth Opens New HQ in Frisco," *WFAA*, March 8, 2024, https://www.wfaa.com/article/news/local/california-company-ruiz -foods-opens-new-hq-north-texas-frisco/287-96568a6b-a38e-45c7-b55a-558eae9dd717; Ruiz Food Products, Inc., "Ruiz Foods Celebrates Grand Opening of Frisco Headquarters Office," news release, March 6, 2024, https://ruizfoods.com/newsroom/ ruiz-foods-celebrates-grand-opening-of-frisco-headquarters-office/.

9   Frank Lopez, "Dinuba's Ruiz Foods Moving Corporate HQ to Texas," *Business Journal*, May 24, 2023, https://thebusinessjournal.com/dinubas-ruiz-foods-moving-corporate-hq-to-texas/.

10   Tessa McLean, "California Businesses Are Leaving the State at Double the Rate of Previous Years," *SF Gate*, November 4, 2022, https://www.sfgate.com/local/article/California-businesses-leaving -the-state-17553168.php; Joseph Vranich and Lee E. Ohanian, "Why Company Headquarters Are Leaving California in Unprecedented Numbers," Hoover Institution Economics Working Paper No. 21117 (Hoover Institution, Stanford University, September 14, 2022): 2–4, https://www .hoover.org/sites/default/files/research/docs/21117-Ohanian-Vranich-4_0.pdf; Edward Ring and Steve Hilton, "From Worst to Best: How California Ended up with the Worst Business Climate in America, and What It Will Take to Turn Things Around," California Policy Center, April 30, 2024, https://californiapolicycenter.org/reports/worsttobest/.

11   "The Wealthiest Californians Are Leaving the State," Spectrum News 1, January 22, 2024, https://spectrumnews1.com/ca/la-west/la-times-today/2024/01/22/wealthy-residents -leaving-california.

12   Bethan Moorcraft, "'We're Leaving!': Rich Americans Are Ditching California and 'Taking Their Tax Dollars with Them'—and Now the Tax Rates They're Fleeing Have Been Raised Even Higher," *Yahoo Finance*, March 1, 2024, https://finance.yahoo.com/news/leaving-rich-americans -ditching-california-163000441.html; Mehdi Punjwani and Sierra Campbell, "Average Salary in the U.S. in 2024," *USA Today*, September 26, 2024, https://www.usatoday.com/money/blueprint/ business/hr-payroll/average-salary-us/.

13   Don Lee, "The Wealthiest Californians Are Fleeing the State. Why That's Very Bad News for the Economy," *Los Angeles Times*, December 19, 2023, https://www.latimes.com/business/story /2023-12-19/the-wealthiest-californians-are-fleeing-the-state-why-thats-very-bad-news-for -the-economy.

14   Ariana Cohen, "California Ranks #1 State Wealthy Americans Are Moving Away From," CBS8, July 24, 2023, https://www.cbs8.com/article/news/local/california-ranks-1-state-wealthy -americans-are-moving-away/509-81f48f7d-9e67-46f9-b999-ad7b60c213dd; "The Blue-State Wealth Exodus Continues," *Wall Street Journal*, July 3, 2024, https://www.wsj.com/articles/ blue-state-exodus-irs-data-income-7c878e40.

15   Lee Ohanian and Joseph Vranich, "California Business Exits Soared in 2021, and There Is No End in Sight," Hoover Institution, October 25, 2022, https://www.hoover.org/research/ california-business-exits-soared-2021-and-there-no-end-sight; Dale Buss, "Best & Worst States For Business 2023: Where The Boom Lives On," *Chief Executive*, accessed August 21, 2024, https://chiefexecutive.net/best-worst-states-for-business-2023-where-the-boom-lives-on/.

16   Moorcraft, "'We're Leaving!'"

17   Susan Haigh, "Tax the Rich? Liberals Renew Push for State Wealth Taxes," *Associated Press*, January 20, 2023, https://apnews.com/article/politics-california-state-government-connecticut -massachusetts-hawaii-04d5178b6c0f9c603b29631631e1cd2c.

18   Dan Latu and Kelsey Vlamis, "Why LA's Richest Are Ditching Their Mansions—and Where They're Moving To," *Business Insider*, January 15, 2024, https://www.businessinsider.com/ where-las-wealthy-are-moving-2024-1.

19   Richard A. Epstein, "The Wealth Tax Is A Poor Idea," Hoover Institution, January 24, 2023, https://www.hoover.org/research/wealth-tax-poor-idea.

20   "California and the QSBS Tax Exemption," *QSBS Expert*, accessed September 1, 2024, https://www.qsbsexpert.com/california-and-the-qsbs-tax-exemption/.

21   Levi Sumagaysay, "'Wouldn't Be Where I am Today:' California's Small Business Owners Fight to Save State Aid," *Cal Matters*, June 14, 2024, https://calmatters.org/economy/2024/06/ small-business-program-california-cuts/.

22   Zelda Roland, "How Did Hollywood End Up in…Hollywood?" *PBS SoCal*, November 7, 2017, https://www.pbssocal.org/shows/lost-la/how-did-hollywood-end-up-in-hollywood.

23   Matt Stevens and Christopher Kuo, "States Have Spent $25 Billion to Woo Hollywood. Is It Worth It?" *The New York Times*, March 21, 2024, https://www.nytimes.com/2024/03/21/arts/states -hollywood-film-tax-incentives.html.

24   Ryan Zickgraf, "How Tax Breaks and Cheap Labor Built the Hollywood of the South," *Atlantic Civic Circle*, August 8, 2023, https://atlantaciviccircle.org/2023/08/08/how-tax-breaks -and-cheap-labor-built-the-hollywood-of-the-south/.

25   Eliana Dockterman, "How Georgia Became the Hollywood of the South," *Time*, July 26, 2018, https://time.com/longform/hollywood-in-georgia/.

26   Dockterman, "How Georgia Became the Hollywood of the South."

27   "Driving Economic Growth," Motion Picture Association, accessed August 15, 2024, https://www.motionpictures.org/what-we-do/driving-economic-growth/.

28   Ivan Ehlers, "Opinion: Studio Productions Keep Moving Out of Los Angeles. We Need to Stop the Bleeding," *Los Angeles Times*, May 21, 2024, https://www.latimes.com/opinion/story/2024-05-21/film-tv-los-angeles-california-entertainment-labor-jobs.

29   Jared Walczak, Andrey Yushkov, Katherine Loughead, "2024 State Business Tax Climate Index," Tax Foundation, October 24, 2023, https://taxfoundation.org/research/all/state/2024-state-business-tax-climate-index/.

30   Edward Ring and Steve Hilton, "From Worst to Best: How California Ended up with the Worst Business Climate in America, and What it Will Take to Turn Things Around," California Policy Center, April 30, 2024, https://californiapolicycenter.org/reports/worsttobest/.

31   Ring and Hilton, "From Worst to Best."

32   Ring and Hilton, "From Worst to Best"; Alexander Hall, "Restaurant Owners Warn New California Law Will Make Menu Prices Skyrocket: 'Crippling to Everybody,'" Fox Business, February 21, 2024, https://www.foxbusiness.com/media/restaurant-owners-warn-new-california-law-will-make-menu-prices-skyrocket-crippling-everybody.

33   Jonathan Vankin, "CEQA: The Surprising Story of the State's Keystone Environmental Law," *California Local*, February 14, 2024, https://californialocal.com/localnews/statewide/ca/article/show/94237-ceqa-california-environmental-quality-act-housing-gavin-newsom/#:~:text=Scott%20Wiener%2C%20a%20state%20senator,a%202023%20editorial%2C%20the%20Los.

34   "CEQA Is Too Easily Weaponized to Block Housing and Slow Environmental Progress," *Los Angeles Times*, January 30, 2023, https://www.latimes.com/opinion/story/2023-01-30/editorial-ceqa-is-too-easily-weaponized-to-block-housing-and-slow-environmental-progress; Ring and Hilton, "From Worst to Best."

35   M. Nolan Gray, "How Californians Are Weaponizing Environmental Law and How to Fix It," *The Atlantic*, March 12, 2021, https://www.theatlantic.com/ideas/archive/2021/03/signature-environmental-law-hurts-housing/618264/.

36   "CEQA Is Too Easily Weaponized," *Los Angeles Times*; Ring and Hilton, "From Worst to Best."

37   "California Travel-Related Spend & Visitation Forecast (June update)," Visit California, June 10, 2024, https://industry.visitcalifornia.com/research/travel-forecast.

38   Patricia Kirk, "Costly Regulations Putting Some California Coastal Hotel Projects Over the Financial Tipping Point," *Hospitality Investor*, December 6, 2023, https://www.hospitalityinvestor.com/development/costly-regulations-putting-some-california-coastal-hotel-projects-over-financial.

39   Sherry Karabin, "Hotels Face Increased Regulations," *San Fernando Valley Business Journal*, December 4, 2023, https://sfvbj.com/real-estate/hotels-face-increased-regulations/.

40   Bryan Wroten, "Los Angeles Housing Law Adds More Hurdles to Hotel Development: High Barriers to Entry Make Construction Harder to Justify Financially," *Hotel News Now*, January 19, 2024, https://www.costar.com/article/521716799/los-angeles-housing-law-adds-more-hurdles-to-hotel-development.

41   Roger Dow (former president and CEO of the US Travel Association), interview with the author, May 1, 2024.

42   William S. Laufer and Matthew Caulfield, "Wall Street and Progressivism," *Yale Journal on Regulation*, January 16, 2020, https://www.yalejreg.com/bulletin/wall-street-and-progressivism/.

43   Nicholas Kristof, "What Have We Liberals Done to the West Coast?" *The New York Times*, June 15, 2024, https://www.nytimes.com/2024/06/15/opinion/progressives-california-portland.html.

44   LA4LA, "Public-Private Partnership 'LA4LA' Launches to Accelerate Affordable Housing," press release, July 11, 2023, https://www.la4la.org/news/press-release-public-private-partnership -la4la-launches-to-accelerate-affordable-housing; "Mayor Bass Wants Wealthy Angelenos to Pay for Homeless Housing: LA4LA Initiative Urges Private Sector Donations to Fund Conversion Projects," *Real Deal*, April 16, 2024, https://therealdeal.com/la/2024/04/16/ las-mayor-bass-asks-the-wealthy-to-pay-for-homeless-housing/.

45   "When All Institutions Contribute Every Person Benefits," LA4LA, accessed September 1, 2024, https://www.la4la.org/invest.

46   Karen Bass, "Change In LA: Homelessness Down In City of L.A. for First Time In Years Following Urgent Action Taken By Mayor Bass and Partners," Office of the Mayor, City of Los Angeles, June 28, 2024, https://mayor.lacity.gov/news/change-la-homelessness-down -city-la-first-time-years-following-urgent-action-taken-mayor-bass.

47   Stephen J. Cloobeck (@stephenjcloobeck), "It Was a Joy to Attend the Grand Opening of the Eaves Development Last Night, a Housing Project That Will Help Get Many Families off the Street in Los Angeles," TikTok video, July 12, 2024, https://www.tiktok.com/@stephenjcloobeck/ video/7390860736974556447.

48   *The Return on Investment of Brand USA Marketing Fiscal Year 2023*, Tourism Economics, March 2023, https://www.thebrandusa.com/sites/default/files/Brand%20USA%20ROI%20(FY2023)%20TE -Oxford%203-1-2024%20(1).pdf.

49   Tierney Sneed et al., "How the Supreme Court's Blockbuster 'Chevron' Ruling Puts Countless Regulations in Jeopardy," CNN, June 30, 2024, https://www.cnn.com/2024/06/30/politics/chevron -ruling-explained-supreme-court-meaning/index.html.

50   J. Mark Gidley et al., "White & Case Global Non-Compete Resource Center (NCRC)," White & Case, October 7, 2024, https://www.whitecase.com/insight-tool/white-case-global -non-compete-resource-center-ncrc#legal-challenges.

51   Meghan Bartels, "A Supreme Court Ruling May Make It Harder for Government Agencies to Use Good Science," *Scientific American*, June 25, 2024, https://www.scientificamerican.com/article/ supreme-courts-chevron-deference-decision-could-make-science-based/.

52   Jessica Glenza, "Chevron Doctrine Ruling a 'Gut-Punch' for US Health and Environment," *The Guardian*, July 6, 2024, https://www.theguardian.com/us-news/article/2024/jul/06/chevron -doctrine-supreme-court-ruling.

53   Ezra Rosser, "Trump's All-Out War on the Poor," *The Hill*, February 15, 2018, https://thehill.com/ opinion/civil-rights/374069-trumps-all-out-war-on-the-poor/.

54   Timothy Noah, "Why Republicans Hate It When Poor People Have Food to Eat," *New Republic*, April 27, 2023, https://newrepublic.com/article/172242/republicans-hate-poor-people-food-eat.

55   Anne Kim, "How America Stopped Caring About the Poor," *Washington Monthly*, February 2, 2022, https://washingtonmonthly.com/2022/02/02/how-america-stopped-caring-about-the-poor/.

56   Alex Rogers, "Conservatives Say War on Poverty Failed," *Swampland*, January 08, 2014, https://swampland.time.com/2014/01/08/conservatives-say-war-on-poverty-failed/.

57   Samantha Smith, "Why People are Rich and Poor: Republicans and Democrats Have Very Different Views," Pew Research Center, May 2, 2017, https://www.pewresearch.org/short-reads/2017/05/02/why-people-are-rich-and-poor-republicans-and-democrats-have-very-different-views/; "Most Americans Point to Circumstances, Not Work Ethic, for Why People Are Rich or Poor," Pew Research Center, March 2, 2020, https://www.pewresearch.org/politics/2020/03/02/most-americans-point-to-circumstances-not-work-ethic-as-reasons-people-are-rich-or-poor/.

58   Dylan Matthews, "The 2 Most Popular Critiques of Basic Income are Both Wrong," *Vox*, July 20, 2017, https://www.vox.com/policy-and-politics/2017/7/20/15821560/basic-income-critiques-cost-work-negative-income-tax.

59   Allie Kelly and Noah Sheidlower, "Denver Basic Income Reduces Homelessness, Food Insecurity," *Business Insider*, July 11, 2024, https://www.businessinsider.com/denver-basic-income-reduces-homelessness-food-insecurity-housing-ubi-gbi-2024-6.

60   Meryl Kornfield, "A City Gave People $500 a Month, No Strings Attached, to Fight Poverty. It Paid Off, Study Says," *Washington Post*, March 4, 2021, https://www.washingtonpost.com/nation/2021/03/03/stockton-universal-basic-income/.

61   Stephen J. Cloobeck (@stephenjcloobeck), Instagram video, July 10, 2024, https://www.instagram.com/reel/C9QVrPUy6lv/?igsh=MTc4MmM1YmI2Ng%3D%3D.

62   Please consult the website: https://www.dreamcenter.org/.

63   *Dream Center Annual Impact Report 2023–24*, Dream Center, accessed September 4, 2024, 23, https://www.dreamcenter.org/wp-content/uploads/2023/09/DC_Impact-Report_2023-F-D.pdf.

64   Dream Center, "Los Angeles Dream Center: Sarah's Story of Hope," YouTube video, 4:27, October 27, 2020, https://www.youtube.com/watch?v=rnq_w4uVSOc.

65   *Dream Center Annual Impact Report 2023–24* , Dream Center.

HARD TRUTH #5

1   Piper French, "A Future for Susanville," *Bolts*, May 5, 2022, https://boltsmag.org/susanville-prison-closure/#:~:text=Last%20April%2C%20California%20Governor%20Gavin,of%20the%20state's%2033%20prisons.

2   *City of Susanville Comprehensive Annual Financial Report Fiscal Year 2020*, Susanville, June 30, 2020, 123, https://www.cityofsusanville.net/rooptown/wp-content/uploads/2021/01/Susanville-CAFR-FY-2020.pdf.

3   Ruth Styles, "Inside California's Most Republican Town Where Locals Recoil at Thought of Newsom Presidency as They Launch Bid to Oust the Governor for a Second Time," *Daily Mail*, July 2, 2024, https://www.dailymail.co.uk/news/article-13588765/California-Republican-stronghold-Susanville-recall-Gavin-Newsom.html.

4   Tim Arango, "'Nothing Will Be the Same': A Prison Town Weighs a Future Without a Prison," *The New York Times*, updated January 12, 2022, https://www.nytimes.com/2022/01/10/us/susanville -california-prison-closing.html; Hailey Branson-Potts, "California's Prison Boom Saved this Town. Now, Plans to Close a Lockup are Sparking Anger and Fear," *Los Angeles Times*, June 21, 2021, https://www.yahoo.com/news/californias-prison-boom-saved-town-120053103.html.

5   "California Correctional Center Closure Key Dates," California Department of Corrections and Rehabilitation, accessed September 4, 2024, https://www.cdcr.ca.gov/prison-closures/; Keith Sanders, "Judge Dismisses Suit Filed by California Town to Keep State Prison Open," *Prison Legal News*, March 1, 2023, https://www.prisonlegalnews.org/news/2023/mar/1/ judge-dismisses-suit-filed-california-town-keep-state-prison-open/.

6   David Buchan, "The Red Island in a Sea of Blue: Inside California's Trumpiest Region," *Daily Mail*, July 3, 2024, https://www.msn.com/en-us/travel/news/the-red-island-in-a-sea-of-blue-inside -california-s-trumpiest-region/ss-BB1pjWWvl; Arango, "'Nothing Will Be the Same.'"

7   "Cruel and Unusual: A Guide to California's Broken Prisons and the Fight to Fix Them," *ProPublica*, May 28, 2019, https://www.propublica.org/article/guide-to-california-prisons.

8   "Actions to Reduce Population and Maximize Space," California Department of Corrections and Rehabilitation, accessed September 4, 2024, https://www.cdcr.ca.gov/covid19/frequently-asked -questions-expedited-releases/; "76,000 California Inmates Now Eligible for Earlier Releases," *Spokesman Review*, updated May 1, 2021, https://www.spokesman.com/stories/2021/may/01/76000 -california-inmates-now-eligible-for-earlier-/.

9   The population was projected to continue to drop through 2028: Nigel Duara, "Closing Prisons: Why Newsom Didn't Have That Option in Budget Trims," *CalMatters*, May 12, 2024, https:// laist.com/brief/news/criminal-justice/california-is-spending-more-money-on-fewer-inmates -why-isnt-newsom-closing-more-prisons; *The 2024-25 Budget: California Department of Corrections and Rehabilitation*, Legislative Analyst's Office, February 22, 2024, https://lao.ca.gov/Publications/ Report/4852.

10   French, "A Future for Susanville."

11   Anabel Sosa, "Newsom Has Approved Three California Prison Closures but Resists Pressure to Shutter More," *Los Angeles Times*, April 1, 2024, https://www.latimes.com/california/story/2024 -04-01/newsom-already-closed-three-california-prison-but-is-resisting-pressure-to-shutter-more.

12   Joe Mathews, "Susanville, California, Is Being Punished for Town's Business of Punishment," redding.com, March 31, 2022, https://www.redding.com/story/opinion/contributors/2022/03/31/ closing-wrong-prisons-susanville-california-employment-jobs-economy-gavin-newsom-joe -mathews-column/7233449001/.

13   Joe Mathews, "Governor Newsom Needs to Be Smarter about How He Shuts Down California Prisons," *San Francisco Chronicle*, April 3, 2022, https://www.sfchronicle.com/opinion/article/Gavin -Newsom-needs-to-be-smarter-about-how-he-17052560.php.

14   "California Supports Workers and Fosters Bottom-Up Economic Resilience in Lassen County," State of California Labor & Workforce, accessed October 9, 2024, https://www.labor.ca.gov/2022/ 12/01/california-supports-workers-and-fosters-bottom-up-economic-resilience-in-lassen-county/.

15   *First Look: Understanding the Governor's 2024–25 May Revision*, California Budget & Policy Center, May 2024, https://calbudgetcenter.org/resources/first-look-understanding-the-governors-2024 -25-may-revision/#:~:text=Introduction,the%20shortfall%20by%20%2417.3%20billion.

16   Nigel Duara, "California Is Spending More Money on Fewer Inmates. Why Isn't Newsom Closing More Prisons?" *Laist*, May 12, 2024, https://laist.com/news/criminal-justice/california -is-spending-more-money-on-fewer-inmates-why-isnt-newsom-closing-more-prisons.

17   Mikhail Zinshteyn and Sameea Kamal, "Digging Out: Newsom Outlines Plan to Cover State Budget Deficit," *CalMatters*, January 10, 2024, updated January 13, 2024, https://calmatters.org/ politics/2024/01/newsom-budget-california/.

18   Kristen Hwang and Nigel Duara, "As California Closes Prisons, the Cost of Locking Someone up Hits New Record at $132,860," *Cal Matters*, January 23, 2024, https://calmatters.org/justice/ 2024/01/california-prison-cost-per-inmate/#:~:text=It%20also%20recently%20contributed% 20$1,from%207%25%20to%206%25.

19   Hwang and Duara, "As California Closes Prisons."

20   Lindsey Holden, "California Democrats Want Gavin Newsom to Close More Prisons Over Cutting Child Care, Welfare," *Sacramento Bee*, May 15, 2024, https://www.sacbee.com/news/ politics-government/capitol-alert/article288497115.html.

21   Hwang and Duara, "As California Closes Prisons."; Duara, "Closing Prisons."

22   Duara, "Closing Prisons."

23   *The 2023-24 Budget: The California Department of Corrections and Rehabilitation*, Legislative Analyst's Office, February 16, 2023, https://lao.ca.gov/Publications/Report/4686.

24   Vik Jolly, "California to Examine Medical Staffing at State Prisons and Hospitals. Here's Why," *Sacramento Bee*, May 21, 2024, https://www.sacbee.com/news/politics-government/capitol-alert/ article288595445.html.

25   "Cruel and Unusual: A Guide to California's Broken Prisons and the Fight to Fix Them," *ProPublica*, May 28, 2019, https://www.propublica.org/article/guide-to-california-prisons.

26   Simone Weichselbaum, Andrew Blankstein, and Alexandra Chaidez, "California's Prison-to-Homelessness Pipeline," NBC News, July 18, 2023, https://www.nbcnews.com/news/ investigations/californias-prison-homelessness-pipeline-rcna93975.

27   "Executive Order N-79-20," Executive Department State of California, September 23, 2020, https:// www.gov.ca.gov/wp-content/uploads/2020/09/9.23.20-EO-N-79-20-Climate.pdf; "Governor Newsom's Zero-Emission by 2035 Executive Order (N-79-20)," California.gov, January 19, 2021, https://ww2.arb .ca.gov/resources/fact-sheets/governor-newsoms-zero-emission-2035-executive-order-n-79-20.

28   Nadia Lopez, "Race to Zero: Can California's Power Grid Handle a 15-Fold Increase in Electric Cars?" *Cal Matters*, January 17, 2023, https://calmatters.org/environment/2023/01/ california-electric-cars-grid/.

29   "How Roads Are Funded," San Diego County Government, accessed September 7, 2024, https://www.sandiegocounty.gov/content/sdc/dpw/roads/roadfnd.html#:~:text=For%20every %20gallon%20of%20gasoline,fund%20called%20the%20Road%20Fund.

30   Kate Murphy, "Pumping Gas in California Is Getting Pricier," *Axios*, July 3, 2024, https://www.axios.com/local/san-diego/2024/07/03/gas-tax-california-pricier-cost-per-gallon.

31   Grace Toohey, "California Offers $400 to Test Gas Tax Alternatives," *Governing*, May 15, 2024, https://www.governing.com/finance/california-offers-400-to-test-gas-tax-alternatives.

32   "EVs Are Heavier Than Gas Cars, but Are They Harder on Roads?" Tickle College of
      Engineering, March 11, 2024, https://ctr.utk.edu/evs-heavier-than-cars-are-they-harder-on
      -roads/#:~:text=So%2C%20how%20much%20heavier%20are,vehicles%20because%20of%20
      their%20batteries. They also cause more safety issues: Nathan Bomey, "EVs Are Much Heavier
      Than Gas Vehicles, and That's Posing Safety Problems," *Axios*, April 28, 2023, https://www.axios
      .com/2023/04/28/evs-weight-safety-problems.

33   Jeanne Kuang and Nicole Foy, "California Built a Safety Net for Undocumented Immigrants.
      Now Deficits Could Leave Some Behind," *Cal Matters*, July 11 2023, https://calmatters.org/
      california-divide/2023/07/undocumented-immigrants-california/; "Overview: Public Benefits for
      Noncitizens in California," ILRC, February 2024, https://www.ilrc.org/sites/default/files/2024-02/
      CA%20Public%20Benefits%20for%20Noncitizens%20.pdf.

34   Don Lee, "Why California's Surge in Immigration Is Lifting Our Economy," *Los Angeles Times*,
      July 31, 2024, https://www.latimes.com/business/story/2024-07-31/what-the-crisis-at-the-border
      -has-meant-for-californias-economy.

35   Mary Kekatos, "California Becomes First State to Offer Health Insurance to All Undocumented
      Immigrants," ABC News, December 29, 2023, https://abcnews.go.com/Health/california-1st
      -state-offer-health-insurance-undocumented-immigrants/story?id=105986377.

36   Tim Ranzetta, "California's Personal Finance Education Requirement Is a Commitment to Future
      Generations," CNBC, July 2 2024, https://www.cnbc.com/2024/07/02/op-ed-california-financial
      -literacy-law-is-a-commitment-to-the-future.html.

37   "AB-2927 Pupil Instruction: High School Graduation Requirements: Personal Finance (2023–2024),"
      California Legislative Information, accessed September 7, 2024, https://leginfo.legislature.ca.gov/
      faces/billNavClient.xhtml?bill_id=202320240AB2927.

38   Sharon Epperson, "More Than Half of U.S. High School Students Will Take a Personal Finance
      Class Before Graduation, Following the Passage of a New Pennsylvania Law," CNBC, December
      16, 2023, https://www.cnbc.com/2023/12/16/more-than-half-of-us-high-school-students-will
      -take-a-personal-finance-class-before-graduation-following-the-passage-of-a-new-pennsylvania
      -law.html.

39   Ranzetta, "California's Personal Finance Education Requirement."

40   See, for example, the semester-long Next Gen Personal Finance offering, available at
      https://www.ngpf.org/courses/semester-course/.

41   David Palmer (former CEO of Diamond Resorts), interview with the author, August 8, 2024.

42   This paragraph and the previous one draw on my book *Checking In: Hospitality-Driven Thinking,
      Business, and You* (Greenleaf, 2018), 56–86.

43   Martha C. White, "More Hotels Facing an Uncertain Future," *The New York Times*, April 13, 2009,
      https://www.nytimes.com/2009/04/14/business/14hotels.html; Roger Yu, "More Hotels Are
      Facing Foreclosure, Bankruptcy," *Deseret News*, March 6, 2009, https://www.deseret.com/2009/
      3/6/20305612/more-hotels-are-facing-foreclosure-bankruptcy/.

44   Palmer, interview.

45   Mike Flaskey (former CEO of Diamond Resorts), interview with the author, April 12, 2024.

46   Palmer, interview.

47   Aliss Higham, "Property Tax Anger Is Growing Across America," *Newsweek*, updated January 29, 2024, https://www.newsweek.com/property-tax-anger-american-poll-1864769.

48   Cameron Huddleston, "Survey: Only 18% of Americans Believe Their Tax Dollars Are Being Spent the Right Way," *Yahoo Finance*, July 1, 2024, https://finance.yahoo.com/news/survey-only-18-americans-believe-233858435.html.

49   James Reinl, "Auditors SLAM California's $24 BILLION spend on shelters and rent subsidies, with little to show but 53% rise in homelessness to 180,000 this past decade," *Daily Mail*, updated April 10, 2024, https://www.dailymail.co.uk/news/article-13292861/California-audit-shelters-rent-homelessness.html.

50   Flaskey, interview.

51   Palmer, interview.

52   French, "A Future for Susanville."

HARD TRUTH #6

1   Ramin Setoodeh, "'The Apprentice' is still Donald Trump's proudest moment," *Washington Post*, June 17, 2024, https://www.washingtonpost.com/style/power/2024/06/17/trump-apprentice-book-setoodeh/.

2   Bill Pruitt, "The Donald Trump I Saw on *The Apprentice*," *Slate*, May 30, 2024, https://slate.com/culture/2024/05/donald-trump-news-2024-trial-verdict-apprentice.html.

3   Republican voters in 2016 who were fans of the show tended to trust him more than other such voters did, as an academic study has shown. Philip Bump, "'The Apprentice' and the Creation of Leader Donald Trump," *Washington Post*, May 24, 2024, https://www.washingtonpost.com/politics/2024/05/31/trump-apprentice-campaign/.

4   James Poniewozik, "Donald Trump Was the Real Winner of 'The Apprentice,'" *The New York Times*, September 28, 2020, https://www.nytimes.com/2020/09/28/arts/television/trump-taxes-apprentice.html.

5   Manuela López Restrepo, "Press 1 for More Anger: Americans Are Fed Up with Customer Service," NPR, March 15, 2023, https://www.npr.org/2023/03/15/1163723617/customer-service-satisfaction-survey-freakout-shortage-2022; "Almost Half of Consumers Feel Customer Service Has Worsened Over Past 3 Years," *CX Today*, April 19, 2024, https://www.cxtoday.com/voice-of-the-customer/almost-half-of-consumers-feel-customer-service-has-worsened-over-past-3-years/; "Customer Service Is Getting Worse—and So Are Customers," *The Economist*, September 28, 2023, https://www.economist.com/business/2023/09/28/customer-service-is-getting-worse-and-so-are-customers. Consider health care as a case in point: Deb Woods, "What Over 2 Million Patients Say About Their Healthcare Experiences," Physicians Practice, April 23, 2024, https://www.physicianspractice.com/view/what-over-2-million-patients-say-about-their-healthcare-experiences.

6   Ivana Saric, "Americans Are Giving to Charity at Lowest Level in Nearly 3 Decades," *Axios*, June 22, 2023, https://www.axios.com/2023/06/22/charitable-giving-donations-income.

7   "American Volunteerism Continues to Decline, Studies Find," *Philanthropy News Digest*, December 12, 2023, https://philanthropynewsdigest.org/news/american-volunteerism-continues-to-decline -studies-find; "Americans Can Fix Their Fraying Society," *Washington Post*, July 4, 2024, https:// www.washingtonpost.com/opinions/2024/07/04/united-states-volunteer-decline-charity-july-4/.

8   Matt Seyler, "Military Struggling to Find New Troops as Fewer Young Americans Willing or Able to Serve," ABC News, July 2, 2022, https://abcnews.go.com/Politics/military-struggling -find-troops-fewer-young-americans-serve/story?id=86067103.

9   Christianna Silva, "Freemasons Say They're Needed Now More Than Ever. So Why Are Their Ranks Dwindling?" NPR, November 28, 2020, https://www.npr.org/2020/11/28/937228086/ freemasons-say-theyre-needed-now-more-than-ever-so-why-are-their-ranks-dwindling.

10   Robert D. Putnam, *Bowling Alone: The Collapse and Revival of American Community* (Simon & Schuster, 2000).

11   As some have pointed out, the trends since 2000 seem to be nuanced and not entirely grim: Alexandra Hudson, "*Bowling Alone* at Twenty," *National Affairs* 61 (Fall 2024), https:// nationalaffairs.com/publications/detail/bowling-alone-at-twenty.

12   Leslie Davis and Kim Parker, "A Half-Century After 'Mister Rogers' Debut, 5 Facts About Neighbors in U.S.," Pew Research Center, August 15, 2019, https://www.pewresearch.org/ short-reads/2019/08/15/facts-about-neighbors-in-u-s/.

13   Marc J. Dunkelman, *The Vanishing Neighbor: The Transformation of American Community* (W.W. Norton, 2014); E. J. Dionne Jr., "Where Goes the Neighborhood?" *Washington Post*, August 10, 2014, https://www.washingtonpost.com/opinions/ej-dionne-where-goes-the -neighborhood/2014/08/10/8a137cde-1f39-11e4-ae54-0cfe1f974f8a_story.html; "Are America's Communities Disappearing?" *VOA Learning English*, April 8, 2021, https://learningenglish .voanews.com/a/are-america-s-communities-disappearing-/5843120.html.

14   Daniel A. Cox, "America's 'Friendship Recession' Is Weakening Civic Life," American Survey Center, August 24, 2023, https://www.americansurveycenter.org/newsletter/americas-friendship -recession-is-weakening-civic-life/. See also "Our Epidemic of Loneliness and Isolation: The U.S. Surgeon General's Advisory on the Healing Effects of Social Connection and Community," Office of the Surgeon General, May 2023, 13, https://www.hhs.gov/sites/default/files/surgeon-general -social-connection-advisory.pdf.

15   "Our Epidemic of Loneliness," Office of the Surgeon General.

16   "Robert Putnam Knows Why You're Lonely," *The Daily*, podcast audio, July 13, 2024, https:// podcasts.apple.com/us/podcast/the-daily/id1200361736?i=1000662102883. As other observers have pointed out, the trends since 2000 might be more nuanced and not entirely grim: Hudson, "*Bowling Alone* at Twenty."

17   "Our Epidemic of Loneliness."

18   "Our Epidemic of Loneliness."

19   "Our Epidemic of Loneliness."

20   "Robert Putnam Knows Why You're Lonely," *The Daily*.

21   "The Decline of Empathy and the Rise of Narcissism, with Sara Konrath, PhD," *Speaking of
Psychology*, podcast audio, episode 95, American Psychological Association, accessed September 18,
2024, https://www.apa.org/news/podcasts/speaking-of-psychology/empathy-narcissism.

22   Karen Sloan, "Civility Is on the Decline, ABA Civics Poll Finds," *Reuters*, April 28, 2023, https://
www.reuters.com/legal/government/civility-is-decline-aba-civics-poll-finds-2023-04-27/.

23   "Mark 4:25–41," Bible Study Tools, The Message translation, accessed September 19, 2024,
https://www.biblestudytools.com/msg/mark/passage/?q=mark+4:25-41.

24   Brandon Keim, "Kindness Breeds More Kindness, Study Shows," *Wired*, March 8, 2010, https://
www.wired.com/2010/03/kindness-spreads/.

25   "Real Examples of Big Money's Power to Sway Politics," Free Speech for People, October 5, 2022,
https://freespeechforpeople.org/real-examples-of-big-moneys-power-to-sway-politics/.

26   Jack Caporal, "Congressional Stock Trading: Who Trades and Makes the Most," *Motley Fool*,
updated April 2, 2024, https://www.fool.com/research/congressional-stock-trading-who-trades
-and-makes-the-most/.

27   Jenn Hatfield, "More Than 80% of Americans Believe Elected Officials Don't Care What People
Like Them Think," Pew Research Center, April 30, 2024, https://www.pewresearch.org/short
-reads/2024/04/30/more-than-80-of-americans-believe-elected-officials-dont-care-what-people
-like-them-think/.

28   Andy Cerda and Andrew Daniller, "7 Facts About Americans' Views of Money in Politics,"
Pew Research Center, October 23, 2023, https://www.pewresearch.org/short-reads/2023/10/23/
7-facts-about-americans-views-of-money-in-politics/.

29   Monster.com, "When I Grow Up," Facebook video, 0:32, posted by Media Samosa,
February 10, 2022, https://www.facebook.com/mediasamosa/videos/monstercom-when-i
-grow-up-1999/479999587067656/.

30   Alan Davis and Morris Pearl, "Billionaires Say They Can't Give Their Money Away Fast Enough:
Here's How," *Nonprofit Quarterly*, July 14, 2021, https://nonprofitquarterly.org/billionaires-say
-they-cant-give-their-money-away-fast-enough-heres-how/.

31   MacKenzie Scott, "Pledge Letter," Giving Pledge, May 25, 2019, https://givingpledge.org/
pledger?pledgerId=393.

32   Net worth as of 2024: Matthew Lee, Brian Trelstad, and Ethan Tran, "$15 Billion in Five Years:
What Data Tells Us About MacKenzie Scott's Philanthropy," *Harvard Business School Working
Knowledge*, December 19, 2023, https://hbswk.hbs.edu/item/mackenzie-scotts-15-billion-pledge
-what-the-data-says-about-her-epic-giving; "MacKenzie Scott," *Forbes*, accessed September 20,
2024, https://www.forbes.com/profile/mackenzie-scott/?sh=7876a6c4243d.

33   Scott has been known for simply finding grantees and writing them checks, although she recently
held an "open call" grant application process: Kalie VanDewater, "The Impact of MacKenzie
Scott's Open Call Grants," *NonProfit PRO*, April 16, 2024, https://www.nonprofitpro.com/article/
the-impact-of-mackenzie-scotts-open-call-grants/; MacKenzie Scott, "384 Ways to Help," *Medium*,
December 15, 2020, https://mackenzie-scott.medium.com/384-ways-to-help-45d0b9ac6ad8.

34   Isaiah Thompson, "How MacKenzie Scott Is Giving Her Money Away," *Nonprofit Quarterly*,
February 20, 2024, https://nonprofitquarterly.org/how-mackenzie-scott-is-giving-her
-money-away/.

35   Alan Schwarz, ed., "Customer Experience All-Stars 2024," *Forbes*, February 20, 2024, https://www.forbes.com/lists/customer-experience-all-stars/.

36   I describe these examples in my book *Checking In: Hospitality-Driven Thinking, Business, and You* (Greenleaf, 2018), 96–101, 114–19, 158–59.

37   Patrick Duffy (former chief experience officer at Diamond Resorts International), interview with the author, June 6, 2024.

38   Steve Bell (former Diamond Resorts executive), interview with the author, April 23, 2024.

39   Duffy, interview.

40   "Mandatory Service Around the Globe," National Commission on Service, December 6, 2018, https://medium.com/@inspire2serveUS/mandatory-service-around-the-globe-c05e11810cfc; "Countries with Mandatory Military Service 2024," World Population Review, accessed September 20, 2024, https://worldpopulationreview.com/country-rankings/countries-with -mandatory-military-service.

41   "Which Countries Have National Service and How Does It Work Elsewhere?" *Sky News*, May 26, 2024, https://news.sky.com/story/which-countries-have-national-service-and-how -does-it-work-elsewhere-13143261.

42   Steve Cohen, "The Need for a Mandatory National Service Program," US Naval Institute, *Proceedings* 147, no. 4 (2021), https://www.usni.org/magazines/proceedings/2021/april/need -mandatory-national-service-program.

43   Steve Cohen, "Americans Support Mandatory National Service," *The Hill*, October 15, 2023, https://thehill.com/opinion/campaign/4253664-americans-support-mandatory-national-service/.

44   Beth Nichol et al., "Exploring the Effects of Volunteering on the Social, Mental, and Physical Health and Well-being of Volunteers: An Umbrella Review," *Voluntas* 35 (2023): 97–128, https://doi.org/10.1007/s11266-023-00573-z.

45   "The Joy of Giving: How Giving Can Improve Your Own Well-Being," Andrews University, accessed September 20, 2024, https://www.andrews.edu/services/development/annual/the-joy-of -giving/index.html.

46   "New Research Reveals Linkages Between Volunteerism & Social Connections," Do Good Institute, January 11, 2024, https://dogood.umd.edu/news/new-research-reveals-linkages-between -volunteerism-social-connections-0.

47   National Center for Biotechnology Information (NCBI), "TMPRSS2 Transmembrane serine protease 2 [Homo sapiens (human)]," *Gene*, National Library of Medicine (US), National Center for Biotechnology Information, updated October 1, 2024, https://www.ncbi.nlm.nih.gov/gene/7113.

48   Taylor Romine and Eddie Sun, "Before Las Vegas Mass Shooting, a Friend of the Gunman Implored Him Not to 'Shoot or Kill Innocent People,' Newspaper Reports," CNN, April 8, https://www.cnn.com/2023/04/07/us/las-vegas-2017-shooting-stephen-paddock-letters/index .html; Serge F. Kovaleski and Mike Baker, "Gunman in 2017 Las Vegas Shooting Was Angry at Casinos, New F.B.I. Files Show," *The New York Times*, March 30, 2023, https://www.nytimes.com/ 2023/03/30/us/las-vegas-shooting-gunman.html.

49   "Bringing National Certification to Nevada: Stephen J. Cloobeck Regional Center for Disaster Life Support Receives National Certification," Touro University Nevada, June 21, 2019, https://tun.touro.edu/about-us/news-and-stories/2019/june/bringing-national-certification-to-nevada.php; Shelley Berkley (former US congresswoman), interview with the author, April 29, 2024.

50   Berkley, interview.

51   Ken Ritter and Rio Yamat, "Las Vegas Shooting Suspect Was a Professor Who Recently Applied for a Job at UNLV, AP Source Says," *Associated Press*, December 6, 2023, https://apnews.com/article/campus-shooting-las-vegas-unlv-55ca455e2d00f1126cc1dbf4cc29139e; Ken Ritter and Rio Yamat, "UNLV Shooting Suspect Had List of Targets at That Campus and Another University, Police Say," *Associated Press*, December 7, 2023, https://www.nbclosangeles.com/news/national-international/vegas-shooter-who-killed-3-was-a-professor-who-failed-to-get-a-job-at-unlv-sources-say/3285691/.

52   Ritter and Yamat, "UNLV Shooting Suspect Had List of Targets."

53   Jacob Slavec (former team member at Diamond Resorts), interview with the author, August 15, 2024.

HARD TRUTH #7

1   John Regan, "The World's Strongest Man," *Waltham Boy* (blog), January 6, 2017, https://walthamboy.wordpress.com/2017/01/06/teddy-achilles/.

2   Amber Hye-Yon Lee, "Social Trust in Polarized Times: How Perceptions of Political Polarization Affect Americans' Trust in Each Other," *Political Behavior* 44, no. 3 (2022): 1533–1554, https://doi.org/10.1007/s11109-022-09787-1.

3   David Brooks, "America Is Having a Moral Convulsion," *The Atlantic*, October 5, 2020, https://www.theatlantic.com/ideas/archive/2020/10/collapsing-levels-trust-are-devastating-america/616581/.

4   Jedediah Britton-Purdy, "We've Been Thinking About America's Trust Collapse All Wrong," *The Atlantic*, January 8, 2024, https://www.theatlantic.com/ideas/archive/2024/01/trust-democracy-liberal-government/677035/.

5   "The State of Personal Trust," Pew Research Center, July 22, 2019, https://www.pewresearch.org/politics/2019/07/22/the-state-of-personal-trust/.

6   Adella Pasos, "How Much Do Americans Spend on Security Systems?" Medium (blog), July 27, 2022, https://adellapasos.medium.com/how-much-do-americans-spend-on-security-systems-80ac5489bf50#:~:text=Nearly%2021%20billion%20dollars%20each,year%20on%20home%20security%20systems; Rob Gabriele, "Home Security Statistics 2024," SafeHome.org, August 27, 2024, https://www.safehome.org/data/home-security-statistics/.

7   Lydia Saad, "Personal Safety Fears at Three-Decade High in U.S.," *Gallup News*, November 16, 2023, https://news.gallup.com/poll/544415/personal-safety-fears-three-decade-high.aspx.

8   Anagha Srikanth, "Shocking New Study Shows Segregation Growing Worse in Surprising Parts of US," *The Hill*, June 29, 2021, https://thehill.com/changing-america/respect/equality/560711-shocking-new-study-shows-segregation-growing-worse-in/.

9   Alvin Chang, "White America Is Quietly Self-Segregating," *Vox*, updated July 31, 2018, https://www.vox.com/2017/1/18/14296126/white-segregated-suburb-neighborhood-cartoon.

10   Georgetown Institute of Politics and Public Service, "Battleground Civility Poll: New Poll Shows Near Universal Concern Over Level of Political Division and High Levels of Self-Segregation," news release, July 28, 2022, https://politics.georgetown.edu/2022/07/28/battleground-civility-poll -new-poll-shows-near-universal-concern-over-level-of-political-division-and-high-levels-of-self -segregation/; Daniel A. Cox et al., "Socially Distant: How Our Divided Social Networks Explain Our Politics," American Enterprise Institute, September 30, 2020, https://www.americansurvey center.org/research/socially-distant-how-our-divided-social-networks-explain-our-politics/.

11   Anna Brown, "Most Democrats Who Are Looking for a Relationship Would Not Consider Dating a Trump Voter," Pew Research Center, April 24, 2020, https://www.pewresearch.org/short -reads/2020/04/24/most-democrats-who-are-looking-for-a-relationship-would-not-consider-dating -a-trump-voter/; Nicholas Jacobs and B. Kal Munis, "Place-Based Resentment in Contemporary U.S. Elections: The Individual Sources of America's Urban-Rural Divide," *Political Research Quarterly* 76, no. 3 (2022): 1102–1118, https://doi.org/10.1177/10659129221124864; Mike Allen, "Rot of Nation's Core Values Quantified by Single Poll," *Axios*, March 28, 2023, https://www.axios .com/2023/03/28/america-core-values-economy-poll.

12   Robert P. Jones, "Self-Segregation: Why It's So Hard for Whites to Understand Ferguson," *The Atlantic*, August 21, 2014, https://www.theatlantic.com/national/archive/2014/08/self-segregation -why-its-hard-for-whites-to-understand-ferguson/378928/.

13   Tara Suter, "New Survey Finds Agreement on Most Core American Values," *The Hill*, April 3, 2024, https://thehill.com/homenews/campaign/4572036-new-survey-agreement-most-core-american-values/.

14   "Is America More United than You Think? What Readers Told Us," *Newsweek*, January 10, 2024, https://www.newsweek.com/2024/01/19/america-more-united-you-think-what-readers-told-us -1858707.html

15   Gary Fields and Amelia Thomson Deveaux, "Yes, We're Divided. But New AP-NORC Poll Shows Americans Still Agree on Most Core American Values," *AP News*, April 3, 2024, https://apnews .com/article/ap-poll-democracy-rights-freedoms-election-b1047da72551e13554a3959487e5181a.

16   "What Makes Americans Proud and Angry?" McCourtney Institute for Democracy, Penn State, accessed September 14, 2024, https://democracy.psu.edu/poll-report-archive/what-makes -americans-proud-and-angry/.

17   Carl Smith, "Is American Polarization a Reality or a Political Strategy?" *Governing.com*, October 2, 2023, https://www.governing.com/politics/is-american-polarization-a-reality-or-a-political-strategy.

18   Karl Vick, "The Growing Evidence That Americans Are Less Divided Than You May Think," *Time*, July 2, 2024, https://time.com/6990721/us-politics-polarization-myth/.

19   Susan K. Urahn and Michael Dimock, "Americans Hate Divisiveness. We Need to Demand More From Our Leaders," Pew Trusts, December 12, 2023, https://www.pewtrusts.org/en/about/news -room/opinion/2023/12/12/americans-hate-divisiveness-we-need-to-demand-more-from-our-leaders.

20   Smith, "Is American Polarization a Reality or a Political Strategy?"

21   Luxuan Wang and Naomi Forman-Katz, "Many Americans Find Value in Getting News on Social Media, but Concerns about Inaccuracy Have Risen," Pew Research Center, February 7, 2024, https://www.pewresearch.org/short-reads/2024/02/07/many-americans-find-value-in-getting-news -on-social-media-but-concerns-about-inaccuracy-have-risen/; Julia Mueller, "Most Americans Say Media Increases Political Polarization: Poll," *The Hill*, May 1, 2023, https://thehill.com/homenews/ media/3981449-poll-media-increases-political-polarization/.

22   Steven Lee Myers, "How Social Media Amplifies Misinformation More Than Information," *The New York Times*, October 13, 2022, https://www.nytimes.com/2022/10/13/technology/misinformation-integrity-institute-report.html.

23   "Industry Ethicist: Social Media Companies Amplifying Americans' Anger for Profit," CBS News, November 6, 2022, https://www.cbsnews.com/news/tristan-harris-social-media-political-polarization-60-minutes-2022-11-06/.

24   "How Solutions Journalism Rebalances the News," *Solutions Journalism*, accessed September 14, 2024, https://www.solutionsjournalism.org/impact/how-solutions-journalism-rebalances-news.

25   Adam Gabbatt, "FBI Data Shows US Crime Plummeted in 2023 but Experts Warn Report Is Incomplete," *The Guardian*, March 19, 2024, https://www.theguardian.com/us-news/2024/mar/19/fbi-data-shows-us-crime-plummeted-2023#:~:text=Crime%20in%20the%20US%20fell,violent%20crime%20declined%20by%206%25.

26   Lauren Aratani, "Majority of Americans Wrongly Believe US is In Recession—and Most Blame Biden," *The Guardian*, May 22, 2024, https://www.theguardian.com/us-news/article/2024/may/22/poll-economy-recession-biden.

27   Mike Flaskey (former CEO of Diamond Resorts), interview with the author, April 12, 2024.

28   "Pavlovian Influence: We Trust Strangers That Look Like People We Know," *Technology Networks*, updated January 30, 2018, https://www.technologynetworks.com/neuroscience/news/pavlovian-influence-we-trust-strangers-that-look-like-people-we-know-296964.

29   Diana Orcés, "How Comfortable Are Americans with LGBTQ Friends?" PRRI, September 7, 2023, https://www.prri.org/spotlight/how-comfortable-are-americans-with-lgbtq-friends/.

CONCLUSION

1   "Social Determinants of Health," Health.gov, accessed October 9, 2024, https://health.gov/healthypeople/priority-areas/social-determinants-health.

ABOUT THE AUTHOR

STEPHEN J. CLOOBECK is the founder and former CEO and chairman of Diamond Resorts International—a business that grew to become the second-largest vacation ownership company. A busboy turned entrepreneur with more than thirty years' experience across every aspect of hospitality, he is the author of *Checking In: Hospitality-Driven Thinking, Business, and You*. He is the former chairman of the State of Nevada Athletic Commission.

Cloobeck was appointed by former Commerce Secretary Gary Locke to serve as the inaugural chairman of the board of Brand USA Inc., a US government-formed nonprofit corporation with the sole mission of promoting travel to the United States. In 2004, he was appointed by former Governor Kenny C. Guinn to Nevada's Standing Committee on Judicial Ethics and Election Practices. A native of Encino, California, he currently resides in Southern California.